Naked Cinema

Sally Potter has written and directed seven feature films (*The Gold Diggers, Orlando, The Tango Lesson, The Man Who Cried, Yes, Rage* and *Ginger & Rosa*) in addition to short films and documentaries for television. She has also directed opera. Her background includes work as a dancer, singer, lyricist and performance artist. Her films have received over fifty international awards, including two Oscar nominations, and she was made an OBE in 2012 for services to cinema.

by the same author

ORLANDO
THE TANGO LESSON
THE MAN WHO CRIED

NAKED CINEMA
Working with Actors

SALLY POTTER

FABER & FABER

First published in 2014
by Faber & Faber Ltd
Bloomsbury House
74–77 Great Russell Street
London WCIB 3DA

Typeset by Faber & Faber Ltd
Printed in England by CPI Group (UK) Ltd, Croydon, CRO 4YY

A CIP record for this book
is available from the British Library

ISBN 978–0–571–30499–8

FSC
www.fsc.org
MIX
Paper from
responsible sources
FSC® C101712

2 4 6 8 10 9 7 5 3 1

Contents

Introduction

Why 'Naked Cinema'?

Audiences enter the world of a film through its complex surfaces and structures, whether they are elaborate or minimal, realistic or fantastic. But invariably it is the human in the frame who guides us through the labyrinth of feeling and visual information; it is because of him or her that we want to know what happens next. The intimate, powerful relationship between audience and actor may feel natural, but it is a construction, the end result of many working processes. This book attempts to strip away the mystique and look at how we come to feel we know actors intimately and what it is that they and the director have to do to arrive at an apparently seamless and effortless result that feels 'true'.

Believing that transparency – a willingness to reveal what you know – not only strengthens your own practice but also, curiously, evokes further mysteries beyond language, is what lies behind the title of this book. Just as actors themselves often feel emotionally naked in front of the camera – and know that this is necessary – this book aims for a similar state of openness. I will begin by revealing my own hand; some parts of the story that led me to become a director.

I grew up loving actors and acting. My grandmother had studied singing in the 1920s, then worked in variety in Charlot's Revue in London's West End before becoming a more 'serious' actress (she used the term proudly), playing ingénue parts in productions such as *The Ghost Train*. She stopped when she gave birth to my mother at the relatively late age – for that period – of thirty-three. As a child I was entranced by her stories of life in the theatre and often played with the black metal box of greasepaints which she had kept intact since her years on the boards. It was the gleam in her eye when she recounted the camaraderie, the thrill of stage fright, the feat of memory she had achieved when she was asked to step into a lead role only three days before opening night – and managed to be word-perfect – that entranced me. It wasn't just the buzz and glitter she evoked, the late smoky nights in Soho after a show, the fans at the stage door (including her own beau, who became my grandfather). It was also the look in her eye that suggested she had touched something mysterious and essential: a sense of purpose, a wicked irreverence for what was considered proper in pursuit of what she felt to be true.

Beatrice Fox – 'Hunny'

She remained an entertainer throughout her life, but her stage was limited to the home, where she shone: laughing, telling stories, creating domestic beauty, but above all caring for others. She served, with a sense of duty and out of love, but for me she was a queen. I wished I had seen her on the stage. I would have led a standing ovation. Hunny, my Hunny! For that was the name I knew her by. Her stage name was Beatrice Fox, but the name Hunny evoked sweetness, bees, the good creatures who make all life possible.

My mother too dreamed of a life on stage, but her ambition was to be a singer. She gave birth to me when she was still a teenager, swiftly followed by my brother Nic, and was only able to study professionally when she reached her thirties. She aimed at opera, but a short-lived career touring the provinces singing in the chorus of an ice-skating show deflated her longings. She became a devoted music teacher and continued singing, passionately, in amateur opera troupes. Nic and I were often in the heartbreakingly sparse audience, witnessing the love and vigour, the energy and desire that amateurs demonstrate, doggedly, in pursuit of excellence.

Nic became a rock musician at sixteen, and was backing Chuck Berry on bass guitar at the Albert Hall by the time he was eighteen. And my father, though his *métier* was design and the properties of wood – some of my earliest memories are of playing in the saw-dust in his workshop while he worked, humming happily, late into the night – loved music, especially Beethoven. He would conduct to recordings as if the phrasing of the orchestra was in his hands. Years later I watched as he came alive when he stood up to address a crowded hall of students, lecturing on modernism. It wasn't just the excitement of the ideas that ignited his passion, it was the thrill of being watched, being heard, and being able to deliver. I saw the circuit of energy between performer and audience in which the speaker articulates, for himself and for those listening, ideas and experiences that had somehow previously remained vague, a dull outline. I was once again witnessing a form of theatrical presence, the occupying of an ancient space, an arena.

When we were tiny, I coerced my brother into participating in shows performed in our bedroom. Our bunk beds were the stage, a blanket used as a curtain. My mother and perhaps a lodger or two were the audience. At primary school I wrote plays and bossed around an often bewildered, but willing group of ten-year-old participants. And then at fourteen I was lent an 8mm camera and put the viewfinder to my eye. Framing the world – in black and white

– made my heart beat faster and clarified my sense of purpose, without my consciously knowing for a moment what that was. But I announced to a largely cynical and uninterested world that I was going to be a film director.

The road to this intoxicatingly thrilling and powerful place would prove to be more arduous and full of obstacles and deviations than I could ever have imagined. I left school at sixteen to prove I could honour my ambition, joined the London Film-makers' Co-operative (there was no film school at the time that accepted undergraduates), devoured hour upon hour of films from Warhol to Eisenstein, and, by and large, taught myself the rudiments of shooting and editing on out-of-date 16mm film stock in the ramshackle but extremely lively 'Arts Laboratory', a collectively run, idealistic endeavour. The results – the no-budget school of film-making – were abstract, anti-narrative and very short. But unlike many of the 'structuralist' film-makers in the co-op (whose passion, borrowing heavily from linguistic theory, was decoding the 'language' of cinema), my efforts always involved looking at people. I wanted to see the human face, the human body, illuminate the frame.

A foundation year at St Martin's School of Art taught me how to look – really look – in hour upon hour of life drawing. I joined a 'happenings' group. We performed on the London Underground and called it 'guerrilla theatre'. A few more years of washing up and chopping carrots in the steamy infernos of restaurant kitchens to earn money whilst painstakingly labouring at my 'underground' cinematic works (including several 'expanded cinema' events, which consisted of live action simultaneous with projected footage), led me circuitously to spend a year studying dance and choreography at The Place in London. Friends and family were puzzled. Dance? What did that have to do with cinema, with my stated ambitions? Nothing, on the surface, but a great deal underneath. It was attending class, day-in day-out, in whatever I 'felt' like doing, that taught me self-discipline. It was the collaborative endeavours of dancers working together in the rehearsal studio that taught me about the evolution of form in a process shared with others. And it was the crafting of my relationship as a choreographer with dancers that began to teach me how to direct performers. How to use their unique qualities. How to search for their genius. I stayed on at The Place for another couple of fruitful, physically demanding years.

With Jacky Lansley in Limited Dance Company, 1974

The decade that followed began with forming a dance company ('Limited Dance Company', co-directed with Jacky Lansley and so-called because it featured a limited amount of dance) and then morphed rapidly into a series of collaborations and solo shows in the world of performance art. These were sometimes played out in small theatres and art galleries, but above all in public spaces. We explored 'real-time' in slowly unfolding events or performance marathons and 'real-space' by putting on shows in swimming pools, ice rinks, squatted houses, abandoned warehouses, all of which became our arena. In cinematic terms, we were working 'on location'.

Berlin, 1976   *Death and the Maiden*, 1975

The audiences were enthusiastic but the spaces and places were inherently limited to one self-selecting type of crowd. Watching Patti Smith play live in Central Park to a huge, mixed audience, one hot summer afternoon in New York, on a stop-over in the middle of a performing and teaching tour of US art colleges, sparked in me a burning desire to occupy a larger stage.

I joined a music group, drawing on my mixed bag of skills as a performer, and embarked on several years of touring in Europe playing the festival circuit. This was an all-female group of improvising musicians – known as FIG – playing in heavyweight jazz festivals in France and Germany and in Communist Party festas across Italy. We occasionally shared the bill with such luminaries as Miles Davis and Chet Baker, but were musical anarchists and political renegades in the context of such virtuosos. I was by far the least skilled, musically, in this group and, later, in mixed ensembles, but developed a nice line in improvised lyrics – a kind of wild, deconstructed rap. Looking out at a sea of faces, feeling the power and attention of an enormous crowd, taught me more about timing, projection and presence – let alone stage fright – than any academic course could ever have provided.

FIG on tour, 1981

I called all these experiences cumulatively an immersion in 'avant-garde show business', because whilst the musical and theatrical forms we explored were far out on the edge, always pushing against convention, the audiences were sometimes huge and their expectations of being entertained were palpable. We simply had to deliver.

By the time I was back in London at the end of my twenties, having moved house multiple times, from squat to squat – a penniless and merciless way of keeping a roof over my head, for my line of work certainly did not pay – my performance collaborator Rose English and I had landed in a Georgian house in Bloomsbury that had previously been occupied by junkies for years. We barricaded ourselves in the house one freezing Christmas, cleaned the syringes out of the stinking lavatories, lit the fires, and assessed the situation. I decided to try again to do what I really wanted to do: make films. I would do it with what I had – nothing but raw experience – and where I was: an abandoned building that had once housed a sweatshop in the attic. This is where I filmed *Thriller* (1979) – a long (by my standards) short film that mashed up opera (*La Bohème*) film noir (*Psycho*) and linguistic philosophy (Marcuse,

Lacan, etc.), initially for no budget at all. The four performers were
Rose English and three ex-dancers from The Place. I edited the
resulting material through the nights in borrowed cutting rooms
and the film was finally shown at the Edinburgh Film Festival.
Its surprising success led me to venture into my first feature film,
The Gold Diggers (1983), co-written with Rose English and Lindsay
Cooper, the composer. And since then, by and large, film-making,
my first love, has been where I have continued to work.

Colette Laffont in *Thriller*

Along the way, restlessly seeking a deeper understanding of the
invisible worlds within, I studied meditation and peer counselling.
These practices helped me understand the inner lives of others, the
suffering and mental chaos, the longings, the inherent beauty in
each individual and the hidden dramas in every human life. Essential information for a writer/director and useful tools for relating to
actors and understanding their vulnerability.

This leapfrog through my autobiographical back-story – the rag-
bag mixture of the autodidact – is by way of providing a context
for all that follows in this book. My education as a film director has

been an intensely practical one. I have had no formal training in any aspect of the craft of cinema. Any ideas I have developed about working practice – my own and with a variety of performers – have evolved out of hands-on experience. They are conclusions drawn – often painfully – from some very public mistakes. I have also learnt, however, that the word 'mistake' is not necessarily pejorative. It's another word for risk-taking, which can lead to some very exciting discoveries.

So why write a book about working with actors?

It all started quite modestly as written responses to questions in a forum on my website. This was in the relatively early days of Internet traffic (before Facebook, Twitter, etc.) and it seemed at the time that I was the only film director who opened herself to direct dialogue on a website with the random self-selecting individuals who posted their questions. The traffic intensified, as did the debates. By and large the questions initially came from film students, screenwriters and a few directors (both aspiring and those with more experience), and from actors – all of whom expressed a need for a deeper understanding of each other's work. As the net widened, the threads were joined – no less enthusiastically – by a broader group. I gradually developed the idea for the book during so-called 'masterclasses' and repeated Q&A sessions following screenings of my films around the world, when I discovered that there are many people, working in a variety of professions, who are simply curious to know: just exactly what does a film director do with actors? What does the work consist of? How do you get them to do what you want? The confusion is a little wider than that: many people don't know what film directors do at all, either on set or at any other point in the long and varied processes involved in making a film. Even the editor of a respected film magazine was quoted as saying that once there's a shot list (literally, the list of shots you hope to achieve that day), the director doesn't really have to do anything else; the film somehow 'makes itself'. I wonder if he was ever on a film set?

Nevertheless, it is an understandable confusion. Making a film is a collaborative process, involving a great many people (look at the average end credits and start counting), each of whose work is crucial, yet the director is often seen as the 'author' of the film, even when he or she hasn't written the script. This authorship takes the form of decisions. Many, many decisions. The director works through the work of others, making choices, guiding and shaping the result at every moment; details of design, costume, location, camera and performance: every aspect of cinematic language, and these multiple choices then add up to a whole, a directed vision. The degree to which these choices are conscious and consistent is the degree to which the director has a coherent 'voice'.

For many people, however, this work remains confusingly invisible. They see the end result – the seamless consequence of the director's choices – but above all they see the actors. Almost everything else – sound, camerawork, design and music – is absorbed subliminally. As a director you learn about this phenomenon by the questions people ask once the film is complete. In my case, the first question film fans – and many journalists – often ask is: 'What was it like working with *x*?' (Whoever the 'star' was in the film they've just seen). More detailed questions about other aspects of the craft will come from those closer to the medium, but the fascination remains similar: a need to penetrate this mysterious working relationship, to find out what really goes on behind the scenes. And above all a longing to know – really know – the actor, and how it is that he or she has come to feel like an intimate friend.

How is this apparent intimacy between actor and audience achieved? Much of the answer lies in the actor's ability to be truly present at the moment of shooting; to arrive in the here and now at the word 'action'. The best actors achieve a sort of emotional transparency that invites an audience into the unfolding experience. But other clues lie in how the actor's work is supported and shaped by those behind the camera and in particular, the subtle alchemy of the relationship with the director. The influence of this relation-ship applies at every level of film-making, from the lowest budget to the enormous studio machine.

Not every part of this book will appear at first sight to apply to film-makers working – as I started out – on a shoestring. Some of the chapters in this book refer to members of a crew (hair and make-up artists, designers and so on) that a low-budget film-maker may not be able to afford. However, whether you are working with a crew of hundreds or doing it with a few friends, the same issues will apply. As soon as you point a camera at someone they become a performer. Even in a documentary, people tend to start performing 'being themselves'. And how the director relates to the performance, mirrors it, shapes it, edits it or just watches it, will profoundly influence the result. The more that this director/per-former relationship can be refined, clarified and strengthened, the more precisely the final film will be able to be shaped, in subtle and dramatic ways.

Strange as it may seem, I have learnt that many film directors are afraid of actors. Afraid of their power, afraid they might not be able to get what they want from them, afraid they won't gain their respect, afraid the actor will 'act up'. They may even, on occasion, refer to the actors as 'cattle' or 'soft props'. This all stems from ignorance of the actor's process and his or her deeper needs: needs that must be met in order to deliver a performance.

At the beginning of my full-time working life as a film director, following the decade in my twenties of choreography, music and performance art, I was obsessed by the visual, structural and con-ceptual aspects of cinema. I rejected conventional ideas of character and narrative. Despite having already experienced many fruitful and intense collaborations, I did not fully understand just how much time and energy – psychic, physical, mental and emotional – you have to invest in your relationship with an actor on film in order for it to work. You need to have respect for the actor's process and precise knowledge about what it consists of in order for your writing or your directing to come alive.

So what are the significant differences between acting for the cinema and other modes of performance? Performance artists often think of themselves as an image, or living object: the catalyst of an event, rather than a 'character'. Performance is seen as 'doing' – an activity that is being watched in real time rather than a part being played in imaginary time and space. In fact theatricality is sometimes sneered at and the idea of 'acting' can be seen as another word for pretence. Performance – when it is seen as art – is intensely visual and is often conceptual rather than representational.

Performing in *Berlin* on ice, 1976

Dancers also work in the sphere of the abstract – shaping movement through time and space in relation to both sound and silence – though, paradoxically, through a form of total physicality. Dance is a mercurial, top-to-toe, bone-and-muscle art-form. Musicians occupy the most metaphysical performance zone of all, in which a skilful relationship with an instrument is developed in the service of pure sound. The body of the musician is, in some sense, intentionally invisible, however interesting he or she may be to watch. For all of these artists working in the medium of performance, narrative is secondary and 'realism' is irrelevant. For these art-forms occupy their own reality and work to illuminate the here and now, evoking mysterious, ephemeral and non-verbal levels of existence rather than telling stories or pretending to be somewhere, someone, or something else.

Many aspects of these related disciplines apply to cinema as well. However, whilst cinematic 'truth' is not necessarily wedded to naturalism, feature films – and therefore also film actors – almost invariably work with story, character and authenticity of performance; something that needs to look, sound and feel 'real' on its own terms. Suspension of disbelief, acceptance of the imaginary as actual, and the transposition of the actor into the body and 'self' of another in a film builds on the history of storytelling, a reflection of (and means of reflecting on) what seems to be real. Despite increasing globalisation, this 'reality' is of course culturally specific and is linked to the visual and dramatic codes audiences in different countries find familiar and comprehensible. Bollywood musicals and Nordic minimalism, whilst being different facets of a cinematic prism, nevertheless rest on different assumptions about what is entertaining and meaningful for their respective audiences. But all films seem to aim at the same feeling of connectedness with the experiences unfolding on screen, as portrayed by actors.

To understand what it takes for the actor to occupy this space of connection – and potentially, what can help make him or her become an extraordinarily powerful presence on screen – a director has to become more observant than a detective. You have to learn to be more flexible and adaptable than you thought possible. You have to accept that you will make mistakes, to feel sometimes like a servant and at others like a tyrant. Mystifying the process – or your own role – will not help. But putting your focused attention on this aspect of your work, which is part technical, part personal, and often invisible (even to the actor), will open doors in ways you never thought possible. It is an area of the director's work that is difficult to learn except by doing it; and yet it is a complex bundle of skills that, once identified, can be endlessly refined.

This book does not attempt to examine other directors' ways of working with actors. It has no scholarly pretensions, no footnotes or references. I have limited its scope to my own direct experience. I learnt how to work with actors – following my work with dancers, performance artists and musicians – by trial and error, eventually including experience of acting on film myself in *The Tango Lesson* (1997). My past experiences as a choreographer, directing opera and working with musicians on stage and in recording studios have all helped. But I have learned that working with actors on film is a unique discipline.

From my first experience of pointing an 8mm camera at a face when I was fourteen years old, through multiple experiences with 'unknowns' and well-known actors until the present day, I continue to be entranced by actors, by the working process we share, and by the metaphysics of representation in such a physical medium. Cinema exists in time. Though it is constructed with great care and precision, it is not an object. You can't hold it or touch it. It must be projected through light. It eventually becomes a highly crafted and distilled experience, designed to capture and illuminate a moment, or series of moments. And these moments of height-ened experience are mostly embodied by the actors.

What you record on film (or digitally), however, is not necessar-ily what you see with the naked eye while you are shooting. The lens is more precise, ruthlessly microscopic, unforgiving. It can also hide, camouflage, distort. It reads light but doesn't always record experience. By the time the recorded image is embedded in the finished film it will have undergone an extraordinary number of changes. Changes in structure, cuts in scenes or sequences and also the choice of takes can tilt the whole film violently in one direction or another. Even by cutting in or out a microsecond earlier or later, a performance can be radically altered. In the later stages of the work on the image, skin tone can be changed in the grading suite; a glint in the eye exaggerated. The director is in control of all these changes, but can't edit or refine material that is not there. He or she can only work with the performance the actor has delivered.

Learning how to 'read' what the camera is seeing and recording, rather than just what you 'feel' experientially at the moment of shooting, comes from experience. Watching something that seemed extraordinary at the time but looks flat on screen, or the converse, something that felt small or banal but looks fascinating, is a great teacher. Through a process of observation of what happens when you attempt to transfer theatrical excitement – the thrill of the 'live' event – onto the screen, I have learned about the crucial differences between live performance and acting for the camera. Theatre and cinema are closely related, but the demands on the actor and what the camera will 'read' are very different. Navigating these shifts and discovering how to recognise and solve the inevitable problems that arise during the speed and intensity of the working process has taught me about the necessity of a flexible, individual approach to actors. There are no rules that apply to everyone. I have become deeply suspicious of any 'method' that attempts to be universally applicable.

Working under the extreme pressure of a shoot, often exhausted, and knowing that what you do will be there for ever (or for as long as celluloid or digital information turns out to last), brings with it a heightened awareness (or panic); also a need for speedy reactions and quick results, both for actors and directors. As a film director you learn to look for what works, and may not even have time to figure out why.

This book will, I hope, bring some clarity to the process. What I describe – the lessons learnt from my experience on films with budgets both (fairly) big and non-existent or very small – may or may not work for every film-maker, and may not apply to every actor. Experienced actors and directors may well feel I am stating the obvious. This book is certainly not intended to prescribe a way of working. At best it may serve as a tool to sharpen awareness and improve what you do, however you want to do it, whether you are working in film, or in a parallel medium, and whether you agree with me or, on the contrary, clarify your own views by arguing with mine. For ultimately, this is a book that examines different facets of working practice, and – vitally – of working relationships, covering some of the practical tools of the trade as well as the finer points of working psychology in what is a profoundly social medium.

I have structured the chapters in chronological order, following the sequence in which a film is made. They cover the various processes involved in the period known as 'pre-production', then the shoot and finally post-production and beyond. However, the only process covered in any depth is performance; looked at mostly from the director's point of view, but with an attempt to describe and understand the actor's as well. The director's work on the script, cinematography, design, music, sound mix and all the other vital, massively varied and detailed aspects that go to make up this mongrel medium (any of which can often easily preoccupy directors to the exclusion of any detailed work with the actors) are not described in this book, except inasmuch as they impact on the work with the actors.

As I wrote, I found I was often addressing some invisible individual: possibly an aspiring director, searching for clues about how to do better work – or how to work at all. I gradually realised that I might also be addressing my younger self, sharing information that I craved at the time but could only find out by having a go, blindly. I also discovered, while writing, that I was finding out what I really thought about what I was doing, more or less intuitively, in the hurly-burly of my film-making in more recent years. As film shoots get shorter one has to work faster and there is less and less time for reflection. The act of trying to write it all down, simply and clearly, began to clarify what was achieved largely by just getting on with it. I'm still trying to sort out whether I agree with myself, as many of these chapters do not really provide answers but rather ask ongoing questions. But this aspect of the writing process – who I am talking to – explains the tone of address throughout.

A word about audiences. A film needs to be watched. It still exists, in some platonic sense, if it languishes on a shelf or in a digital file without an audience. But it is only when it is seen that it fulfils its purpose. Making a film is like having one half of an imaginary conversation. The act of receiving, experiencing and digesting it is the other half. When you make a film, striving day after day for months or, more usually, years, you live with a hope that it will land, one day, in other people's consciousness, in a way consistent with your intentions. Only when you watch it for the first time with an audience do you begin to sense if you have succeeded. And if you keep your ears open you will hear the audience talk about . . . the actors. They are your ambassadors, your messengers, your gatekeepers. You need them and you need to understand them. But they also need you. You create the arena in which they can work, you invite them in to it, and the end result is in your hands. It's a profoundly interdependent relationship.

I have at times heard directors and actors express fear and dismay at the prospect of revealing their secret processes. The fear is that by breaking the mystique, something delicate, mysterious and instinctive will be destroyed. I have my superstitions too, but I would argue that clarity makes us more robust. In attempting to find accurate words to describe and honour the process, nothing will be lost. Mystification of working practice reduces it to private ownership, or perhaps an inherent gift, rather than something that can be learned. Sharing information makes us all stronger. If you believe, as I do, that learning is an infinite process – that you never 'arrive' – and that even instinct can be consciously refined, then the attempt to elucidate working practice can only help everyone get better at it.

Nevertheless, at every stage of writing this, I have had feelings of doubt and trepidation. In particular, I puzzled over how to give concrete examples of what I was talking about, by referring to experiences with particular actors. Whenever I tried to, it felt like a betrayal of trust. There is something extraordinarily private in the relationships I have forged with each of the actors I have worked with. It is a point of principle for me to never gossip about any of them. Whilst I am happy to praise them, I never offer salacious anecdotes or 'revelations'. I have included some examples of working practice with individuals where I felt it was necessary to be more specific, but eventually I decided the best strategy to overcome this deliberate obstacle of confidentiality would be to interview some of the actors I have worked with, to draw them out and let them use their own words to talk about the process as they see it. In this way no confidentiality would be broken, and there would also be a variety of points of view that would bring to life some of the concepts I explore. I interviewed the actors after I had finished writing most of the following chapters. Some of what they have to say echoes my own conclusions. Sometimes their views contradict my own. So much of the working process is a question of perception. And our work is so grounded in relationship, the sheer magic of collaboration, that dialogue really is everything.

So in that spirit I offer up what I have learned so far, alone and together with my beloved actors, and hope it will be useful.

Part One

Preparation

I

Embodiment (the actor's work)

Actors are what most people 'see' in a film. Audiences don't look at the camera-work, the sets, the lighting, the design, the structure of the story – any of the multiple cinematic choices that the writer, the director and his or her team have laboured over – with anything resembling the same amount of attention they give to the actor. This is a testimony to the inherent power of the actor's trade. When an actor seems fully to occupy the screen it becomes very close to the experience of having intimate access to someone you love. Many people even experience the actors as the authors of the film – as somehow having created their own characters, or written what they say. (Sometimes, of course, they have.) The better the script – more generally thought of as the real 'authorship' – and the clearer and more powerful the direction (directors too are seen as 'auteurs', at least in the European tradition), the more likely an audience is to have the experience of watching something 'real' unfold in present time. But it depends on the actors' ability to be fully 'there' at the moment of shooting; fully occupying the cinematic space and inviting us in to join them.

On screen, whatever else is going on, the human being will always dominate the field of vision. The human face is invariably the focal point, the zone of emotional identification, an endless source of fascination. When projected on a big screen the sheer scale of the image may take us back to a primal, infantile relationship with the looming faces of those whose love and care we depended on as babies. We merge, seamlessly, with these adored beings; experientially we take them inside us and we become them. Or perhaps the fascination is just an appetite to know more about our own species; an intense form of curiosity. The magnetic appeal of the human face applies across the whole cinematic spectrum, from every independent low-budget work of fiction to the biggest blockbuster. Even the most elaborate special effects cannot compete, in the end, with something that directly touches the experience of the viewer. The emotional (and intellectual) connectedness that most of us long for in a film, as in life, usually comes via the face, body and voice of another human being, in this case the actor.

It is in this sense that the actor embodies the writer's work and the director's vision. He or she 'carries' the film with his or her physical presence. However adventurous the cinematography and whatever the director may do later in the cutting room and in post-production, with music, colour grading and sound effects – or any of the other subtle ways it is possible to help a performance – the material has to have been offered up by the actor in the first place. Without that, there is nothing. So for a director, understanding how to work with actors is, in many ways, the most important, delicate and powerful skill he or she must develop. And this skill must be developed amidst a maelstrom of activity. You have to do your most subtle work and be most eagerly attentive when you feel pulled in a thousand different directions by an army of people. As director you may well be exhausted before you even begin the shoot, as pre-production work is equally demanding and will have been going on for months, often after years of struggle in what is known as 'development hell' – the long, arduous battle to get a film financed. Once the shoot begins, the juggernaut of the film-making machine keeps relentlessly moving forward. There is little or no time for contemplation. You work fast, using your instinct. So the key to keeping on track is preparation. And this vitally necessary, meticulous preparatory process – the research and development of a clear vision of how the film will look and sound – becomes your armoury in the battle to do good work.

The preparation for your work with the actors really begins with the script, long before you meet the cast or even know who they will be. If you are a writer/director you will have laboured for months or years, refining images, characters, story and structure. You will have worked and reworked every scene, developing tension and contradiction, distilling the narrative to its essential elements, and writing the dialogue. A common misconception is that a script largely consists of what people say. Whilst this is true of most plays, cinema is a profoundly visual medium. Every image in a film script is described and evoked, as well as every action and the environments in which it will all take place. The screenwriter invents – or finds – a world. The screenwriter who understands actors also develops an architecture of the unsaid. What people may be feeling and thinking but not saying – the inner contradictions – needs to be mapped out. This is as important as the words that are spoken, if not more so, for the depth and complexity of the final film.

Once the script is 'there', and the search for financing and the wheels of the production machine start to turn, the director shifts his or her attention to the crucial question of casting. This is a thrilling and often terrifying moment, for the abstract vision is about to become real. Your film, which has only existed in your mind or on the page – whether paper or electronic – is about to have a body.

Quentin Crisp as Queen Elizabeth I in *Orlando*

2

Casting (crossing the magic line)

Here, and throughout this book, I am assuming that the choice of cast (and all other 'creative' decisions) ultimately rests with the director. This assumption is based on the largely European tradition of director-driven film-making, because that is the process I know at first hand. In the United States many films are producer-driven, at least in the first instance. This means, in practice, that the producers may initiate the original idea, option a book, commission the script, attach some lead actors, and then hire a director. This way of working sets up a drastically different dynamic between the director and the actors, and of course shifts the sense of authorship of the film as a whole from the director to a producer or production company. Both methods have validity and have historically produced great results. But the choice of cast – including surprising choices – sets a tone, a direction, from the outset, that has ramifications throughout the entire ensuing process. For many directors, therefore (as in my own case), control of casting is absolutely key.

There's a good reason why the first question many people ask about a film is, 'Who's in it?' If you accept that a film will often stand or fall on the quality of the actors' performances, then casting can be seen as the single most important set of decisions you make as a director. Not only the actors' skill, but also the relationship that you are able to build with them and the clarity with which you are able to communicate, are the factors that will determine the extent to which the script and your directing is going to come to life on the screen.

The actor becomes the carrier of all your hopes and has to replace the abstract ideal you will have carried in your mind for months or years. The actor's face and body is always going to be different in practice from the one you imagined when you were writing (if you are a writer/director), or the fantasy you had as a director when you first read someone else's script – unless of course you already knew who you wanted and ended up with them. Even then, at the definitive moment of casting you are crossing the magic line – from a platonic ideal, to complex human reality. I have heard some directors describe this as the beginning of a long series of inevitable compromises, or even disappointments, for nothing can ever live up to the perfect fantasy. My own experience, on the contrary, is that casting can be an ecstatic moment of transformation from the abstract to the concrete, from a thought or a hope to a real person. Your imagination finds its human form in a mysterious and thrilling moment of transition.

But if it is so crucial, how do you learn to choose the right actor? How do you know when you have met the one you need? Part of the answer – the conscious, methodical part of the process – lies in careful, extensive research into the actor's previous work. The other part lies in knowing how to identify your instinct – and listen to it – even when you don't consciously understand why, for example, you're feeling trepidation at a safe, obvious choice or excitement about a risky one. Perhaps a role resonates perfectly with an actor's physicality or with their own personal or professional history (the so-called 'baggage' they bring to a part), but nevertheless you feel something is missing. Or, when you meet, an actor may seem to offer him- or herself to the working process with a quality of generosity that is inspiring and invigorating, even if he or she doesn't seem like a perfect 'fit' with the role.

The casting director

Turning the long imagining of your dream cast into a reality takes time and a lot of research, during which a director's best ally is a good casting director (if you can afford one, of course). The work of a casting director is a source of mystification to most people outside the film industry. What he or she does, essentially, is recommend a variety of possible actors for each role, based on the script and on discussions with the director and producer. Some directors (and producers) already know who they want for certain roles – or think they do – but a casting director may come up with a surprisingly different suggestion that works better. He or she may initiate a hunt for unknown actors and will organise auditions, based on a wide, detailed knowledge of a huge number of actors. He or she will also be a sounding board for the director, a co-conspirator in the often lengthy process they will share; a source of solidarity in moments of disappointment, and inspiration in moments of uncertainty. The process begins in pre-production and may even continue into the shoot. Organising a shooting schedule that works for everyone in the cast – each of whom may have multiple other commitments – is a complex art-form in its own right, and sometimes actors are lost in the process. Last-minute juggling and emergency casting rethinks are familiar experiences for most directors.

The relationship with a casting director can be intensely creative. It is the place where both of you can be caustically honest, airing your doubts before you commit yourselves to an irrevocable decision. It is, by definition therefore, a private discussion. In my own experience (working mostly with London-based casting director Irene Lamb and with Heidi Levitt in Los Angeles), many long conversations are had, many DVDs are viewed, long days of auditions are sweated through. Lists are written and discarded, revised and revisited. We brainstorm again and again, we lay out images of actors in different combinations, to get a feeling of a possible ensemble, the effect of one presence on another. It is a collaborative process but the final choice must ultimately be the director's. No decision is taken lightly, whether over the lead roles or the so-called minor parts. I am even a fanatic about extras and will study photos of faces for crowds.

Rather in the way that all football fans are highly opinionated about the formation of the ideal team, everyone (including audiences) seems to have an opinion about casting. And this process begins early in the development of a film. People will read a script and think they can 'see' someone in a role. Producers or financiers often want the faces that they think will 'sell', for obvious and understandable reasons. Even a low-budget film costs money and is a substantial investment with uncertain returns. The film does not yet exist except in the imagination of its makers. No one knows how it will turn out. Known faces appear to anchor this imaginary world in some kind of reality or to offer a guarantee of success. This may lead to an absurdly narrow 'A' list, with other actors insultingly labelled as 'B' or 'C' categories. This view of reliable 'marquee' names has taken a battering in recent years, as a big name does not necessarily guarantee big box office. But the myth of the equation – stars equal success – lingers on. It is possible to miscast for these kinds of strategic financial reasons, or over-cast (big names in small roles which can unbalance a film). The best casting decisions feel both surprising and inevitable, as if no other actor could play the role.

Once you have finally arrived at the ideal choice, the actor will be sent the script, or part of it. Then – if the actor is interested – there is an audition or face-to-face meeting. You talk, and feel each other out. And then you agonise, alone or with the casting director and maybe the producers. Eventually you take the plunge. Once you have offered an actor the part, then you are responsible for that choice and must move forward with certainty and commitment, so it is vital to dispel in advance any doubts you may have. But the decision-making process can be fraught with anxiety, for so much is riding on it. The bare bones of the procedures involved don't begin to describe the intensity of making the choices.

Instinct

In the end the decision to offer a role to an actor is often intuitive. As a way of identifying my own instinct, I have learnt to trust my gut. When I meet the right actor, something starts to flutter in that part of my body. Indeed, often my body seems to know before I can rationalise why. Intuition or instinct is perhaps a very rapid form of thought, happening faster than you can hear yourself think in words. It can be confusing, because sometimes fear or excitement feels very similar to instinct. But genuine instinct doesn't seem to be really an emotional state, though it may bring feelings with it. More often it is a sober but speedy state of non-analytical clarity.

Tilda Swinton during preparation for *Orlando*

Sometimes a long decision-making process about casting is irrelevant. As a writer/director, you may think you know who you want to work with even before you write a word of a screenplay (I wrote *Orlando* (1992) with Tilda Swinton in my mind's eye, for example). Or perhaps the script is nearly finished and you suddenly remember a person you have seen in a film or a play, or met at a party. Their image or presence has stayed with you for years before you get to work with them. In that sense, from the actor's point of view, a warm or interesting encounter is never wasted, even if at the time it does not seem to lead anywhere. These initial casting ideas – the images of who you think you want whilst you are writing – are worth pursuing, vigorously. But they are also worth throwing away. Perhaps they served their purpose during the long, arduous development of an idea but are no longer relevant.

But what happens if you are sure, instinctively, about an actor, offer the role, and he or she then turns it down? I have found it best not to try to persuade an actor to take a part, though it's very tempting to go after them in hot pursuit. How can they not see it's perfect for them? The universe starts to feel out of balance when your passionate certainty is met with indifference or rejection. But the most useful philosophical approach is to assume that if they don't want to do it, then it probably isn't right, for them or for you. It is certainly more constructive to assume there will be somebody else who is better or more appropriate. If you take this attitude, not only do you avoid bitter disappointment, but the hunt for the right person becomes like a hunt for buried treasure.

Casting famous actors

Casting famous actors brings its own demands: on the budget, on everyone's expectations, and on your working practice. Despite the pervasive and ever-growing influence of the Internet – now the biggest source of consumption of the moving image – and the rapid development of excellent writing and performance for television (once considered the poor cousin of movie-making), cinema remains an enduring and monumental form. It is still widely perceived as the biggest arena of the imagination in which to discover – and also to remember – who we are and why we're here.

This power is partly due to the sheer size of the projected image.

Experientially we sit in the dark, we enter the world of light and are enveloped by it. The actors who work in this arena are projected onto the screen, project themselves into a huge cultural space and are projected onto, emotionally, by a mass audience. These familiar, haunting and powerful two-way projections in this dense, distilled form often have real value, humanly and aesthetically. The dim, vague outline of experience becomes sharp. A film can feel like an awakening from the torpor of everyday life. But this is not the same as the false, glittering value to which cinema and famous actors are so often elevated. The cult of celebrity and worship of fame is a distortion of cinematic power and a measure of most people's feelings of invisibility. It is also a consequence of the audience's imaginary intimacy with 'stars'.

As the 'face' of cinema, well-known actors have to deal with the stresses of celebrity as well as enjoying its privileges. They can be taken off-course by its excesses. With fame comes power, of a sort, but also certain kinds of human loss. People become inauthentic around those who are famous. Interactions become stilted or invasive. People project their hopes and fears, their desires and their resentments onto the famous face. They feel they know the person they have gazed at on the big screen, for hours at a time, in the darkness, safety and anonymity of the cinema. These projections (the pun is significant) can take extreme forms: worship or hatred; adulation or envy; or a mixture of both. Any form of projection is unstable and has little to do with the real person. Audiences will confuse the role with the actor, or the way they look with who they inherently are. Actors themselves can become confused about their true identity and their intrinsic value as human beings.

All this means that the actor develops both a need for 'real' relationships and an acute sense of inauthentic, exaggerated, or needy interactions. The director may be just as subject to fantasies and projections about the famous actor as anyone else. This will be an impediment in developing a relationship. So decoding fame, understanding its complexities, and being responsible for your own weird behaviour around someone famous is an essential part of your task.

It doesn't help to start throwing your weight around as a director to prove how unimpressed you are. Nor does it help to be cringingly humble and reverential. I have fallen into both traps at times and they don't go anywhere useful. It is important to reach past your own projections onto the individual actor, beware of being inappropriately intimate (feeling you know the person better than you do), and remember to concentrate on what you are there to do, which is to make something bigger than both of you: the film.

'Oscar-winning' actors may be useful and impressive to financiers but these forms of recognition are not necessarily important for the director. What really counts is that you respect your actors, have genuine admiration for their work and are not over-impressed by their celebrity or their awards. Without this attitude you won't be able to do your best work – and neither will they.

If you approach a very well-known actor to play a part, it will most often be with a definite offer. It is rare to find a 'star' who is prepared to audition, either formally or in the disguised setting of a 'meeting'. (On the other hand, some actors might well want to audition you.) American actors are sometimes more open, modest and matter-of-fact than British or European actors about the audition process. It is not seen as a humiliating test but rather an opportunity to try something out that might be interesting. (Elle Fanning, Christina Hendricks and Alessandro Nivola all generously auditioned for *Ginger & Rosa* (2012), for example, even though they are all distinguished, experienced actors.)

The quality of your initial encounters with actors will give you a preview of how the work might unfold. I have only once ignored the painful reality of a difficult first meeting, to my cost, hoping the dynamic might change 'later'. Actors tend to show themselves to you right away – perhaps everyone does – and it is wise to take note. As a director, your ability to inspire confidence in any initial encounter, even if you are less experienced than the actor, is crucial. And however famous the actor is, it is you – and you alone – who will be responsible for the film as a whole, so you need to keep your head, trust your gut and honour your role, even if you don't feel up to it. You and the actor may both secretly be feeling fraudulent, in any case, and undeserving. These are just feelings, though they have their place. A healthy distrust of fame and of your own authority means you are reaching towards authenticity in your relationship, right from the start.

Later, on set, you will need to remember that, in addition to all your other time-consuming and demanding directorial responsibilities, you must have something to give to the actor, even when he or she is very well known, older than you, or much more experienced than you are. Your gift to them may not come in the form of directorial 'instructions' but by creating a space in which they can work freely, or by daring to be an accurate mirror for them. Sometimes you just need to get out of the way, stand back and admire. But nevertheless you cannot 'abandon' experienced actors and expect them to do it all, just because they can already do it so well. With care and courage a director may, at any level of experience, be able to help a great actor discover something new and become even greater.

3

Auditions (what really happens)

Auditions are the standard way of meeting a variety of actors for smaller parts, and are often the only way to discover new people for lead roles too. Auditions are a difficult process and a peculiarly artificial way to meet people. It takes care and artfulness to run them. The actor can feel humiliated by a process in which most of those turning up will be turned down. He or she may feel judged by unclear standards, unsure whether to push him- or herself forward; whether to try and resemble the part being cast, or, on the contrary, to hold back and 'be himself'. (As every actor knows, though, what we mean by 'self' can be changeable and subject to multiple influences: ultimately, the idea of 'self' is an illusion. For this reason, incidentally, the instruction 'just be yourself' is worse than useless as a direction at any moment in the working process.)

The director and casting director, meanwhile, are themselves often feeling anxious in the audition room, well aware of the discomfort of the actor, trying to be compassionate human beings and yet also having to be ruthless in pursuit of the right choice for the part. And although auditions are inherently an unstable experience, they are often an eerily accurate guide to any future working relationship. There are always clues in the quality of interaction. So, from the director's point of view, it is a process that demands alertness and focus. You don't want to miss any quality in the actor. You are searching, passionately, with curiosity and optimism. Many factors can make an audition seem to 'work' and suddenly feel worthwhile, rather than an agonising slog. It is always a relief when an actor has a sense of humour, is willing to do anything you ask without false 'pride' and is aware of the job the director is trying to do. That way you feel, 'There is no resistance here: I can work with this person.' Anything seems possible.

But there has to be the right fit for the role as well – or the right look, or age and so on – and these factors may mean an actor is turned down for the part, despite he or she clearly being excellent in every way. One hopes that an actor will not take rejection personally. A meeting is never wasted. One remembers a face, a warm encounter, an intelligent exchange. I have often called people back for something else, another time, another film. From the actor's point of view, therefore, it may be helpful to think of an audition as a useful way of saying hello. It can also be approached as a meditation: an exercise in being fully present and open to every suggestion. By being generous with his or her energies in this way the actor can use the audition to learn something new about his or her limits and how to move past them to discover hidden abilities. With this attitude, whatever the outcome, there will have been something of value in the experience.

Elle Fanning auditioning for *Ginger & Rosa*

Many actors worry about how to behave at auditions and place a lot of emphasis on doing and speaking. It is often more effective to take attention away from 'doingness' . . . i.e. stop worrying about 'performance' and put your attention on relating to the other people in the room. In this way the actor will come into the present and 'be'. This sense of 'presence' is, in any case, the apparently mysterious quality most directors are looking for on film. The director and casting director can help with this by trying to put the actor at ease, but sometimes everyone just has to accept the tension in the room and attempt to look past it.

The director may be so preoccupied with trying to visualise a series of actors, one after another, in a role they have imagined for so long, that a state of anxious torpor starts to pervade the room. This is partly because, in reality, the director often knows within seconds of an actor walking into the room whether or not he or she is right for a role. There is already enough information to make an intuitive decision. Out of politeness and human decency the director then attempts to have a conversation to draw the actor out. First impressions are not always right. But a kind of animal instinct takes over during the process. It's not just the look, or tone of voice. It's a kind of energetic emanation that you become aware of: multiple small signals that tell you whether this might work or not. And you have to trust this instinct, for later on, in the shoot, it will become your most important asset.

4

Money (and other exchanges)

Once the casting choices have been made in principle, the producers start to work on the deals with the actors' agents. At this point, the distorting demon of money starts to come into play, too. Money is a live issue at every stage of film-making. Films are expensive to make – often extremely expensive. They are high-risk enterprises and no one knows if they will succeed financially. If an actor is well-known the financiers hope that this will guarantee some box-office success, which puts enormous pressure on the actor and can also correspondingly greatly unbalance the fee structure of the cast and crew. In fact, the economic exchanges in a film, including wildly varying levels of payment to individuals, are often a deeply distorted reflection of their true value, just as the economic success or failure of the finished film is not necessarily a true measure of its inherent value, aesthetically, politically, cinematically or humanly.

Once the film is financed, the producers may control the budget and payments, but are usually constantly monitored by the financiers. Cinema is an art-form that has to be run like a business. But the end product is volatile and the structures of power and control are complex. Though the producers may employ the actors, technically, the director (at least in the European tradition), is also effectively the actor's employer, by virtue of choosing him or her, even though he or she does not control their payment and may not even know what it is. (I deliberately keep myself uninformed about actors' fees.) This contradictory balance of power remains even if, ironically, the actor is paid a great deal more for a few weeks' work than the director is paid for a year: it can lead to some complicated underlying dynamics.

The correct, creative allocation of the money in the budget to ensure the vision of the film is realised in its entirety and to its fullest potential – or sometimes just to scrape by and make it at all – is a huge part of the producers' work. A good producer is a vigorously creative and adaptable force in the evolution of a film. But in certain instances, at the low-budget end of the spectrum, directors may need to convince actors to work with them when they can't pay them very much, or even anything at all. This can feel extremely awkward.

Within the film industry as a whole (as within most industries) there is an exchange of cash for labour. If you can give people money for their time, they will give their time to you. A wage or fee enables them to live their lives in the way that they need to do. On the surface it is a very simple equation (though who ultimately profits from this exchange in an industry that aims to make a profit is another question, a bigger one than can be addressed here). Nevertheless, if you can give actors reasonable money for their time then, at least in that basic sense, you don't have to ask yourself how to convince them to surrender themselves to what may well be an extremely demanding experience. But sometimes, despite the best combined efforts of you and your producers, there is still little or no money available to pay anyone. You are then in the low- or no-budget zone of film-making, increasingly familiar to anyone starting out, or indeed anyone wanting to take what are perceived as risks in a self-confessedly 'risk-averse' industry.

As a consequence, the reality of many independent film-makers' existence is that you often have to ask favours of people. (I have done it many times over.) In these instances you have to think of it as an exchange, asking yourself what you can give to a person that will make it worth them giving their time and energy to you. For example, if you are asking actors to work for free for a day, what can you give back to help them feel valued rather than exploited? Perhaps you can give them roles of a kind they've never had before, or at the very least an interesting working experience. You can make them feel involved in the development of a script, a respected collaborator. Or perhaps you can look at them in a way that they have never been looked at before, giving them a quality of attention as an actor they may always have wanted but never received. In these circumstances they won't care (so much) that you can't pay them, because they've been given experiences that are, ultimately, more valuable to them than money. I have found that most people would rather work for nothing on an interesting idea than get paid to work on rubbish. But actors have to eat and pay the rent. You can't be greedy with their energy or make unrealistic demands. You have to earn the trust of actors (and of other collaborators) by respecting their time. It is rare to be able to ask somebody to work with you full-time for a year for no pay, for example. Part-time, maybe, if the desire and motivation is there. But as a rule you have to be sensitive to certain limits.

Whatever the nature of the exchange of work for money – historically always unstable for all artists: think of the great composers and their 'patrons', or starving painters whose work makes millions for others after their deaths, or black musicians whose riffs and melodies were appropriated by the white rock 'n' roll industry – you always have the choice to focus on value of a different kind. For some actors the development process itself is what thrills them: a pleasurable adventure, with all its twists and turns.

I have been blessed again and again by an attitude of generosity on the part of actors during these long unpaid periods. Tilda Swinton, for example, frequently stood shoulder to shoulder with producer Christopher Sheppard and me during a five-year process of raising money to make the 'un-makeable' *Orlando*. It was an epic adventure which demanded a lot of stamina, as one financial catastrophe succeeded another. This hidden process, and the quality of friendship and solidarity in adversity that evolved in the relationship, became part of the feeling of the finished film.

With Tilda Swinton trying to fund-raise for *Orlando*
in New York City, 1989

Simon Abkarian, likewise, gave himself unstintingly to the
development process of *Yes* (2004), long before any financing
was in place, and his role became the richer for it. And the entire
cast of *Rage* (2009) was paid pro rata – i.e. every actor, known or
unknown, was paid the same minimum daily rate. This produced
an atmosphere of collegiality, generosity and mutual respect.

Wrestling with film financing and attempting to create a just and
fair allocation of funds is something that has preoccupied me from
my very first feature. *The Gold Diggers* – made with an all-female
crew, in part to open up a 'closed-shop' industry – had an entirely
egalitarian fee structure. We were all – cast and crew alike, including
Julie Christie – paid a flat rate of £25 per day. I discovered, eventually, that this so-called equality worked against those of us who put
in many more hours, but that's another matter. The principle was
what counted at the time, and a desire for the politics of the process
to reflect the ideas embedded in the end product, for the themes
of the film included the relationship between high finance and
film-stars – between banking and what is considered 'bankable'.

Julie Christie outside the Bank of England in *The Gold Diggers*

Whatever the budget and whatever pay scale you are working on, it is crucial as a director that you communicate to your crew and actors that the true value of their collaboration cannot be measured in money, or by its lack. This is not to justify an unjust distribution of wealth in what can be a ruthless and exploitative industry. But the real economy of a creative collaboration is a gift economy. Each gives to the other what they can, and willingly. When an actor's time starts being measured only in cash you have a problem. It's the default position people take when they feel undervalued, in an industry that takes economic distortion as the norm.

I once received a post about the budget of *Rage* on the forum of my website. The writer, hearing that *Rage*, widely advertised as a 'low-budget' film, had cost a million dollars, said, 'I just don't find it very interesting or justifiable that "only" a million dollars was spent on this film. That doesn't impress me.' The post ended with the question: 'Must art steal from life in order to enrich it?'

As the budget figures for films are often quoted but rarely ana-lysed or discussed, I was grateful for the opportunity to try to explain how it is that a minimalist film like *Rage*, (aesthetically naked, in the sense of a form being laid bare) and considered ultra-low budget by Hollywood standards, can nevertheless end up costing $1 million, which for most people sounds like a huge sum of money. I wrote a long, detailed response explaining how this figure broke down. An abbreviated version of my response is as follows:

> Money is so often the root of all divisiveness and misunderstanding, and film budgets are no exception, so I am going to try and be as clear, detailed and transparent as possible. First, the million-dollar figure is the true cost of finishing the film, not the sum raised for shooting it. We struggled for some months to bring the budget down as low as possible, to follow a 'no waste' principle, to be as joyfully minimalist in the process of its making as the script intended the film to be as a viewing experience. We borrowed money to finance the development and eventually took out a second mortgage on my flat in London in order to get it off the ground. A private individual who had never been involved in movies before enjoyed the script and decided to invest $300,000. A second person invested $25,000. Between them this was just enough to cover the actual cost of shooting the film, covering the hard costs of renting a small amount of equipment, a studio (a small space in Harlem) and paying each of the fourteen actors the same Equity/SAG minimum for just two days' work each, and the small crew at the union minimum rates.
>
> The two producers and myself deferred our fees. This means that during the working process itself you don't get paid, and then, in theory, when the film is sold, following payment of the sales agent's commission and expenses, and whatever repayment has been negotiated with your investors, you get your fee, or part of it, somewhere down the line. But the reality of 'independent' film-making, outside of mainstream genres, is that this very rarely happens. I have accepted deferment of my fees as the cost of working on films which are for me a personal, poetic and political necessity. This is not the kind of thing one advertises, as for most people the idea of sympathy for the financial woes of film-makers is, understandably, a laughable concept.

Having decided to go for it and make the film for the cash available without exploiting anyone – except, arguably ourselves – we had, nevertheless, a film in the digital can and a theoretical budget for finishing it. This is where the million-dollar figure comes in. On paper, if everyone was paid, including the costly post-production laboratory expenses of taking a digitally filmed movie through to 35mm print and commercially projectable digital format, with the sound mixed in a large enough studio to survive in a big cinema, we arrived at the sum of a million dollars.

Arguably, one could make a film cheaper by doing it digitally from start to finish, involving almost no one else, and putting it out on the Internet. This may be the way forward for some types of film, and we discussed it as a strategy for *Rage*. However there is a counter-argument to the digital cottage-industry approach. Even a film like *Rage*, by having such a small crew (I operated the camera myself, for example) does in a sense steal work from others who would otherwise be employed in one capacity or another. A film is not a solitary process, like writing a book or painting. It is a collaborative medium, an interface of art and industry, and therefore money is involved for those people – from sound recordists to editors to lab technicians – who depend on being paid to eat and pay the rent.

As for your question 'Must art steal from life in order to enrich it?' Taken literally, I don't think that the money that went into *Rage* was 'taken' from anywhere else. Global economies lurching in and out of recession seem to indicate that there is not a finite fund of money with a limit, but rather a mutable process of financing in crisis. Money seems to be a fiction that depends, in the capitalist system, on confidence. With *Rage* I hoped that one of the central themes of the film – the way in which the pursuit of profit impoverishes us all – might have its own subtle impact and do its work in the slow and strangely immeasurable way that art functions. And I believe that art is not theft but gift, even if the gift seems unwanted when it is first offered.

This response to the comment on my website applies primarily to low-budget film-making, but has wider implications. Once you start examining the ethics and morality of the economics of film-making, you are led inexorably into a wider argument about the value of labour involved in creating art of all kinds. Whilst many people in the film industry would rather think of the endeavour as a business – and there's no business like show business – it can never be unproblematically described as utilitarian. A film is not food, medicine, or transport. Actors and film technicians are not cooks, doctors, or road-builders. But if you believe that music, dance, performance, literature and films feed, heal and transport us in another sense that is equally but differently necessary to our survival, then those who work towards excellence in those spheres also deserve to be paid.

The question of exactly how much it makes sense to pay people, on both sides of the camera, remains open. The larger the budget, the more these sums are driven by a quasi-objective notion of what an actor, for example, is 'worth'. This is measured in terms of how many people a marquee 'name' seems to draw into the cinema, and therefore how many tickets are sold. But the recipe for commercial success is, in fact, uncertain and somewhat mysterious. A large advertising budget will attract a large audience by stimulating an appetite, and a familiar face may be a draw, but the equation is not precise. Nobody really seems to know why one film succeeds and another does not. This provides a sound reason for developing your own criteria for what works and has inherent value. Most actors would rather be valued for what they can give than for what they can earn.

The gift

There is another definition of 'gift' that does not relate directly to money, but is an additional aspect of the hidden 'economy', or underlying structure, of film-making and other art-forms. There are many myths about the nature of individual ability – particularly that some people are inherently gifted, or talented – and very little understanding about the circumstances that nurture gifted-ness. Interestingly, in the film industry, actors (and directors) are referred to as 'the talent'. This terminology implies that all the others are 'merely' technicians or administrators, but without a spe-cial, magical 'gift'. This split, between the art and the craft involved in making a film, probably has its roots in class division, but is also a mystification of the hard work and cultivation of good habit that goes into achieving excellence in any sphere.

'It will take ten years of work, day in and day out, whatever you feel like, before you can call yourself a dancer,' said the dour, authoritative teacher in her long black dress in my first day of class at The London School of Contemporary Dance. The ten-thousand-hours principle seems to hold good. When you dig around you find that everyone who seems 'talented' has worked for it, regularly, long and hard. The 'gift' will also have been helped by circumstance: a supportive individual, encouragement at the right moment, or a 'lucky break'. It is also, in another sense, mysterious and sacred. We all – every one of us – have untapped potential, 'given' in some sense, but rarely honoured. It is the cultivation of the habit of working at it that makes the difference.

It may help an actor who is not pushing out to his or her poten-tial, or who is abusing or neglecting the physical body in some way, to think of him- or herself as a 'sacred vessel'. It is a phrase I have occasionally used. What right have you not to honour this gift? How can you consider depriving us all of what you have to offer? This way of thinking can lift someone out of the kind of self-doubt that leads to apparent laziness.

5

Why all preparation is gold-dust

Once you have cast an actor, and the deals have been done, you enter a period of preparation with him or her that can be short – very short – or if you are lucky or persuasive, a little longer. Rarely, or almost never, is it as long as the rehearsal period for the theatre. Furthermore, a bigger-budget film does not necessarily buy more time with your actors, in fact possibly the contrary. But however long or short it is, this period of preparation is gold-dust for a director.

Whether the preparation takes the form of phone calls, texts, emails, meetings, dinner, hair and make-up tests, costume fittings, more formal rehearsals or just hanging about in each other's presence, you can learn precious and important information about the actor at every moment. If you watch carefully you will see when he or she comes alive and when he or she closes down. You will notice what gives energy or what seems to take it away. You can observe when an actor becomes anxious, and take note of your own anxieties when they arise. You will discover individual qualities and specific skills that you may be able to incorporate into the work. All your observations will become 'material' for you and are invaluable information. It's one of the upsides of a long and difficult development process, if you have cast the film early on but the financing falls through, or some other obstacle presents itself. The side benefit, in the midst of the stress and uncertainty of it all, is the potential to develop a relationship of solidarity with the actors and to learn a great deal about their commitment to you and the film, as well as strengthening your own stamina and persistence.

However long the preparation time turns out to be and however many guises it may take, once you start shooting there are bound to be many surprises – for film actors often only truly ignite once the camera starts turning. But during the preparation you will, like a detective, have amassed many vital clues that will help you to make the film you envision. A huge part of this process is something that can sound nebulous: helping to create a 'space' for the actor in which he or she can do their best work. This space is, however, very real. Every actor wants to transcend his or her limits, and dreams of delivering a performance at a new level – more subtle, deep, or surprising. By investing your directorial energy in finding out how to enable this to happen – creating this space – you will, to exactly the same degree, be helping your film to reach its own zenith. Above all, you will be building a relationship with your actors: a shorthand, a basis of trust.

Bonding with the actor

People sometimes ask me, 'How do you bond with an actor?' The answer is that it is not a magical process, it's exactly how you make a relationship with anybody. This is not always easy, especially if you feel shy (as I often have done), inadequate, or under immense pressure; but there are some simple, practical steps that are essential ingredients.

First, every relationship starts with making eye contact, however fleeting. So whenever you meet, look your actor in the eye. It's a way of saying, without words, here I am and there you are, and my attention is with you. If you are avoiding the actor's gaze, fiddling with papers, or speaking on the phone, you are giving a message that you are not capable of focus and may not be capable of watching the actor with the relaxed precision he or she will need later. The right look is not a glassy fixed stare, however. It's just a genuine form of benevolent visual regard. It tells the actor you are interested in them and what they have to give.

Second, you need to be respectful. In a working environment people arguably need to be respected more than they need to be loved; in fact, respect can be thought of as a deeper form of love. But this has to be authentic. A posture of phoney respect is an insult; true respect is born out of knowledge, both of the individual and of the working process you are entering into together. It also requires knowledge of the consequences of your directorial demands. Your clear and sober understanding of the actor's complex working needs will be experienced by him or her as an attitude of respect.

Third, you need to be warm. For some actors a physical expression of warmth, such as a hug, is a way to relax and feel close. It makes him or her feel safe, reassured and wanted. But for others, touch can feel intrusive or disturbing. They may wince and tighten if you try to hug them and you must quickly make a mental note of this. For these individuals, enforced intimacy feels invasive. Actors, like most people, give you clear messages about their needs; you have to be sensitive and alert to their messages, in whatever way they are communicated. There is no right or wrong way to be, but there is always appropriateness for the individual.

If you follow these simple principles – make eye contact, be respectful, and be warm in ways that are appropriate to the individual – you have the basis for 'bonding': a word that really means connecting in an open, relaxed and trusting way. Then you can move forward into a focused working relationship.

All of this will place demands on your abilities to deal with your own anxieties so that you can relax and concentrate on other people's needs, rather than your own. The actor's needs, in particular, are more important than yours. Not humanly more important, of course, but strategically more important in this particular working process. Stress for an actor will show in their face. It can ruin a performance. The furrows in your own brow do not matter in the same way. As director you have to get used to this dynamic, which can feel unequal and even unfair. You are unlikely to be praised or reassured by anyone in your crew or cast at any point along the line, however well you do, or however much stress and pressure you are under. It is your job to reassure them, not the other way round. It's part of your role, and you have to rise to meet it.

With Simon Abkarian on the set of *Yes*

In all communications, especially at the beginning of a relationship with an actor, it is vital not to become defensive, especially if you feel insecure. They may want to challenge you, to ask awkward or difficult questions that seem to imply criticism, but may prove to be part of an essential dialogue. You have to be 'big' enough to be open, to listen well, and to show the actor with your facial expression what kind of attention and communication they will be getting from you later on during the shoot. Listening attentively with a respectful and warm expression, even if you are feeling nervous, goes a long way. Plus, if you stop concentrating on your own anxieties and instead concentrate on the actor and what they are doing or saying, you will be able to decipher the subtexts or coded messages they are delivering more adroitly and respond appropriately.

6

Working one-on-one

Though this was something I had often done instinctively for years, it took a while for me to learn that it really was a golden rule: build your relationships one-on-one. This applies to your key crew (your heads of department: designer, cinematographer and so on), and crucially, to your actors. If you try to make a relationship with a whole group of people at once you are entering a completely different dynamic: the actors will then be watching each other, perhaps competing or comparing themselves. They may start adapting what they do to the other actor's methods or ways of behaving or performing. You will be dealing with a confusing array of messages and dynamics. The actors will eventually work with each other, in rehearsal or on set, in any case. They will feed off each other, give to each other and be inspired by each other. It's a huge part of their working process. But first they need to get to know you.

In order to have an open line of communication with each actor, you must relate to him or her first and foremost as an individual. Even if you can't have any formal rehearsals, it is vital to organise a private meeting in which you address the actor's concerns, invite questions, take every worry seriously (and act on them), express your own hopes and expectations, and listen to theirs. This inter-action will form the basis of all future interactions, on and off the set. You can begin to develop a unique shorthand with each actor, you will amass vital information that they will only share with you in a private encounter, and you will begin to win the actor's trust, the most vital ingredient in your working relationship.

In *Orlando*, the episodic structure of the story meant that many actors only worked for a few days when we were already some way into a highly pressured shoot. Formal rehearsals were out of the question under these conditions. I noticed, however, that even a brief private meeting repaid itself many times over. The quality of time spent seemed more important than quantity. If you have to, you can go a long way, fast.

On *Rage* each actor worked alone with me during the shoot, as I was operating the camera and the crew was minimal. I discovered that such intense individual focus was extraordinarily productive in finding a way through to each actor's unique qualities. Directing whilst holding the camera in your hands (and to your eye) is a relatively rare experience, but teaches you both about how the camera 'reads' performance and also how vital the presence of the camera-operator is for the actor.

With *Ginger & Rosa* the working process was quite different. I would not be shooting it myself (I worked with the agile, brilliantly intuitive Robbie Ryan as cinematographer). But I spent a great deal of time before the shoot, working one-on-one with Elle Fanning and Alice Englert and eventually with all the main actors. I was going to be demanding an extraordinary degree of openness from each of them. Elle, in particular, was going to have to tackle some very emotionally demanding scenes. Though already professionally experienced, she was still only thirteen years old. The only way to make this work, and be responsible, was to build real closeness and trust. It wasn't hard to do as Elle was extremely responsive, but without this private time together before the shoot I'm not sure the atmosphere would have been safe enough on set to work at such a deep level.

There's another reason why working one-on-one is so crucial. Cinema is ultimately an intimate medium. Whilst it may – or may not – be experienced collectively in a huge, dark auditorium, it must invite each member of the audience into a private relationship with what's happening on the screen. The level of professional intimacy you can build with the actor, the extent of your inclusiveness in the vision of the film and the warmth of your 'invitation' to them to fully participate, will eventually translate into a quality of intimacy in performance. The camera will 'find' and record the actor's openness – their quality of 'invitation' – which is a quality of relationship you have ignited in them. Each member of the audience will, in turn, experience it as their own.

Photographing Lily Cole for *Rage*

7

Holding the space for the actor

Being the first audience

The director must function as the first, most attentive, respectful and loving audience the actor will ever have. Even if you hope that you (or the writer) have already written a beautifully constructed part, in reality it is a kind of ghost shape, a spirit, which the actor is going to inflame, manifest and become. But he or she needs your help, whether this is active or simply a form of bearing witness to their evolving process. Either way, the power of attention you are able to muster will greatly assist the actor to embody the role, flesh it out, and bring it alive. As you watch the actor in the first read-throughs of the script, even if you do not feel perfectly focused and completely enthusiastic about what they are doing, you must try to be; the actor will appreciate even an imperfect attempt. It is partly about creating an atmosphere of trust and openness in which risks can be taken. Under these conditions, actors feel that they can go beyond their usual limits and become more of whom and what they really are, both as actors and as human beings. If you are truly attentive and non-judgemental they will know that they can make mistakes and that this is not a disaster. The so-called mistakes are often, in reality, vital learning tools, to be welcomed rather than feared. Many apparent errors bring surprising and interesting gifts in their wake.

As director, in these earliest read-throughs of the script with an actor, even if you are alone in a room together, you will come to embody the gaze of the first-night crowd in a theatre or the cold, all-seeing eye of the camera during the shoot. Either way, for the actor the experience of the first read-through is subjectively similar to standing alone on an enormous stage. It's a terrifying moment. But there is really only one person who matters in the audience and that is you, the director. For in the film-making process you represent all the others. For better or worse, you are the filter, the critic, the mirror, the guide. This first read-through is therefore a moment both of power and of responsibility.

At this moment you have to learn to look at actors with an understanding of their experience of vulnerability, a vulnerability inherent in this level of exposure and scrutiny. And you have to use your eyes to look beyond how they are performing in that moment to see what they can become. You have to try to visualise their potential, see what they're reaching for, the limits they want to overcome, the performance of a lifetime that they want to discover. In short, you have to look at their innate genius and not at their inevitable stumbles along the way. They want to see in your eyes that you are genuinely attentive, both to what they can give now and – crucially – to what they might be able to give in the future. A good actor will sense if you are only partially present, perhaps because you're so preoccupied with a multitude of vital directorial decisions: an unresolved design problem, or maybe the fact that the scene as a whole is not working at all and needs to be scrapped or rewritten.

Attentive looking

Developing an attentive, intelligent gaze is a disciplined process and takes practice. Your mind may wander to the next scene or your next meeting, a location that has just fallen through, an unresolved costume issue or some other more pressing question. Or perhaps you can see the actor is going off track. A voice has emerged that is too theatrical, a posture that is too exaggerated; the actor is tense, or having trouble remembering the lines. An attentive gaze is not a sloppy or therapeutic one. It's not necessarily permissive, in the sense of 'anything goes', it's more about being in the present and alert. It seems to involve repeatedly making the decision to focus only on who or what is in front of you. And to really focus. Pretending to look whilst actually thinking about something else will not work.

With Joan Allen on location for *Yes*

Once you can achieve this way of looking – which is a relaxed gaze of unconditional respect and understanding – and become the best audience that the actor has ever had, then you have the basis of an extraordinary working relationship. By looking so attentively, you create a safe space in which the actor can inhabit a role and freely explore beyond his or her habitual boundaries. It may feel, for both of you, that you are entering an unknown arena together; it can feel like a dangerous space. But as a director your job is both to define and to hold this invisible space. To make it safe. It is an act of psychic responsibility which no one can see but everyone can sense.

This space is often defined by the quality of your silence. It may be expressed in a glance of complicity. A warm look, a smile or just an expression of focused seriousness will often be more helpful than anything you could say. It doesn't mean you stop thinking. On the contrary, the more you apply your intelligence to what is unfolding in front of you the more 'held' the actor will feel. The silent presence of active intelligence – what it feels like to be thought about well – is extraordinarily powerful.

Put yourself in the actor's shoes

It can be extremely useful for a director to experience – at least once – what it feels like to be on the other side of the camera. Even trying it in private with some friends, armed with a small digital camera, will be illuminating.

It might happen like this. Nominate a friend to be 'director'. Then learn a speech, have somebody fiddle around with your hair just before a take (so you know what the pressures of people working on your appearance feel like), and then, while shooting, have some people in the room scrutinise you critically while others seem hardly to notice you are there. (That's what the crew behind the camera can feel like to the actor.) Having done it once, get the 'director' to ask you to do it again – perhaps faster or slower; louder or softer. That's what it feels like to be bombarded by so-called 'direction'.

You will learn a lot. You will discover your need for approval, the immediate gnawing insecurity about how you look. You will feel how much you need someone to give you clear instructions but not boss you about. You may wonder why they are pointing the camera up your nose, you may forget your lines, or where to stand. Or you may feel so triumphant that you got through it at all that when you look at the material afterwards you will be devastated to see that you kept touching your hair, or frowning, or looked completely unconvincing. You may seem entirely disconnected from the text, obviously concentrating just on remembering the next line. You will understand how clear, careful communication from an object-ive director is crucial, and also how difficult the actor's work is.

It really helps to put yourself in the actor's shoes in this way, even if only in your imagination. It will motivate you to become a clearer communicator, a kinder person, a more efficient director who knows when to speak and when to shut up. It also helps you identify when the problem is the actor's and when the problem lies in your own directorial choices of camera position, costume, tim-ing, and so on. You will learn that creating an atmosphere of ease and emotional relaxation helps actors to function better, whereas tightness, unkindness and anxiety will limit what they can do.

Another interesting experiment is to try performing without a director, alone in a room. If you set up a camera and try the same exercise, performing a speech, deciding for yourself where and how to deliver it, you will note how it feels speaking into empty space with just an inanimate camera as your witness. (This has, of course become part of the 'confessional' language of reality television and video blogs, and tends to produce a very consist-ent and now over-familiar kind of result, one with its own laws, conventions and arm's-length camera angles. The raw and appar-ently amateurish result has become synonymous with 'reality' but is in fact as fictional a construction as any other more elaborate performance.) Having tried this, note what happens when you ask someone to come in and watch you, silently but attentively and respectfully, as you do it again. You will soon experience the force-field of another human intelligence in the room. (This is also interesting to try for any actor who doubts that the director is 'doing' anything if they are not giving instructions and appear to be 'only' watching).

My own apprenticeship in all these areas came about when I decided to act in *The Tango Lesson* (which I also wrote and directed). As an ex-performance artist and dancer and an already fairly experi-enced feature-film director, I thought I understood the actor's craft

and hoped I could handle acting alongside the challenge of directing the other performers and making the usual multitude of directorial decisions. Nothing prepared me for the extreme vulnerability
of being in front of the camera, with a large crew but no director
to turn to between takes. I found I was searching for an open,
non-judgemental face; a steady gaze that would let me know that
what I was trying to do had been witnessed. Someone who would
reassure, or challenge me intelligently. Someone who would hold
me, silently, in their field of vision. Penny Eyles, the script supervisor, gave me good, straightforward feedback when she could, but
she also had many other things to do. Most of the time when I
looked out, everyone on the set was busy. I felt utterly alone.

Of course, I could blame no one for my solitude. I had chosen
to put myself in this position and was consciously working with
my own awkwardness and loneliness as a necessary quality in the
role I had created. I wanted to explore subjectivity in cinematic
storytelling, by making the director a visible part of the story being
told (as every director seems to need to do at some point in their
life's work, for we need to reflect on the all-absorbing activity to
which we have devoted our lives).

All films have invisible hands and minds controlling the fictional
world which appears real or seamless. There is a hidden, silent nar-
rator. We accept the 'eye' of the storyteller as quasi-objective, or
neutral (especially in documentaries), but of course it is not; there
is always a point of view at work. In *The Tango Lesson* I wanted
to meditate on the 'reality' of this so-called objective realism, by
showing the process of a film's making unfold, albeit in fictional
form. I hoped to make the process transparent by exposing the persona of the storyteller to the light, with all her needs, vanities and
longings. And my own real longings – to dance again, experience
the magic of embodiment once more and explore the director/
actor relationship on screen, rather than behind the scenes – would
function as research and be the engine powering the story.

But when I saw the rushes, my heart sank. I had done what I set out to do and had thoroughly exorcised my dancer fantasies in the process. But I knew I could have done so much better – even at performing being a parallel or semi-fictitious version of myself – with a good director. I would never again underestimate the necessity of the director's gaze in the actor's process.

Between takes on location for *The Tango Lesson*

8

Rehearsals (why, not how)

In film-making a formal rehearsal period is a luxury (unlike theatre, where it is thought of as an absolute necessity). In some cases the first time you work with an actor may be on the set. And some directors may favour this way of working, to capture what they perceive as an authentic spontaneity. Some actors feel the same way, fearing that rehearsal will kill the spark, take the life out of their performance. They fear they may lose their best moment in the rehearsal room: the freshest take, the most spontaneous gesture, the danger of being 'in the moment' which can produce the most alive cinematic performance. So as a director, you have to make judgements about whether or not to rehearse formally, if indeed you have the luxury of this possibility. Sometimes you will find you have a cast with wildly different needs, some of whom crave rehearsal and others of whom resist it. In this instance you need to devise a flexible strategy. This is further complicated by the fact that an actor's resistance to any particular way of working may be based on habit and familiarity, or fear, rather than a deeper need.

The only way to arrive at good judgement about all this is through observation of what works for the individual. If you begin by building a relationship, one-on-one, and think of every meeting, every exchange (even on the phone) as a form of 'rehearsal', giving the same amount of energy and attentiveness to every encounter with the actor, however apparently casual it may be, you will soon learn to discriminate between genuine self-knowledge and destructive resistance.

Every actor will start subtly 'offering up' material once they feel the director's gaze, if it is respectful and open enough. With this way of operating, the strict boundaries of 'rehearsal' start to dissolve and it all becomes part of a continuum, leading up to and continuing throughout the shoot. Sometimes a conversation over a meal, a stroll around a location, or a joke shared during a car journey can be as helpful as more apparently focused work. What matters is to enter a zone of attentive observation at all times, and remember that essentially what you are doing is building trust.

If you do have a formal period of rehearsal you need to remind yourself that its purpose is to open things up, not close them down. For the actor it is the time to find out why the character is doing or saying something, not how to deliver it. A rehearsal period that tries to set everything in stone and then shoot it without changing anything is almost bound to look fake and feel lifeless. Rehearsal should, on the contrary, be about breathing life and confidence into an evolving and ever-deepening process.

There are no rules and no generalisations about how to achieve this. Each actor is a unique being and the goal is to try to find the key that will help unlock the door to the secret room he or she needs to enter (or, sometimes, to break out of). For some the key will be through the nuance and detail of appearance: you enter through the outside. For others the process needs to be interior: you work from the inside out. Some actors can become breathtakingly courageous in the raw privacy of the rehearsal room and share many personal details that must remain – by agreement – for ever confidential. Others need to 'save' that kind of exposure for the moment of the shoot and will reveal themselves only through the words and actions of the character they are playing.

Actors who started out in the theatre tend to want rehearsal and know very well how to use it to improve their work. A rehearsal – whether structured formally or informally – becomes a place of safety, where they can try out ideas without fear of failure: I often invite people to start by doing it 'wrong' to explore their limits, the range of possibilities. It can be humiliating for an actor to be criticised in front of the crew on the set, whereas a gentle unravelling of something that doesn't yet work in the safe and protected environment of the rehearsal room can be exhilarating. When things get sticky it's helpful to remember that every actor wants to do their best and will welcome an opportunity to take the necessary steps to get there.

Rehearsal also creates a space for the actors to bond with each other and to find a common rhythm and language of performance. This too can have its pitfalls. Actors can start adjusting their performance to 'match' someone else's, or start playing for laughs, or to please each other. As director you have to keep your eye on the vision of the film as a whole, the development of the character on screen rather than in the rehearsal room, and a scale of playing that will work for the lens rather than the eyes and ears of others in a room.

There are other invaluable reasons for rehearsal, too, for the director. You can learn things in the rehearsal room that you may not spot again until the cutting room, when it's all too late. You will suddenly notice holes in the story, gaps in the arc of a character, lines that don't ring true or themes that have not been properly developed. It is a good moment to be open to seeing these problems and finding a way to sort them out, often with the help of the actors. This will, in the end, make for a more fluid and relaxed shoot. When their instincts are recognised by the director, the actors will experience themselves as collaborators in a process in which they too have responsibility for the final result.

Under the difficult, speedy and pressurised conditions of a shoot, it helps immeasurably if you and the actors already have a mutual understanding of the goals of the film – and ideally of each scene and moment within a scene – and a shorthand way of communicating about things that work or don't work. This common language emerges from the kind of deep preparatory work that can usually only be achieved in protected conditions. It begins one-on-one and then develops when you put people together.

Finding the frame of meaning

Above all, actors need to find a way to anchor themselves in a genuine impulse in the scene: a reason for speaking or being silent; a
reason to reveal themselves or remain hidden. When you know
why you are doing something – or not doing it – you become free.
The canvas of how you do it is limitless. Rehearsal can help create
sure ground with clear boundaries, in which to find this freedom.
In effect, in rehearsal you can discover a frame of meaning. This
frame of meaning can then work in parallel with the visual framing
– literally, the lens: exactly what you are looking at, and how – but
also the production design and every aspect of the visual world of
the film. Carlos Conti, my long-time production designer, often
speaks of the design as a character in the film, or as a space which
holds the performances. By thinking in this way the cinematography, design and performances then eventually become one, a
united whole.

I experienced the steps involved in this process very forcefully
when in rehearsals for a pivotal scene in *Yes*. The story follows
the arc of a love affair between an American woman and a Mid-
dle-Eastern man in the years of hate following the traumatic events
of 9/11. Joan Allen and Simon Abkarian played the protagonists.
The scene – set in a bleak car park at night in London – is the
moment in the story when the East/West conflict between the two
characters reaches its zenith. We had already worked through the
scene many times and I had rewritten parts of it as world events
changed tumultuously around us. During our rehearsal period
the US and UK invaded Iraq and then, two days before our final
rehearsal, declared themselves to be the new occupying power.

In the rehearsal room Simon, Joan and myself talked and talked,
and eventually wept, about what this might mean, for the future
of relations between East and West, and what it might take for
people from such different cultures and religions to listen to – and
really hear – each other's point of view. In the process of talking

about the power of listening, we discussed our own experiences of being listened to and not listened to: the unheard stories, the grief and rage of not having our experience understood – for Simon, as a man from the Middle East, and for Joan and myself as women. These conversations proved to be profoundly important as a way of identifying the true arc of the scene and the point at which, by really listening to him, Joan's character would create the space in which Simon's character would be able to reveal the wounds behind his aggression. In this way, our conversations veered seamlessly between the extremely personal and the broadly political, as well as covering more conventional analyses of the precise meanings and implications of certain words and phrases in the script.

In this instance, I made an intuitive (and risky) decision to open myself up in the rehearsal room as a way of 'giving permission' for the actors to open themselves up as well. This was not a moment for a divide between 'detached' director and 'emotional' actors. I felt we needed to be in it together. But – simultaneously – a part of me was always watching and noting: is this helping or hindering them in their process? When I shared my experience – or even my tears – and saw something mobilising in their performance, I continued, but I stopped as soon as it started to eat into the space they needed to occupy in order for it to work.

It is vital to cultivate this kind of detachment, even when you are entering the actor's arena as a form of solidarity, or to demonstrate your willingness to share extremes of emotion – otherwise it becomes a theft of their working space. The actors need to know that you are using your intelligence at all times and not just indulging your own needs. This work – for them and for you – may be experienced as cathartic and illuminating, but the goals are quite different from any therapeutic process. You are intensely engaged, together, in excavating deep feeling and thought, to serve a specific goal: the depth and quality of the final film. You are discovering the frame of its meaning.

Working with children and young people

Working with young actors is really, at its core, no different from working with adults. All the essential processes – building a relationship and a basis for trust, working on the text, the character, tracking his or her inner life, thoughts and feelings, identifying the arc of change in a scene – apply equally to all actors. The only meaningful difference, and one to be aware of, is the uneven balance of power that comes with a difference of age. Younger people can be exploited and often suffer from a lack of true respect in a working environment. They are sometimes patronised, humiliated or teased in hurtful ways. They may try too hard to please you, which brings a forced quality to the work.

The preparation period, including rehearsal, is where you can demonstrate a respectful attitude and awareness of the challenges they are facing. You can create an atmosphere of warmth and safety in which the younger actors can reveal any difficulties, seek out the information they need, and also gain permission to 'shine' in an authentic way.

On a tour of film studios with a group of independent film-makers in the mid-1980s, shortly before 'perestroika' in the then Soviet Republics, we were given the opportunity to visit a children's art museum in Yerevan, the capital city of Armenia. I was entranced as a museum guide led us through the echoing galleries, speaking respectfully and knowledgeably about each artist's use of colour and composition. Some of the artists in question were as young as eight or nine, but the seriousness of their relationship with their work was not in question. It was not seen as a fluke or a lucky accident, it was real work, executed with skill and passion, comparable to the work of artists of any age.

I try to apply this way of looking when working with children or young people. I have always found them to be serious, eager and utterly professional when given due respect and proper attention. They want their work to be as good as it can be, for their own self-respect. They sometimes seem to feel freed from constraint when relieved of the double burden of having to 'perform' being a 'child actor' as well as concentrating on the work in hand. Most of them long to just get on with the job.

Paradoxically, the strict rules concerning child actors' hours during a shoot (taking a break every hour, being chaperoned, continuing with school lessons with a tutor if shooting takes place during term-time) can benefit everyone. When filming *Ginger & Rosa*, Elle Fanning, who was thirteen at the time, regularly left the set to study maths, science, or literature. I used her breaks to prepare the next set-up, or rethink the scene, or take care of whatever was pressing, and she invariably reappeared full of zest and freshness from having put her attention elsewhere for a while. Her youthful enthusiasm, boundless energy and appetite for learning – she was especially open to finding out how to really use the rehearsal process – was infectious and inspiring to everyone.

Elle Fanning, Annette Bening, Oliver Platt and
Timothy Spall between takes of *Ginger & Rosa*

9

Finding the 'look' (hair, make-up and costume)

Appearance is mysterious. In the surface of things we can find both truth and lies; appearance can reveal or it can camouflage. The way someone looks, including what they wear, contains a wealth of detailed information that cannot be expressed as clearly in words, for the eye can read extraordinary amounts of information with lightning accuracy. The camera picks up every minutia of this information, in a surprisingly volatile way, depending partly on the conditions of light (which is why one has to take the necessary time to observe – and correct – the effects of light on the actor's face during the shoot).

Quentin Crisp preparing with make-up artist Morag Ross for *Orlando*

Knowing how a performance can be enhanced – or even destroyed – by any number of appearance-related issues means that the concern of an actor, whether male or female, about appearance is entirely justified. It is sometimes perceived, however, as a matter of vanity. This is a misunderstanding of the actor's work. To state what should be obvious: the actor's physical self is the medium he or she is working with. Each detail speaks, in its own way, of character, mood or historical reference. The wrong detail can distract from a brilliant performance. A stray hair or an over-loud tie, if inappropriate, can become the focus of attention rather than what is being said. The right detail, on the contrary, can be phenomenally articulate and take us in a nanosecond to an understanding of the character and where he or she is coming from. A character who looks overgroomed or overdressed hints at inner anxiety, for example. Obviously dyed hair in an older character communicates fear and resistance to ageing. This work on the outside – the look, in all its forms: clothes, hair and make-up – is crucial. Paradoxically, proper attention to every aspect of appearance at the right moment frees the actor from worrying about appearance at the wrong moment. The apparently trivial concern can have profound implications.

Timothy Spall during a costume fitting for *Ginger & Rosa*

For these reasons it can be rewarding and informative as a director to spend time with an actor during hair and make-up experiments and costume fittings. (This may sometimes have to be negotiated delicately with the relevant heads of department, for whom this moment can be a valued private process of discovery with the actor.) By the time fittings begin you will already have had long, detailed meetings with your costume designer; you will have discussed the clothes as a reflection of character, and what fabrics or tailoring might work for the specific actor's body-shape and colouring. You will have developed how the arc of the story may be expressed through the changes in clothes the characters are wearing. You will have thought about the overall colour palette of the clothes in relation to the production design. You will have imagined clothes as a signal of class, of aspiration, of age and desire. And of course your designer will have researched the clothes and hairstyles in relation to the period the story is set in.

Cate Blanchett in *The Man Who Cried*

But once you see the difference in practice between the choice of one outfit and another, you will see, vividly, how 'clothes make the man'. You can gain a huge amount of vital information by being present at this moment. You can laugh with delight and applaud or you can quickly nip a wrong direction in the bud. Above all, you can learn a great deal about the actor's own vision of the role. Watching Johnny Depp try on a series of hats, or Cate Blanchett transform herself in a succession of dresses in front of a mirror, for example (when preparing for *The Man Who Cried* (2000)), was extremely instructive. In both cases watching them find the right clothes was like watching them walk through the mirror into the film.

Understanding the importance of hair and make-up is also crucial. Because these parts of the visual 'design' of the character are closest to the actor's face, they are extremely visible on screen (even when designed to look so natural as to be invisible). A sequence of tests and revisions in advance of the shoot will reward you many times over. You, the actor and the hair and make-up artists will gain immeasurably valuable feedback before it is too late to change the look.

Even on a very tight schedule on *Rage*, Morag Ross (hair and make-up), Es Devlin (costume) and I worked with Jude Law through a long sequence of tests – including many looks that did not work – until we felt we had 'found' the physical persona for his character, Minx. It was going to be a big leap for Jude to dress convincingly as a woman and in this case his inner work on the character was dependent on appearance, with which Minx was obsessed. Once you have done this kind of meticulous, detailed research and experimentation with an actor and arrived at a look you are all confident about, you can move forward into the shoot speedily and with great freedom.

Jude Law – one of the 'looks' for Minx in *Rage*

Incidentally, your choice of hair and make-up artists is crucial from another point of view as well. These are the members of the crew that the actor will interact with first thing every morning, and who will come physically closest to them many times during the day as they do 'checks' between takes. The nature of this relationship with the actor will be a secret key – or sometimes an impediment – to the actor's role, and will also affect the actor's relationship with you, in ways you may not understand. In addition, the work of the make-up artist is sometimes – mistakenly – seen as secondary on set, an annoying hold-up to the shoot. It is important for any director to make sure they respect and appreciate make-up artists' work. In the cutting room (and on the big screen) I have time and time again come to appreciate the subtlety and importance of their fine, detailed efforts (and occasionally agonised when they are not).

Anxiety about appearance

An actor's anxiety about appearance (rather than their perfectionist and necessary desire to achieve the right look) is a different issue.

Some actors – whether male or female – are hampered in their work by a constant low-level drone of anxiety about what they're going to look like on the screen. They fear that their nose looks too big or their hair is unruly; perhaps they saw themselves once in an ugly light, or a critic wrote something hurtful about their weight. The sources of anxiety can be endless. The actor fights the feeling because he or she feels ashamed of it, so it becomes an un-admitted private agony and instead is projected onto costume, hair or make-up which may, in fact, be working very well.

For a female actor these feelings can link into some of her deep-est private fears about her value as a human being. The actor, sub-ject in life and on screen to intense scrutiny – to an invasive and often cruel degree – may carry in an exaggerated form the pressure of how we're all judged by our looks. Most women will admit to feelings of never being quite the right age, shape, or weight. This has fuelled the pervasive cult of cosmetic surgery to correct sup-posed faults, and a widespread fear of ageing. It seems that even the most celebrated beauties of all time usually hated something about their appearance. I have repeatedly been astonished by how self-critical famous female actors are about details of their bodies. Male actors also experience these anxieties about appearance, as the male body is increasingly subject to critical scrutiny in advertise-ments and on screen.

The question for the director is how to recognise and deal with this phenomenon when it's in front of you. You may notice that the actor can't seem to concentrate when you're trying to work on a scene. On careful questioning you discover that it's because he or she is worrying about their weight because of a costume that feels too tight. At this point you need to check whether this is just a needless anxiety, or a valid concern. Actors understand the interconnection between exterior and interior life. What the cam-era sees – and amplifies – on the screen will fundamentally affect how the audience responds to the role and the performance. So you need – at least in the first instance – to treat it as an issue deserving of time and respect. The perceived problem, however trivial it may at first sight seem to be, may be the obstacle preventing that actor from delivering the performance of his or her life and it's your job to figure out how to remove the obstacle.

So what do you do in practice? If you discover that hair is the issue (as it often seems to be), you might say, 'let's spend some time just talking about your hair.' The look of relief, if you've hit the right note, can be extraordinary. Indeed, it may be a detail that turns out to be the key to unlock the other apparently larger issue in the scene that you wanted to deal with, which, if you had kept hammering on verbally about it, you were never going to reach.

Another approach is more general, if the actor's anxiety is more diffuse. You might say to that person, 'I'm going to take complete responsibility for your physical appearance on the screen. I'm always going to be aware of it, so that you can relax and forget about it.' I made this promise to one female actor who I gradually came to realise was haunted by insecurity about her looks. She was an internationally celebrated beauty, but thought she only looked good from certain angles, or with her hair a certain way. Years of flattery and inauthentic attention had left her swimming in doubt. A commitment of the kind described, stated out loud and then honoured in practice – you must keep your promise – can liberate actors from shackles that have inhibited their performances for years.

10

Finding the character (secret key or red herring?)

Often finding a 'character' is not so much a matter of building something up, as trying to strip parts of the apparent 'self' of the actor away. What we call 'character' (or sometimes personality or identity) in daily life is often a series of habitual constructions, ways of behaving or appearing. A 'persona' is a creation, not a state of being.

The 'character' you are searching for in a film really needs to be more like a transmitter of experience. This is why people often confuse good cinema actors with their roles: it looks as if they are 'being themselves'. Nevertheless, in the process of arriving at this pure state of presence, the actor and director look for many external clues, which become signposts on the journey. Part of the short-hand used in the process is the concept of 'character'. The actor is playing someone who has lived a different life, with specific – albeit imaginary – memories, desires and habitual ways of behaving.

Each actor has a specific way of approaching a role, empathis-ing with this person who is not them, imagining themselves into their (fictitious) skin. For one actor, the clues to the identity of the character may be found via physical detail and appearance. What clothes do they wear? What kind of shoes? If the actor lights up when you discuss hair or some other physical detail then you know working from the outside in is going to be the secret key.

Another actor might need to know the entire back-story of their character to be able to walk through the door of a room with convic-tion. They might want to know where this fictitious character was born, who their mother was, what their father did, what they ate for dinner the previous night. You can help this process by working out these back-story details with the actor or by preparing material to share if you haven't already written some. (In my case I have generally written lots of background notes about the characters as they evolve during the development and the script. These notes don't appear in the finished script, but they are useful in these conversations.) Many North American film actors work this way – as if they are creating a memory-bank for their characters – and some British actors too. Timothy Spall turned up for our first working session with an entire life history for Mark, his role in *Ginger & Rosa*. It was delightful, funny and insightful, and helped me to understand what he had seen and understood from the script. It was the basis for refining many almost subliminal aspects of the role.

Another actor may be impatient with this process. He or she may find it too literal, an unnecessary amount of detailed information that will never find its way onto the screen. For this actor, there may be something more abstract and overarching that needs to be explored: perhaps an idea in the script they don't understand, or have doubts about. Or they may need to be reassured about what your attitude really is in relation to the core subject-matter. They may be wondering about your political views, or even whether you intend to mock or satirise their character in some way. In this situation you have to find out if there's an issue that you must deal with, for them to be able to trust you and fly. Whatever it is, it's better out in the open, even if it's uncomfortable for you both. It can become a brilliantly constructive analytical conversation about the deeper intentions of the film.

With another actor you might notice that once you start talking about and analysing the character – or talking about any other aspect of the film – they start glazing over. In this instance verbal communication is useless. For this actor you probably need to get physical. The best strategy may be to invite the actor to find a tone of voice, a way of moving, or discover how the character sits or walks, in order to enter into a feeling-state and activate his or her senses. This most obviously applies to ex-dancers or other perform-ers who started out with a physical discipline. They have to get busy and root themselves in the body. Clues may also come via the ears: by listening to the music their character might enjoy. What-ever it is, the process has to be primarily non-verbal.

For another actor (and for some directors), the notion of 'char-acter' is itself a red herring. It's not so much a matter of finding a fictitious self, but rather locating how to inhabit a space with presence. 'Presence' is a mysterious concept, but when you see it you recognise it. Some actors can just stand in a room, on a stage, or on a film set, and seem to fill it with their being without appar-ently 'doing' anything. It takes confidence to inhabit situations and spaces in this way, and it begins by finding an ease with the physical body.

Someone who has designated themselves a 'character actor' (as opposed to a leading man or woman) may discover a great deal by abandoning the idea of character altogether. I have worked with actors where all I do as preparation is spend time looking at them, or perhaps taking photographs of them. Moving through the dis-comfort of being looked at, finding that 'doing nothing' is enough – or more commonly, is excruciatingly uncomfortable – will open a rich vein of awareness. A screen actor needs to be able to tolerate enormous amounts of scrutiny. The camera itself can be experi-enced as a cold, relentless stare. Learning to welcome this without any posture of defensiveness – including 'over-acting' a character – will prove liberating and relaxing. A 'character', for this kind of actor, may have become a hiding place from the discomfort of being looked at (for paradoxically, some actors are shy). Abandon-ing the idea of character for them is like stepping out into the light. They are still playing a role, inhabiting a life-story or situation that is different from their own daily lived experience, but surrender-ing to being looked at means that their own core will also remain visible, instead of being in a state of retreat. This way of becoming 'centred' will root and illuminate their portrait of someone 'other'. The portrayal they are seeking must manifest in their own body and will be animated by their own face. This state of acceptance – of both being and not being the role being played – will enrich it and add depth to the notion of character.

Very occasionally it may help an actor who is having trouble finding who they are playing – what they sound like, how they move – if you demonstrate something, even if you do it badly. In fact as a general principle it's often useful for a director to be prepared to look like a fool. If you are prepared to jettison your dignity, the actor may feel encouraged to take more risks him- or herself. Unexpressed embarrassment is an impediment to everyone. In these circumstances a good laugh at your own expense is extremely useful for both of you.

Sometimes, in the search for whom they are really playing, what the actor really wants is something very simple, but often rare: some private time with you. This actor needs to get to know you as a person and can't figure out how to really connect empathetically with the role – their character – until that happens. The state of connectedness itself has to start with you, or in the space between you. Some actors who get no time with the director may feel chronically alienated from the film and from themselves. If you make the time you will both reap the reward.

To sum up: you observe what works for each individual actor, and take it from there. That means knowing that there are no hard and fast rules. But there is a chain of cause and effect in the development of a role, a character, or simply an actor's presence, and you, as the director, are part of that chain. You are helping the actor to dive into an unknown zone and find the mysterious, transitory and ephemeral otherness of the 'self' they are temporarily occupying.

11

Working with the script

The text

Plays rely primarily on the spoken word, but film – an intensely visual medium – also relies on what you see: action and imagery, spaces and places. These elements of the screenplay must be written and described, equally precisely, in order for the crew to understand what needs to be built, found, lit and filmed. For the actors, whilst their lines are crucial, what is not said must also be understood and, paradoxically, needs to be implied through what is said. So a good screenplay works on many levels: the spoken word, the unspoken subtext, silent gesture, situation, environment and action. It must evoke the finished film in its entirety: not by describing camera angles (which robs the director and cinematographer of their interpretive imagination), but by vividly and economically evoking a world – the world of the story being told.

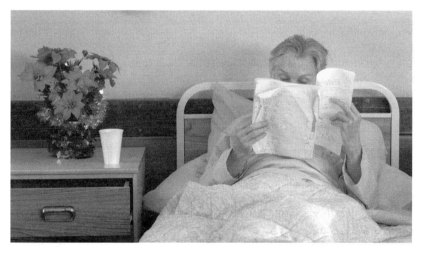

Sheila Hancock studying the script between takes of *Yes*

The work you do with the actor on the text – the things they are going to do and, vitally, the words they are going to say – is one of the most important aspects of your process together. For this reason you must know the script – every word of it – extremely well. In fact, as a general principle, the director needs to know the script much better than everyone else working on the film, for it will become your collective bible and be constantly referred to. As you go through it, again and again, with each head of department and then with each actor, you will discover that each person sees it differently. People necessarily interpret the needs of the script from their own perspective, whether this is camera, design, costume, sound, or performance. Hearing these varying viewpoints will, in turn, clarify your own understanding of what you wrote (if you are a writer/director) or will help illuminate the script someone else wrote and you are now bringing to life. Each meeting with a member of the crew or actor will force you to clarify what you are trying to do.

For the actors to speak lines convincingly and do things authentically, they have to know why they are saying and doing them. This may seem to be stating the obvious, but often enough the actor may find he or she is doing or saying something because it says so in the script, whether or not it seems logical or necessary. Understanding the text may not always be arrived at analytically. It may just 'feel right'. But if it doesn't 'feel' right then the performance is likely to be stiff, awkward, forced or artificial.

If you are lucky enough (or determined enough) to have a rehearsal period – and have decided it is appropriate for the actors you have chosen – then there may be time to unravel every scene, every line, even every word, in order to find its necessity, understand where it is coming from, and anchor the words in the actor's own experience. There will be time to talk about motivation, backstory (where the character is coming from in the fictitious story before the film began) and any other issues arising. But whether or not you do this layered work on the text with the actor, when they are learning the lines they will automatically be doing some version of it for themselves.

Every actor knows that some sections of dialogue are harder to learn than others. This is usually when they stumble across a 'hole' in the script. A hole, or gap, is when the writing tries to disguise an inconsistency in the story or character, or perhaps a cut in a speech, and the actor has to leap across it, trying to make sense of something that does not flow with natural logic. If you don't go through this process with the actor in detail before the shoot it may well arise as a problem on set. The actor suddenly finds, when it's all happening for real, that they just can't make it work. If you gloss over it on set and ask the actor to 'just do it' the problem will then emerge again in the cutting room when you edit the material together. So it is in your interests to identify the problem at the earliest opportunity, when there is still time to fix it. I now relish these awkward moments of realisation.

Or perhaps there will not be any problems, holes, or gaps in the script, but going through it with an actor in a rehearsal or private meeting will deepen your own understanding of the character or the themes in your story by exposing them to the light with the person whose task it is to embody them.

Subtext

Whereas most people watching a film assume that the bulk of the writing consists of the dialogue – and every screenwriter knows that story-structure, character and evocation of imagery make up the real backbone of a script – every actor knows that subtext is what will make their part interesting. Subtext is what is not said, but we feel to be true. The character's thoughts and intentions may even run counter to what is being said. A good writer will structure these unhearable threads every bit as carefully as the spoken word.

You will often find the substance of the character (and the most subtle work of the actor) in this gap between what is being said and what is being thought or felt, but not said. You may find it in the gap between what the character is saying and what they are doing; in the delusions they carry about themselves. In effect this gap is an exploration of the unconscious. The written dialogue will, at its best, imply the thought process of the character, but can rarely spell it out in detail on the page – it would be a very long script if it did.

Some examples of unspoken subtext in my own screenplays include the young Orlando's jolly attempts to push his writing in the face of the sarcasm and obvious rejection by the writer Nick Greene, and Lola's insistence that Dante 'adores' her when we can see it is a doomed relationship in *The Man Who Cried*. The characters know what is going on at a deep level but pride and denial will not allow the difficult truth to rise to the surface. Their silences become more articulate than anything they could say. Similarly, in *Ginger & Rosa* there are several scenes between Ginger and her father, Roland, where what is not being said amplifies the intensity of the underlying feelings. Secrets – and the powerful silences that contain them – can be evoked very strongly if the actors know what it is that they are feeling or thinking but cannot say. Understanding the undertow, the unspoken feeling, will give depth to a performance even without the actor trying to 'show' any of it.

Hearing the script for the first time

If you listen carefully you will learn a lot about any problems or inconsistencies in the script at the very first read-through of a scene. Notice where the actor stumbles or hesitates, or where things seem to flow. Notice where you or the actor might feel too much pleasure in a literary turn of phrase (if it is not relevant to the character), or too little. You will suddenly hear repetitions that had previously passed unnoticed. You may recognise a phrase or theme that really belongs to another character. Beware of such overlaps, because one or the other will end up on the cutting-room floor. (But do not expect the actor to arrive at a fully rounded performance of the text at the first go. In fact I often suggest 'doing it wrong' in order to diffuse tension about 'getting it right'.)

On the second read-through you will start to learn what kind of direction works for the actor. For one actor it may be a great deal of analytical conversation about why the character is saying this or doing that. You may be expected to answer many questions, or discuss in detail the motivation, the reason for each word, each hesitation, or each silence. You may need to clarify the arc of change within the scene, explore how the character is different by the end of the scene compared to the beginning. You will find out – by how the performance is changing – which of your answers to the actor's questions are helpful or unhelpful, which verbal suggestions ignite a spark or seem to close things down.

For another actor this kind of verbal analysis may feel deadening. Too much reasoning, too much verbalising, may feel as if it is killing the life in the scene, obliterating the actor's instinct. The actor may still wish to read it aloud (or you may want them to, for your own reasons), but may not want or need to talk about it. In this instance your silent attentiveness will be far more useful than any phoney or superfluous 'direction'. Your careful listening will start to create the invisible 'space' in which the actor can work, and you will also privately discover vital information about the script itself.

Emotional memory and the 'Inner Score'

For an actor to connect with the inner life of a character, or the deeper themes of a scene, it can be useful – or even essential – to find a way of directly relating the character's experience to a memory of a similar experience in the actor's own life (loosely speaking, this is the famous 'method' approach to acting). Most actors do some version of this, consciously or unconsciously. The memory – which may be different to the substance of the script, but with a relevant emotional tone – will then anchor the scene in the inner life of the actor. An example might be a scene where the character faces a terrible loss, perhaps the death of a child. The actor may not have children or may not yet have faced the death of a loved one. But everyone has faced loss of some kind. By contacting a memory, empathetically grafting the memory onto the experience of the character, it will become easier to locate an authentic, more personal and less stereotyped expression of emotion. Or it may be that the emotion can be felt by the actor but not expressed. Emotional repression might turn out to be the most interesting way to play the scene.

A string of such moments, rooted in the actor's memory-bank, becomes one of the lines in a kind of inner 'score' to which the actor can refer: the equivalent of the musical score a conductor uses to track every instrument in the orchestra and how their parts relate to each other. (This is also a metaphor that applies to the director's work on a film, which is often compared to that of a conductor.) By the time of shooting, this private 'score' will have become quite elaborate, and the actor is, consciously or unconsciously, 'constructing' a complex inner life.

The actor will, on the top line of the 'score', be holding the lines – the spoken words – somewhere in his or her head. The second line will involve physical actions, sometimes predetermined instructions, such as walking to a certain spot ('hitting the mark', which may be necessary if the camera moves are fixed), or timing a move or turn of the head, an entrance or an exit: the 'blocking' of the scene, its choreography. The third line may involve holding an awareness of the arc of the scene – its overall pace and emotional development, a process that may have been clarified and absorbed in rehearsal. The fourth line may be locating or anchoring a moment in the actor's own memory or experience, which will trigger authentic feeling, causing tears to flow, or joy to radiate from the actor's face. The fifth line may be the subtext: what the character is not saying but may be thinking. Keeping awareness of these parallel lines requires extraordinary focus and mental and emotional agility on the actor's part: a blend of total engagement with and surrender to the present moment with, at the same time, a necessary degree of partial detachment, in which part of the actor's awareness is anchored in the crafting of the scene.

Drawing attention to these threads of awareness will not, however, be appropriate for all actors, which is the danger of systematising any 'method'. For some actors it might feel too mental and analytical a process consciously to engage with, even if unconsciously they are doing something very similar. This kind of actor may bring the text to life by unlocking a physical detail in the character's body: a posture, a way of walking, an accent, a turn of the head, or something as apparently simple as anchoring their awareness in their breathing. In the moment of 'enactment' this kind of actor may feel that too much verbal analysis of what they are doing is getting in the way of working instinctively. By forgetting everything else in the moment of shooting, when it eventually arrives, and entering into a state of suspended disbelief or even pure 'being', every word and gesture seems to arrive spontaneously and unbidden. Once again, therefore, the director's job is to observe what works for the individual during preparation rather than impose any particular, preconceived way of doing things.

Finding necessity

An actor may sometimes try to 'do' too much with the text. Ideally, once the actor knows the lines well – knows why something is being said and has found an impulse from within to speak, a kind of necessity – then a quality starts to emerge that feels somewhat metaphysical: 'letting the text speak you', not speaking the text. This becomes a kind of transmission, words flowing through the actor, rather than being pushed, shaped, or forced in any way. (This is also why rehearsal needs to be about the 'why' of a scene rather than the 'how'.)

Needless to say, this feeling of necessity relies on good writing. It's worth spelling out: again and again, at every stage of pre-production, the shoot, the edit, and at every showing of the film, you learn about the primacy of the script. The writing – especially its 'deep structure' – really is the key to the film working, which is why most actors will initially respond to the script above all. But it is also, paradoxically, ultimately only a blueprint. Or perhaps a better metaphor is that of a skin that must be inhabited and then shed. A script is also mutable. It can be changed. A director needs to be alert to when the lines need to be respected – spoken as written – and when a degree of irreverence and flexibility is called for.

Changing more fundamental aspects of the script during rehearsal (and especially during the shoot) can be dangerous. A good screenplay consists of more than spoken words. It is the structure, the emotional and narrative architecture that holds everything together. The writing of this 'deep structure' will have taken place over a long period of time, under solitary, contemplative conditions. Everything in a worked-through screenplay will be there for a reason. If you tinker with that under the turbulent conditions of the shoot, when you may forget why a particular fragment is a necessary part of the whole, you will probably live to regret it in the cutting room. Nevertheless, sometimes you realise, with dawning clarity, that something is wrong and must be changed. The earlier you spot this, the better. And when an actor finds, instinctively, that there is no genuine or necessary impulse from which to speak – or to play a scene at all – this can be as useful to you as a canary who senses problems deep underground before the miners know they are in danger.

12

Rewrites during pre-production (and beyond)

If you are a writer/director you have – at least – one enormous advantage: you can change things when they don't work without referring to anyone else. You don't have to turn to a writer, either in rehearsal or on the set, and say, as tactfully as you can, 'I know you've worked on this scene for years and it looks really good on the page, but in practice it just doesn't work.' Instead, you are quietly and ruthlessly saying this to yourself. You may also have a good idea of how to change it, because the actor has helped you to identify the problem. You can then become a unified channel of writing and directing decisions that will in turn help the actor to deliver something that works.

This state of unified authorship, where writing and directing are indivisible facets of each other, is the working method I am most familiar with. While I am writing a script, I am constantly imagining how to direct it – the pragmatic consequences of every place described, every action, every line to be spoken. While I am directing I am constantly learning about and clarifying the writing, both in the deeper sense of clarifying its meaning and also sometimes rewriting lines and cutting or adding scenes when I realise this is necessary. This double function does, however, also put a double burden of work on you, especially if you are making changes relatively late in the process. It also means that you do not have the advantages of another mind, another vision, to enrich and challenge your own.

If, however, you are a director working with a screenwriter, with all the advantages of this collaboration, you may still need to make changes in the script. In this situation you will need to be able to clearly communicate to the screenwriter the valuable lessons learned in your preparations with the actors. You need to be able to share the reason why something is not working. Either way, it is vital to learn to discriminate between holding true to a vision of the script and rigidly clinging to what you thought was right, when this moment is teaching you otherwise. Defensive rigidity, born of anxiety, is a false comfort that you must do without.

Perhaps you (or the writer) have worked for months or even years on a particular scene, until it becomes the most refined version of which you are capable. Now, in rehearsal – or worse still, on the day of the shoot – when it's already gone through many readings, in which everybody felt it was brilliant, it simply doesn't work. The actor starts to speak, and the opening lines sound like meaningless rubbish. What do you do? As a writer you feel like an idiot. All that work for nothing. How could you have ended up with this piece of trash? Or perhaps you are tempted to feel it's the actor who is useless. You may feel he or she is not managing to make your great writing come alive. Needless to say, this is not a useful train of thought to follow.

This is where alert and flexible thinking must come into play. For it may – or may not – be appropriate to rewrite or drop the offending lines. Perhaps it's something else that needs a rethink. The scene is unfolding in the wrong setting, or the action needs to be directed differently. Instead of shooting the scene looking at the actor's face while they're speaking, you might find that looking at the character's back is more expressive, because it is there that you are going to find a surprisingly muscular expression of the words, and insight into what they are really feeling but trying to hide. Or perhaps it's a different directorial choice: the camera should be looking at the other person in the scene, so that the meaning of the speaker's lines can be reflected in the listener's silent expression. In other words, your shooting choices – where you need the camera to look – may unlock what you were trying to do in the writing.

Your job as director when you hit a problem is to identify its true cause and not automatically assume the problem lies in the script. Experience has taught me that there is often something necessary in the core even of a sequence that isn't yet working, and that it is therefore best to be cautious before you throw it away, or its loss may haunt you later, in the cutting room.

It may turn out, however, when all these strategies have been tried, that the line – or the scene or the image – is wrong, and does need to be rewritten or even cut. At which point, with the crew and production team waiting anxiously, you say alright, let's move on to the next scene. (Your mind is racing, wondering when you can next find half an hour to work on it. Will it be at two in the morning? Or do I need to work this through with the actor in private? Can I reach the script editor to double-check whether this is a vital link that I've forgotten?) You have to be ready to do this kind of thinking on your feet; it is a vital part of your work as director. An attitude of adaptability, flexibility and responsibility is really key: knowing when to change something, when to stick with it and try to make it work, or when to drop it entirely, at any stage of pre-production, the shoot, or the edit. Dance like a butterfly, sting like a bee. You are in the ring, fighting for your film, which has become your life.

I have learned this particular lesson the hard way. Many scenes and lines were cut from *The Man Who Cried* (due to pressures of budget and schedule) that proved to be vital missing links once the film was put together. During the shoot of *Orlando*, however, working against the clock in freezing conditions and falling light, Walter Donohue (my script editor) became the 'guardian' of the script, an independent pair of eyes, and made sure that any cuts made at the last minute were creative and astringent – a form of distillation – rather than tearing into the fabric of the story.

13

Improvisation (finding freedom?)

Improvisation as a way of arriving at character and dialogue has a long and respected history in cinema. John Cassavetes' hugely influential *Shadows* (1959) drew on the spirit of improvisation in jazz. The work of Mike Leigh is another example of the extensive use of improvisation in script development, although it should not be underestimated how much he then shapes the material, following a long and detailed period of rehearsal.

Improvisation at different stages of the process can feel liberating for the actor, but an improvised, natural feel can also be achieved by an actor's ability to enter into the present moment, even with very structured lines. If the character has been written with enough contradictions, layers of complexity, moments of surprise, subtext, and with a good 'ear' for the spoken word, then there is plenty for the actor to work with. If it feels stilted, predictable, unsayable, then the actor may want an opportunity to help the part 'breathe' through improvising around the script. An actor's stated desire to improvise, therefore, can be symptomatic of unresolved problems in the script – a useful piece of information in itself for the director.

I always work through the script with each actor, one-on-one, in a room somewhere, under relaxed conditions, very early in the process, to find out if there are any areas that are not clear, or inadequately written, or somehow don't fit the voice and body of the particular individual. The actor reads his or her part aloud, we talk it through and expose weak areas to the light. Then I go away and make any necessary changes. My aim is to make the writing seem indivisible from the playing, and for the audience to feel that no other actor could have played the part. This liberates the actor to

concentrate on embodiment, on relating his or her unique experience to the text, without stumbling over obstacles in the text or
worrying about the 'fit'. But skilful rewriting may still not be
enough for the part to come alive. This is when improvisation can
be extremely useful, especially during the period of preparation.

Once you are shooting a film the process of in-the-moment writing (which improvisation essentially is) can sometimes create distor-
tions in the broader text. At the time the actor may feel free, inventive
and 'real'. In the cutting room the precision of the original script (if
it was revised and honed as much as it should have been) shows
once again, following the controlled chaos of the shoot. Improvised
deviations, and elaborations, which at the time seemed funny or
brilliant, can often then seem irrelevant, confusing, or long-winded.

Precision in playing – a precision that reflects a worked-through
script – is very satisfying. It can be passionate, for precision is not
a cold concept but a fierce one: the protection of a vision. Wild
and out of control can be good too, if that is a quality you want
your film to have. But the improvisers of genius in the world of
jazz (Charlie Parker, for example) were working with extraordinary levels of skill. They were at one with their instruments, which
became extensions of their bodies, and had such deep knowledge of
harmony that their free, soaring riffs were a form of deep musical
writing that integrated seamlessly with the other lines and the piece
as a whole. They were always listening to each other as intensely as
they were offering up their own solos.

During the years performing in music groups, and also improvising words in performance-art events, I learnt that this form of
spontaneous writing can teach you a great deal about the rigour of
coming into the moment and being alert to those around you. The
audience is witnessing, there and then, the unfolding of a composition, in which their energy as watchers and listeners is almost as
important to the totality of the event as the musicians or performers themselves. For in being heard, the work comes into being.

You can capture this feeling of present-time spontaneity with actors by exploring the 'feeling' of improvisation, even when it is based on a character already written with a story already resolved. What improvisation feels like, when it works, is the freedom to follow an impulse from within. The best moments have a feeling of inevitability, but can also take you by surprise. This feeling, which is dangerous, un-calculated, and alert, can be experienced during sessions of improvising around the text. Once the feeling has been identified, it can be found again during rehearsal with the written lines and can then be recaptured during the shoot.

Joan Allen and Simon Abkarian in *Yes*

Improvisation in rehearsal can have many other useful functions. The actor can start to 'own' the character by getting to know how he or she behaves in imaginary scenes which are never going to appear in the film – the before-and-after moments, outside the frame, even outside the story, but inside the life of the character. This then becomes a private memory-bank for the actor, as if the life has already been lived and the events of the film are the consequences of past actions and experiences. This can allow the actor to feel that he or she can 'breathe' in the unfettered, or even chaotic space in and around the precision of the writing.

The feeling of ownership of the script that ensues has another function too: the actor can subjectively experience him- or herself as the author of the character, and bring this quality of authority to the scenes – what we call 'creating' a character, even when written by somebody else. A writer/director with a good ear may also pick up some gems: a turn of phrase here, a missing link there, which can then be incorporated into the script. The actor's instinct for authenticity is likely to be running high when he or she is, in effect, taking responsibility for the character, and this instinct is invaluable.

Most film actors, however, will find improvisation exercises of the kind often used in theatrical rehearsals both embarrassing and unnecessary. Games, ball-throwing and other types of group work often used to build a sense of ensemble in a stage production can be counter-productive when preparing a film. This is because the actor's energy needs to be focused in a different, more individual way for the lens, whereas stage actors are preparing themselves to become a cohesive group for the collective gaze of an audience.

Improvising the unsaid

Some ways of using improvisation in rehearsal that relate more directly to the needs of a film that I have found useful include asking the actors to riff around a particular speech or section of dialogue to 'loosen it up', or imagining what might have happened or have been said immediately before or after a scene. It is extremely fruitful for each actor to give voice to the characters' secret opinions about the others, or their thoughts and feelings about world events. It's a way of getting to know who the character is, how the actor feels about the character they are playing, or the assumptions they are making about the film as a whole. These were tools we used in rehearsal for *Yes*, which, as it was written in rhyming iambic pentameter, needed to be delivered word-perfect. It therefore became crucially important to 'naturalise' the language by understanding where it was coming from: the unspoken lives of the characters off-screen. We also used this process to great effect whilst preparing *Ginger & Rosa*.

Elle Fanning and Alice Englert on location in *Ginger & Rosa*

When, as with this film, you do not wish the screenplay to plod through lots of explanatory back-story or the characters to say aloud what they are feeling, the actors themselves need to hold this secret knowledge. In a rehearsal of this kind, where the actors can spell out the world of the unsaid, for example by expressing what they imagine their character is feeling about the words or actions of another, they are laying out a road-map that can imbue performances with a quality of subtle authenticity.

Learning how to discriminate between a useful process (which will not alter the written script) and useable material (developed through improvisation) is essential, however, if the film is not to veer off track in the exhilaration of the live, improvised moment.

Part Two

The Shoot

Elle Fanning and camera

14

Acting for the camera (from stage to screen)

Acting for the cinema and acting for the theatre are parallel but subtly different arts. Actors who are magnificent on stage can somehow 'disappear' on screen. The reverse is also true. A charismatic screen actor can seem very ordinary, even diminished, on stage. There are many reasons for this, but with the right awareness the problems of transition from stage to screen can be solved.

Acting on stage is a specific discipline with certain constraints and freedoms. After a period of rehearsal in which the text is analysed, character is developed, movement is blocked, timing refined, and a cohesive ensemble arrived at – all orchestrated by the director – the actor then effectively takes control once he or she is on stage and the show is up and running. Even when the director is watching and giving notes after performances, the actors, in the moment of 'enactment', carry the flow, can be influenced by the mood and responses of the audience, and experience the play in real-time, in the right order, controlling its pitch and the arc of its development.

Effectively the actors stand alone – together – on stage and feel in control of the destiny and delivery of their performance. There are no surprises other than accidents or subtle changes of detail that may arise in the moment, though each and every performance is unique and mutable. There is also a feat of memory involved in learning the text. The actor has to hold the entire play in his or her head and yet deliver it as if it is unfolding in the moment. Furthermore, with the exception of matinées, a play usually happens in the evening, sometimes every evening for months on end. There are many opportunities to refine a role or correct mistakes. There is no 'definitive' performance. There is just another night, another show.

It is an inherently impermanent art-form, which is both its tragedy and a source of mystery and joy.

In cinema, by contrast, the actor usually has to get up very early in the morning, often wait around for hours, deliver a scene in segments, from a script frequently shot completely out of order, without knowing which take will be used, whether certain scenes or lines will eventually be cut, and what music or effects will be on the soundtrack. He or she may never meet some of the other actors, and may have little or no feeling of the film as a whole. Nevertheless, he or she has to be ready at a moment's notice to be 'on'. There may be little or no 'warm-up' into a scene. Despite a varying number of takes, you either get it, or you don't. But this brutally pragmatic process is in the service of something that will become relatively permanent.

All this creates an extraordinary degree of dependence – whether acknowledged or not by the actor – upon the judgement of the director. In many cases the actors have very little control over their final performance on screen. This is one of the reasons some actors may try to exert control in other ways: nit-picking deal points, demanding excessive fees, larger trailers and so on. These demands can often be understood as an attempt to feel powerful in a situation where, in reality, they feel (and often are) relatively powerless. But there is also the potential for their work to reach a huge audience, for many years, even after their own death. An actor's work on film may almost be described as leaving an immortal trace.

One of the first things a stage actor needs to do when working on a film is to relinquish familiar feelings of control of the performance space, and discover a different way to play: a state of surrender, demanding a different relationship with their energy and presence and an utterly different relationship with the audience. Simply put, a stage actor projects energy outwards towards a live audience. This energetic emanation can take many forms, from vocal projection (the best of which is unforced but nevertheless audible in the back rows of the top balcony) to understanding how to angle the body in an unforced way towards the fourth wall and what scale of gesture or detail of body language will 'read' from a distance. The feeling is of reaching out, or projecting – this can be subtle and delicate or large and over the top (as in the case of farce).

This energetic emanation – which you can think of as a sort of cone shape, funnelling outwards from the actor's body towards the audience – can appear diffuse and overblown on camera. Essentially, the greatest screen actors seem to draw energy towards them, exerting a form of magnetic attraction; or sometimes they seem to quietly funnel energy from their body into the lens. They may or may not be consciously aware of doing this, but once you have seen it and learnt to recognise it, it is a palpably different experience on set. The result on screen will be riveting. There is no one else you will want to watch.

Being aware of these different energies is not the same as knowing how to communicate with the actor about what needs to be done for their work to become readable on camera. Here is where trial and error and careful, precise use of language is important. Film directors will often deal with the problem of excessive 'theatricality' (an overblown, forced quality) by saying 'do it smaller', or 'do less'. This is a crude shorthand which is generally understood and may be somewhat effective but doesn't really tackle the root of the problem. It just addresses the scale of the performance.

A helpful direction for an actor who seems to be pushing too hard may be to take their attention away from the exterior and into the interior work of the scene. If they seem to be concentrating on 'showing' a feeling, with a gesture or facial expression that somehow rings false when looked at through the lens, or you sense that the performance is being aimed at a distance (this applies whether the camera is near or far, whether it is a close-up or a long-shot), you can ask him or her to concentrate on the connecting thoughts – the spaces between the lines – and trust that the camera will register this subtle interior work. It's not about doing less – on the contrary, this inner work requires extreme focus – but about showing less.

If, during the shoot, you sense that the actor is playing to the crew – which seems to be the nearest available audience, an equivalent to the theatrical experience – you need to interrupt this dynamic. You can tell by watching the actor's eyes after a take. If they flicker around the crew, looking for reaction, laughter, or approval, you have entered a danger zone. You need the actor to search for your eyes, first and foremost. But this depends on the relationship you have built, and the quality of your attention. A crew will always be an unreliable audience, for they are, by definition, busy with their own preoccupations, and may be tired or even bored by numerous takes. If the actor is trying to please them, the performance will start to become forced, played for laughs, diffuse, and generalised. And the actor may have diluted his or her energy between takes by relating too much to them rather than being 'present' at the actual moment of shooting. This is a hard skill for a stage actor to learn. Their performance moments in a film may be relatively fleeting, in a long day full of distractions. Then it's suddenly over. 'Is that it?' they may feel. 'But I haven't arrived yet.'

The camera and charisma

Stage actors may also not feel at ease with the camera itself. But the lens is, in effect, a stand-in for the eyes of each individual person in the audience in the cinema, and eventually determines how they will experience the film and the actor. The camera – this anonymous piece of metal, with its relatively tiny framing device – is the gateway to untold one-on-one relationships with strangers in the future. It invites intimacy. It is this quality of intimacy in performance, a quality of invitation, rather than projection, which becomes very powerful on screen.

Screen actors can, when working deeply, seem to bring them-selves all the way into their skin, somehow seeming 'full'. A quality of aliveness, of being radiantly there from the core of the body out-wards, comes from deeply resonating with a fictional 'other' who embodies a reality more articulate and distilled than is possible in daily life. The actor 'lets go' into a state of surrender, an empathetic leap. This can, in turn, reveal qualities in the actor that otherwise remain hidden.

We all – whether professional actors or not – consciously or unconsciously develop (or have thrust upon us) over the years a 'self' that we confuse with an essential nature. We do it more or less well, of course, but are often unsure about who we 'really' are. (Anyone who has been told 'just be yourself' when being photo-graphed will recognise the quiet panic that ensues.) The fact is that we create ourselves anew in every fresh situation. An actor does it more consciously, slipping into a parallel skin called a 'character', but drawing on his or her experience in order to render this fic-titious 'other' authentic and believable. It is this that explains, to some degree, the phenomenon of charisma. It is a kind of focused state of being where the essential self comes to the surface and radi-ates outwards. Most of us are in a state of retreat from our own skin. Our nature and qualities are often hidden. An unfettered quality in an actor's face – an access to their 'essence' – helps us to feel we 'know' the person. This is an experience that confronts actors repeatedly when strangers come up to them and treat them as their closest intimates.

Transparency on screen

The quality of 'transparency' on screen is a combination of this inner luminosity or fullness on the part of the actor with appropri-ate lighting and exposure, for we read a lot of emotional informa-tion through skin tone and how it reflects or absorbs light. It is also

about a quality of relaxation – a lack of obstacles to the performance, whether acting habits, physical tics, weird posture, or any
other manifestation of tension. Any number of obstacles – or visual
'noise' – will arise to prevent the blissful state of transparency, and
most actors are eager to shed these obstacles as fast as possible.

You can help with the outer obstacles very easily during the
shoot. If someone's hair, clothes, a shadow on their face or an
object in the background is taking your attention away from the
performance, then you can do something about it, usually with
the help of your crew. If the obstacle is an acting habit, a tic or
over-rehearsed rigidity, you can guide them away from it, or simply
try drawing the actor's attention to the problem if you sense that
feedback will help them correct it. If the problem is one of tension,
you need to use your skills to help the actor relax – a process of
trial and error. It may be a question of verbal reassurance, or a light
touch, even a fleeting shoulder massage. Or perhaps you need to
crack a joke to lighten the atmosphere. If the obstacle lies in the
text – the actor is struggling with lines that feel wrong, redundant,
stilted, or even incomprehensible – then you need to address the
problem directly, either by unravelling it until it's clear, or perhaps
with a careful emergency rewrite.

If the obstacle is still there, then you need to address more subtle
layers in the person. Perhaps this is no longer a question of character, text, or body language but is caused by fear. A quality in the
actor is in the process of becoming visible, once they have stopped
trying to protect themselves with 'technique' or 'doing' too much.
The actor will at this point, begin to feel very vulnerable indeed. It
is as if a veil is lifting and the person is naked.

At this moment of maximum vulnerability for the actor, you
need to be at your most tender, protective and confident. Hold the
space, show with your expression that something good is happening, keep the crew focused and moving forward. Your awareness of
the actor's process will be rewarded by a quality of simplicity and

transparency on screen that is radiant and charismatic; where the actor, unfettered by habit, tension, technique and so-called 'identity', reveals something essentially human. It can be very moving, and usually has little to do with 'emoting', conscious portrayal of character, or any other form of 'doing'. It is a quality of 'being' that the camera can register, as if you can see through the actor's skin to something metaphysical.

Non-professional actors can sometimes achieve this quality of presence precisely because they are unencumbered by rigidities of technique, self-consciousness, attempts at control or awareness of how what they are doing might look from the outside. It's a form of 'beginner's luck'. When you see this quality of transparency and openness emerging with performers, at any level of experience, it feels like an awakening. It takes you back to the very roots of what acting can be: a profound circuit of energy between the watcher and the watched, in which we are reminded that we are alive.

This is when, as a director, you can bathe in a sense of wonder.

Claudia Lander-Duke in *The Man Who Cried*

15

The art of collaboration
(being inclusive, taking responsibility)

Film-making is always a collaborative art-form, but if you are the director you can't remind yourself too often that it is your responsibility – and yours alone – to keep in mind the vision of the film as a whole. You really are the only one who can do this: it is your job to completely envision it, continually adapting and refining the imaginary completed film in your head as it comes together, piece by piece. You are also, therefore, the only person who knows how everyone else's work fits together in the jigsaw. This singularity of vision and responsibility can make directing a lonely occupation, despite the fact that you are working closely with many other people. Film-making may be a collaboration, but it has a leader, and leadership can feel solitary, even when you are surrounded by willing and able others.

Leadership was a problematic concept for me to embrace from a political point of view early in my working life (when collectives were idealised and hierarchies of all kinds abhorred), even though it was clearly necessary when making a feature film, which is always made at speed, with no time to sit and discuss. Decisiveness is everything when every second counts. The confusion between democratic or collective social and political processes and the necessity for an individual voice and leadership in a film – even when many people are working on it together – led to much soul-searching and many passionate arguments at the time. Can a medium that functions as an industry be led by individual artists in a way that is neither exploitative nor oppressive of the skills and initiatives of others? All I knew was that, despite my belief in human equality, I wanted to take charge of the process. I longed to do it; I had to direct. It was a burning passion – an absolute necessity – for me to be able to control the shape and meaning of the work. I also knew, however, that being a director – whilst it meant taking a strong position of leadership – did not mean that I was intrinsically a better or more important human being. Directing was simply a necessary role – arguably the key role in cinema.

The person occupying this role tries to invite others into his or her vision, at the same time guiding the process so that every member of the team sees the imaginary film with the same eyes as it gradually comes into being. The director is also responsible for allocating the limited time available: this means knowing how to prioritise and to pace; how to orchestrate the precious days and weeks during the working process. The first assistant director will organise the shooting schedule and you will be in constant dialogue about moment-to-moment time management, but as the director you will have the last word, for you are the only one who knows whether a close-up is worth lingering over, or whether you 'have' the scene in one wide-shot. You are looking for a quality of 'passionate detachment' in yourself; entirely and intensely engaged, but also striving for objectivity about what is important at any given moment. You must always keep a sense of priority for the good of the film as a whole when you are choosing what to do, whilst making sure there is a feeling – especially for the actors – that there will be time for everything that matters.

Time

One of the most alarming, disorienting things that actors discover when working on a film for the first time is how little time there seems to be for anything, even though they seem to spend much of the day waiting around in a state of suspended readiness. It's easy for the actual moment of shooting to come and go in what feels like an imperfect rush. The director may seem partially absent at the crucial moment, clearly preoccupied with a mass of technical and aesthetic details and continually answering a flood of questions from members of the crew. The actor can suddenly feel alone and the experience can be of an opportunity lost.

Time is the monster on the director's back. Every second on a shoot is crucial and there is always so much to be achieved in any given day in order not to fall behind in the schedule. It can feel like running, with the burning intensity of a sprint, which is exactly what a shoot is: a sprint in the middle of the long marathon of making a film. The writing and development may well have taken several long, slow years; the edit and post-production six intensive and focused months. The shoot itself may be only a few weeks. For many independent film-makers in the last decade or two, shoots have got shorter and shorter. My earliest feature film shoots seemed to average ten weeks, whereas *Ginger & Rosa*, for example, was a mere five. Working at this speed is, of course, a consequence of budget. Economic austerity and a 'risk-averse' cultural mood conspire to make film budgets lower and lower. Some aspects of this are positive. A smaller crew can be more cohesive and the principle of 'no waste', having to concentrate only on what is absolutely essential, can have a usefully astringent effect, aesthetically and dramatically. But it's hard to do your best work when you are running from one scene to the next, on little sleep, without any time for reflection or reverie.

One freezing night I stood on an ice-rink in St Petersburg with Alexei Rodionov, the extraordinary Russian cinematographer I had chosen to shoot *Orlando*. It was his first experience of shooting on a western production and the shortest shoot he had previously done had lasted nine months. We had ten weeks to shoot our story, starting at the end of winter in Russia, catching early spring in England and then the heat of the desert in Uzbekistan. We had to work very fast indeed. Alexei was balancing on a ladder on the ice, adjusting some lights, in a state of near panic. 'This is inhuman,

Sally,' he said to me in anguish. 'Too quick, no time for thinking.'
The strategy I adopted to deal with the time pressure – and the risk
of going off track in a state of thoughtless haste – was to shoot no
'coverage' at all. Every scene was shot almost exactly as it would be
edited. It became an exhilarating discipline and led to some interesting shooting solutions. But I envied what sounded – relatively
speaking – like a state of creative languor in the work process Alexei
had experienced with Elem Klimov on *Come and See* (1985), where
if there was a problem with a sequence, or an actor, they would
simply break for a week or two and rewrite, re-imagine, or do some
in-depth rehearsal. But this was in the days of the state-supported
Soviet film industry, without any commercial pressure in the western sense. Money and time had different meanings.

Given that squeezed budgets are now a reality, and that learning
to use the lack of time as a spur to greater inventiveness is therefore
a necessity, it becomes a question of attitude. We may not be able
to control circumstance (financial constraint or a tight shooting
schedule) but we can control our attitude towards it, and decide
that it can even become an advantage. It is yet another reason for
taking longer – and working deeper – in the preparatory period,
when costs are infinitely lower. In the early one-on-one meetings
with actors, and in rehearsal, you can create an atmosphere of
'slow cooking'. Even a ten-minute exchange with the actor can be
achieved without rushing. For those moments, you can slow the
world down and make the working process feel as languorous as it
needs to. Then, when the heat of the shoot is on, the memory of
the preparatory work will be a form of reassurance. We are able to
run because we have walked, and can walk because before that we
crawled. The first stage, those early thrilling moments of discovering a world, are when you sit and talk with your actor.

Working at speed can be energising, but needs to emerge from a
state of relaxation. A ballet dancer pirouettes and jumps in a burst
of energy after slow, deliberate preparation at the barre, warming

every muscle. Similarly, a film actor needs to have experienced a meaningful and careful 'warm-up' (even if it's some weeks before) in order to be able to seize the moment and arrive, in a state of focused presence, at the word 'action'. This applies to the director as well, of course. The only possible way to be present, alert, intuitive, flexible and inventive in the mad whirl of a shoot is to have engaged in 'slow', thoughtful, detailed preparation on every aspect of the film beforehand.

The balancing act

The director needs to create a mode of working at every stage of the process, fast or slow, in which each person on both sides of the camera feels the film is also theirs. It helps if you try to see the genius nestling within each of the people you are working with, to appreciate them (and their ideas) as much as possible, but also to be very clear about what you are looking for. If you can create an atmosphere of inclusiveness, humanly and aesthetically, people will feel their contribution is respected. They will feel valued, and motivated to give more.

The director's challenge is therefore, at its core, a balancing act. You need to help people to do their best, recognise what gifts they are giving to you and to the film, but at the same time you have to take ultimate responsibility for the entire piece, including the work of others, which may sometimes entail criticising, cutting or demanding changes. In turn, you are the one who will ultimately be held responsible for the result. You may be praised, but you will surely also face criticism once the film is finished, for you are the one who will be held accountable.

Everyone in the collaboration, however responsible they are individually in attitude or deed, relies on you to exercise your judgement, and gives you their trust, both to help them do their best work and to honour the vision of the film as a whole. The feeling you may then have – that it's all down to you – doesn't mean you have actually done everything: on the contrary, you rely very heavily on the work of others; you work through the medium of their work. Nor are you an omniscient god, who has caused every dynamic or feeling in the room. In the attempt to be responsible, you can swing too far and start to indulge in 'magical thinking'. It is not your job to be a therapist (although some of the delicate processes involved may stray confusingly into that area), or to try and change the people you are working with. Surprising qualities may emerge under the pressure of a shoot, but people do not fundamentally change in those short, intense weeks. If you can take a visible attitude of absolute responsibility – whether or not you feel up to it – and never blame anybody for anything that goes wrong, you are going to go a very long way to winning the trust of the actors and everybody else who works with you.

Actors need to see that you know what you're doing in order for them to be able to concentrate on what they're doing. They need to feel confidence in the director to protect them, create a space in which they can let go, or become vulnerable, in the ways necessary to play the role, to really 'be' on screen. If they can't relax because they are worried about your leadership, it will show.

Sometimes a 'testing' of your skill and decisiveness seems to happen and you need to know when to stand your ground. If you don't recognise the phenomenon when it occurs and you are seen to concede everything to an actor's demands, everyone starts to worry. What else might you let go? Sometimes it's important to say no. Not for its own sake, or as a demonstration of power, but to show you are strong enough to protect the film and all the actors' and crew's work in it.

I had one experience of an insecure actor who insisted on telling me where he thought the camera should be placed in a difficult scene. I made the mistake of humouring him, and moved the camera, though I knew he was wrong. It wasted a lot of time and lost

me the respect of the crew and the other actors on the set, which
was hard to win back. In this instance it would have been better to
draw a line and refuse, even if he had then shouted at me – which
was perhaps what he was looking for an excuse to do anyway, as a
way of letting off some tension he was feeling about what he was
being asked to do in the scene.

Gossip

Gossip on set (or indeed at any stage of pre- or post-production)
is a destructive way of communicating, which is one of the reasons
why I have disguised the anecdote above to protect the identity of
the actor concerned. As director you can set a tone about gossip.
Refuse to talk about people behind their back. A discussion with
your costume designer or make-up artist about a problem an actor
is having with their clothes or their face is a different matter. But
even here you need to be careful. It is better not to succumb to the
temptation to download any frustrations you may be having about
the actor to other crew members. It may take effort and self-control
to refrain from any personal comments or criticisms about the person concerned. But if you do not discuss an actor's private life,
do not share anything you have discussed in rehearsal and never
divulge any confidential information, you will be a worthy guardian of a cherished relationship.

Gossip is the last resort of the powerless. If you engage in it you
too will look powerless and untrustworthy. If you set the highest
possible standards for yourself, you have at least a chance that this
will filter through to the crew. I try to nip any rumours or gossiping
by others in the bud, however much 'fun' it may seem to be at the
time.

16

Performing being a director
(your work goes public)

A lot of directors – even quite experienced ones – are secretly afraid of how they will appear to the crew and to the actors. They walk onto the set anxious that their own performance – that of being a director – is not going to be up to scratch. In fact they can be more preoccupied with playing their own role than they are with the performance of the actors. I've caught myself doing this on a bad day. Any actor who's worth their salt is going to sniff that out immediately. They're going to see someone acting being a really serious, thoughtful director, who knows exactly what they're doing, and who is going to demonstrate this by telling everybody what to do and how to do it. Of course, what everyone will really see is a demonstration of a subtext of anxiety.

What the director needs to do is quite simple: be open about what you do and don't know, do and don't want. Communicate clearly and simply, and above all observe the effect of your actions and directions on the actors and other members of the crew. The first moments together with the actors, on the set, are crucial. It's not so much what you do as director as the quality of respectful attention and playful alertness you bring with you during those early hours and days. The actors will be paying attention not only to your behaviour with them but also how you treat your crew.

When you are working, you give out a lot of messages with your facial expression. Directors often forget that actors and crew are looking at their face as well as the unfolding scene on the set. You are so busy and preoccupied that you can feel curiously invisible. In fact, you will be watched all the time when you're working. If you look at an actor with a grim expression, they may well think they've done something wrong. So you have to think of yourself as a vehicle of expression – just as an actor does – with all the warmth and clarity that you can muster. Looking at 'making of' footage can be very telling. I have found, for example, that when I'm concentrating I can be frowning ferociously, which could easily be misinterpreted.

On set with cast and crew of *Ginger & Rosa*

The moment a shoot begins can be an abrupt transition for a director. After months spent alone in a room (if you are a writer/director) and then sitting in endless meetings with your heads of department going over the script, or running about searching for locations, you're suddenly on a set, with thirty people (or more) looking at you while you're trying to figure out where to put the camera or what to say to the actor. Yours is a job that is executed in public, and you have to realise, therefore, that you can be read like a book at any given moment. The tone you set in the human relationships – with your facial expression and way of behaving – is an important part of the work. Of course, at times some relationships will be more demanding of your attention than others and most crew members will understand if you need to focus exclusively on an actor. But whatever else is going on it helps to greet everyone – cast and crew – in the morning before work begins. It is a reminder that you are all in it together and that each individual's work matters. A visible hierarchy of 'importance' creates an unbalanced, destructive atmosphere, whereas simple good manners generate an atmosphere of respect and an acknowledgement of your interdependence.

In a sense, you can invent who you want to be (and how to behave) as a director: the role offers you that opportunity. A lot of who we think we are is really a matter of habit, in any case, rather than anything essential. The Alexander Technique (which focuses on body 'memory' and alignment) is a very useful method for demonstrating this on a physical level. Crooked 'feels' normal or straight; when you change for the better it can 'feel' wrong. Similarly, it can feel strange when we decide to change a behavioural habit or habitual way of looking at the world. One of my mental habits, for example, is to be a catastrophist, imagining everything that could go wrong at any moment. This is not particularly useful on a film set. Sometimes I notice that I have slipped into this state and try to change the habit by saying to myself: 'So far today the set has not caught fire. There have been no visible tragedies. How about deciding that today everything is going to be fine?' This doesn't mean ignoring problems when they arise, but it usually helps me to have a lighter approach towards them.

As a general principle, it comes as a relief to break out of the habitual patterns of how you relate to the world and to other people, whatever they may be. The habits may seem useful, or comfortable, but often function as an invisible prison. If you are 'naturally' shy, for example – something I have also experienced – you can decide to appear open and relaxed, if that's what the situation demands. As Hunny, my grandmother, once said to me – just act the way you want to be, and you will eventually become it. This was a wonderful piece of advice.

17

Looking for happiness on set (an unreliable goal?)

A film shoot, however exhilarating it may be, is often also a stress-ful, exhausting process for everyone concerned. The constant pres-sure of time – as time costs money – means little sleep and no rest. What I've come to realise is that the happy moments, the easy moments, are a bonus, but not a prerequisite, for making good work. A deeper joy is sometimes arrived at through an uncomfort-able or even painful experience.

Pushing past limits – your own and other people's – can cause resentment, tension or even panic to rise to the surface. One has to learn to welcome these feelings – in yourself and in others – as symptoms of something working in productive ways on a deeper level. There are days when you may feel that the crew seems to hate you, where everything seems to have gone wrong, the actors didn't do what you wanted, and you are in despair. But then you find out later in the cutting room, when you look objectively at the mater-ial, that the scene works well – in fact it may even be the best thing you've ever done. So the subjective experience of pain (or equally, of happiness or joy) in the moment may not be relevant. The only meaningful question to ask yourself is: did you do the right thing, or the best that you could, the true thing? Sometimes doing the right thing brings pain with it.

But how do you deal with the pain when it arises in the working process? You have to remind yourself that subjective feeling states are an unreliable guide to excellence, and therefore aiming at fun or happiness on set, for its own sake, is not necessarily very helpful. Instead you need to locate a feeling of being connected with pur-pose or meaning, on a good day or a bad day, on a happy day or an unhappy day. Understanding the causes of your own despair in the work process will, in turn, lead you to be able to deal effectively with difficult feelings the actors are battling with, that may manifest themselves in confusing behaviour.

The corollary of all this, of course, is that just because something was painful, it was not necessarily good. My shoots are often characterised by huge amounts of laughter, rampant displays of affection and sheer joy in the working process. But this is a by-product of the work and our collective enthusiasm, not a goal in itself.

Professionalism and efficiency

True professionalism is about focusing on the job in hand, doing it as well as you possibly can and keeping a sense of priority – the bigger vision of the film as a whole – rather than getting lost in the ups and downs of the process. You need to do what is right and necessary rather than what you 'feel' like. In the attempt to generate a nice atmosphere, keep people happy, or try and make them like you, it is possible to lose sight of the longer view. In order to do your best work there is an overriding need for clarity and efficiency – or even of ruthlessness. The qualities that will help people around you – including the actors – to really relax and respect you (more important than being liked, in the long run) are when they see you doing your job, keeping focused, setting the highest possible standards, and not settling for second-best in any area (for this reason I always ban the use of the word 'compromise' on set). An actor doesn't necessarily want to become your best friend and isn't looking for a quality of 'niceness' but rather one of quiet ferocity in the pursuit of excellence.

Orlando – which I made in this spirit – was the first film where I risked being hated for my perfectionism. I often demanded retakes at the end of long days, insisted on sets being re-redesigned or costumes remade overnight. It was not an easy shoot, but I don't regret any of my unpopular decisions or the extent to which I pushed people. On the contrary, I look back in some amazement at my capacity for ruthlessness in pursuit of a clear vision. At the time I feared I might never make another film. It was all or nothing. I regret the occasional slide, on some subsequent films, into the needy desire to be loved – on occasion, this has led me to compromise on something I knew was wrong.

I had some vivid experiences of the contradictory relationship between feeling and result – and pain and happiness – on the other side of the camera during *The Tango Lesson*. This film was often an extremely painful experience to make, physically and emotionally. The sequence most often played on YouTube, and often imitated – 'Libertango': a tango for three men and a woman (me) – needed to look joyful but was physically agonising to shoot as my feet were so blistered. Tempers were frayed, the atmosphere was thick with hostility and exhaustion and I ended up covered in bruises, with shoes full of blood. But we were all prepared to struggle, painfully, for a result that might communicate some of the deeper joys of dancing together. And I think it does look joyful.

With Pablo Verón, Fabián Salas and Gustavo Naveira in *The Tango Lesson*

18

Communication

In theory, direction and feedback to actors whilst shooting should be a simple, clear process. In practice it can feel complex and difficult. Actors are individual human beings who are trying to find a way of doing what they need to do and at the same time are trying to figure out what you want. They're trying to please you, and at the same time, they hope that you're not going to let them look like an idiot on the screen. You know all this, and yet – suddenly – you see an actor do something that isn't what you want at all. It doesn't fit the scene, it unbalances the dynamic, it's ponderous or too throwaway, it's unfilmable.

When something goes wrong in this way, you have to know how to communicate in ways that will mean something to the actor concerned. It can be a delicate process: discovering what to avoid and what to concentrate on so that they will continue to feel good about themselves and maintain pride in their work, even when you are implying criticism by asking them to do something differently. The first thing to do, of course, is to try to communicate simply and directly what you want instead, which may involve explaining what you think is wrong. If the actor tightens up and becomes defensive, this means the straightforward route is not working and you need to think again.

This is when it can start to get convoluted and you can lose your way. It helps to remember that everybody wants to do their best. The desire to do well is usually the actor's overwhelming wish, and actors are often afraid that they might not be able to deliver. So you may need to reassure them about what they just did whilst gently suggesting another possible approach to the scene. This may feel painful, slow and indirect as a way of correcting something, but may turn out to be a tactful and strategic way to arrive at the best result. It is important, however, to strive never to be dishonest or manipulative. This will backfire, eventually. Sometimes it's better to directly involve the actor by openly sharing your concern about what isn't working. This takes the emphasis away from what the actor is doing and puts the problem into the arena of the relationship between you, one that you can solve together.

You can also ask the actors to help you. Then you're not just asking for a different result, but you're also involving them in locating the cause of the problem and finding a solution. You are including them in the evolution of the piece. They'll feel respected as actors, pleased that their point of view is being heard, and under these conditions they're more likely to give you what you really want. Actors' suggestions are often invaluable; not necessarily as the solution to the problem but by illuminating its root cause. The issue may not be how they are performing a scene but rather that they are being asked to do or say something that they instinctively know isn't right, and that they are then overcompensating for.

There are many occasions when your own instinct takes over, too. An actor is delivering a performance that you know is not working but you just don't know why, and you can't figure out what you are looking for instead. A director may, under these circumstances, resort to vagueness and bluff. I often ask actors for their worst-ever experience with directors (one learns a lot from these anecdotes). My favourite story (from John Wood, who played Archduke Harry in *Orlando*) was about a director who called for another take of a scene and said to him, 'Look, do it again, but better.' Other directors may ask for it faster, on the often false assumption that everything works better when speeded up.

It may be more effective to share your genuine misgivings with the actor. Simply say that something isn't working and you are not sure what it is. Then ask the actor if anything in the scene feels wrong to them too. In the ensuing discussion you will probably find the root of the problem.

Being a mirror

The director needs to learn how to become the actor's mirror, freeing him or her from worry about how things look from the outside. You must become an accurate mirror, not just of physical appearance but also of tone, pace and scale.

This is not as simple as it sounds. At its most basic, it is about being attentive to how the actor looks: hair, make-up and clothes, and how the actor's appearance is affected by light, shadow, lens and framing. If you demonstrate that you are paying attention to these things, and doing something about them when they are not working as they should, the actor will begin to relax and not feel the need either to look in mirrors, or to check takes on the video monitor, both of which are usually symptoms of anxiety or lack of trust in the director's judgement.

At a deeper level, it means becoming a reliable source of feedback about the actor's performance, about what is working and what is not. It is vital to respond after each take, even if only minimally. If the actor is left feeling vaguely insecure and wondering how it's really going, he or she may start to ask the opinion of other people on the set and you find out someone else is inadvertently becoming a second director. However, if you swamp the actor with too much information, he or she will start to feel hemmed in, trapped, unable to let the performance breathe. So you need to gauge how much reflection the actor needs.

Most actors want to know the approximate frame they are working in, the limits of their field of activity. (Full figure, half of the body, or close-up.) They may, however, inaccurately feel that one shot or set-up is more 'important' than another. A close-up is not always the key shot in a scene. A backview, filmed from a distance, may be the most telling, moving shot in a sequence. A reaction shot – one actor listening to another speak – may be the one you end up using in the cutting room. You can be a very effective mirror for the actor in any of these situations. For example you may need to tell them, 'It looks very powerful when you really listen. Don't waste the moment just because it's the other actor who is talking. We're looking at you.'

Many actors dread a high-definition digital close-up. Handled in the wrong way it can become clinical: microscopic detail of pores in the skin doesn't necessarily help you get close to the character. On the contrary, they may push you away. You can give reassurance about this (providing it is honest). I made a point of doing this, for example, on *Rage*, which was filmed digitally and often very close. I always insist on tests of lenses and light in pre-production, using the lead actor's faces, with the resulting material taken all the way up to the final graded result on the big screen. These tests, which can seem slow or pedantic, are an extraordinarily valuable investment of time and energy. As part of the process, the director must educate him- or herself about how lenses really work and how lighting reads on film or digitally. And if you see something that needs correcting on set, don't hesitate to do it. The actor will need to see you really looking at their face and will appreciate it when you insist on taking the time with the director of photography to adjust lighting, lens, or camera position accordingly.

I have learnt a lot about what it's like when people don't do this basic kind of correction from my own experience in press junkets, when being interviewed for television or photographed for newspapers or magazines. I have sometimes been astonished by photographers saying, 'The background looks great.' You realise – with dread about the resulting image – that they are not looking at how the light falls on you but on something behind you. Or you walk into a pre-lit set-up and the cinematographer doesn't even take a moment to adjust the lights to the specific requirements of your face, as if it would be a sign of failure.

This area of painstakingly observant work is not about pandering to vanity, or knowing how to help people look beautiful, but about how to make their work truly visible. Light and shadow fall on facial structures in different ways, and can obstruct or clarify what the actors are doing, the subtle ways they are communicating. A bright reflection on someone's nose can ruin a tender moment. The glitter in someone's eye, lost in deep shadow, can obliterate delicately evoked feeling. It is vital to take the time to make the necessary adjustments to get this right, even when working under extreme pressure of time.

Alexei Rodionov adjusts reflectors during the shoot of *Yes*

19

Fear (your own and the actors')

Occasionally, when you're shooting a scene, an actor will suddenly come up with a protest or demonstration of resistance to the script or your direction. They might say, 'I don't want to say this, it really doesn't feel right for the character,' or perhaps a look or a stubborn expression will pass across the actor's face when you ask them to do something that lets you know that they don't want to do it. They may even refuse outright. What to do? For many directors the immediate sensation is one of panic. You know something's gone wrong, you're not sure what it is, or why, and you don't know what to do about it. The crew is watching, and time is passing.

This is the moment when different parts of the director's brain have to come into action simultaneously. Broadly speaking, one is the analytical, logical part and the other is the intuitive. The analytical approach might be to think: the actor may be teaching me that this line is unsayable, even though I think it is necessary. This is where your own resistance may come into play, for there may be uncomfortable consequences for you if the actor is right. The correct response to this, therefore (whether you say it out loud or not), is to thank the actor because he or she is urgently communicating something to you that you need to know, for the good of the scene and the film as a whole.

It may work to ask the actor, 'Can you help me to understand what it is that's wrong here and how you think it might be better?' If this line of questioning doesn't work, you need to get specific. 'Is it that this isn't consistent with the character? Or is it something to do with the physical position you're being asked to speak in?' Then, if this is getting nowhere, you may realise you need a more private conversation. You take the person aside and ask them if anything is bothering them that you can help with. If they can't volunteer an answer, then start asking in more detail: 'Is something going on that I should know about? Did you have a difficult time with the make-up person this morning in the trailer? Are you unhappy with your costume? Or is it something else altogether?' You act unafraid, listen carefully, you use your analytical ability to get to the root of the problem, and then take immediate action to solve it.

The other approach is more intuitive. You look at the actor and use your senses to feel if the resistance is there because it's going to take them past their own perceived limits, in which case the negativity or refusal is really an expression of their own fear. In this instance your job may be to reassure the person that they can do it and help them go through the pain barrier. This may, in turn, bring up your own fears. You wonder: 'Is this actor going to hate me for ever if I push him or her?' You hope they may hate you today but love you tomorrow. It doesn't matter, either way, if going beyond their limits is going to help them give the best possible performance, which will make the scene and, in turn, the film as a whole, work better.

Sometimes, dealing with an actor's fear means being ready to go through a kind of baptism of fire together. Perhaps the actor needs to weep alone in a room with you, because a scene is pushing them to a place that they can't get to without shedding those tears. So then you have to go into a different mode. You have to be the person who is holding the actor, psychically and emotionally, understanding their process and respecting it. You have to act unafraid and show yourself willing to go to the limits with them, remaining implacable in the face of their feelings, which may include anger with you for pushing them. This is not always easy.

All these potential strategies may be going through your mind in a split second on the set, with many people standing around watching you. Time is precious, and the pressure to gloss over the problem, make a bad decision, not acknowledge what's happening in front of your eyes, is very great. The only rule I know that works under such circumstances is to take complete responsibility for the situation and not blame anybody or anything. Not the actor, the schedule, the writer or the script. Don't blame the budget, nor the lack of time. Blame is useless and takes you nowhere. It's a great relief when you figure that out: it can save a lot of time in the long run which would otherwise be spent indulging this pointless emotion. Instead of seeing a 'problem' when an actor 'acts up', it is more useful to see the actor's resistance as another opportunity to refine the film.

The actor has, in any case, many different experiences of fear. Stage fright seems to be a necessary and useful fear, close to excitement, though it can become disabling if it gets too extreme. Everyone feels fear when they take a risk, and acting is about risking exposure and failure. I try to be kind and respectful of the processes involved in risk-taking but also try not to be alarmed by anyone's fear, including my own. Fear is, after all, just a feeling, albeit sometimes a useful one, either when there is real danger, or as a kind of research: allowing you to empathise with those who live life further out on the edge.

20

Temporary insanity (intensity on set)

Everyone knows that actors sometimes 'fall in love' with one another while working on a film. As with the intoxicating experience of 'falling in love' in so-called 'real life', people suddenly recognise one another's beauty, intelligence and magnetism. In so doing, they also recognise these qualities in themselves. The hothouse atmosphere of a film shoot, the long hours, bustling camaraderie and feeling of vitality at extending oneself beyond any definition of normality, are ideal conditions for seeing the glory, genius and lovability of others. Actors, additionally, are temporarily lifted out of themselves. They are dressed, made-up and visually enhanced in a variety of ways. They are 'free' of their everyday selves and often spend hour upon hour relating intensely – on camera and off – with other actors. They may be acting out a love affair on screen, kissing and holding each other close, with impunity. It's a potent cocktail: a mix of seeing true qualities in working colleagues and entering a fictitious universe in which there is permission – or necessity, for the story – to embody the extremes of longing and desire.

The relationship between actor and director can also become intimate and intense; it can resemble that of a painter and his or her muse, the complexity of a close friendship, or the volatility of lovers. In the brief, delineated frame of time and space that is the journey of the making of a film, it can become extraordinarily passionate; a type of love affair with the process, with the piece of work that you're making together and with each other. This process and the various relationships that can develop – including, on occasion, enmities – can be as confusing from the inside as they are to look at from the outside. A temporary insanity may ensue. I call it 'falling in work'.

With Oliver Platt on his last day of shooting *Ginger & Rosa*

People often mock actors and their 'luvvie' behaviour. The warmth that's demonstrated is, in fact, an expression of the deep state of affection you feel when you join in any endeavour where people are asked to reach into and beyond themselves for a period of time. This feeling of extendedness or even of contact with a 'true' self – the self you want to be but cannot always attain – creates a heightened feeling of closeness, fuelled by the knowledge that it will, soon enough, come to an end. It is a direct consequence of the inherently transitory and impermanent nature of the working process.

Just as in an actual love affair (which, on occasion, it may become) the people involved feel they are seeing the best in themselves and in each other – their true or essential selves. It is precisely the boundaried nature of the experience which is allowing these feelings to surface, which explains in part why relationships which begin 'on set' – whether within the crew or between actors – may not last.

For the director, the intensity of feeling and the memory of the experience continues into the edit: you watch the material again and again and continue to feel connected with the actors and the time you have shared together. For the actor, however, the moment of ending a shoot can be traumatic. It is important to be aware of the moment an actor leaves a set, marking it with appreciation. It will help ease this particular 'ending', which can feel as tragic as the end of a love affair or the dissolution of a family. It will also help when you need to pick up the relationship again, when you have finished the film and it is about to go out into the world.

Looking back, I regret that on my earliest films I did not understand how an actor can feel so rejected at the end of their part of a shoot, as if discarded once his or her usefulness has come to an end. It's easy to forget, because even at the very end of the shoot, the director's work is far from over. The edit always lasts far longer than the relatively short shooting period and you continue your relationship with the actors in their absence, day-in, day-out, for months. The actor is usually only physically present for this 'sprint' in the middle of the marathon of making a film, and may suffer feelings of let-down after such an intense expenditure of energy.

With Julie Christie at the wrap party for *The Gold Diggers*

With Tilda Swinton at the Venice Film Festival for *Orlando*

21

Framing the actor (light and lenses)

When you look at an actor through a lens, whether the camera is basic or sophisticated, you discover information that you cannot always see with your naked eye. The act of framing an actor's face seems to activate a narrative, not one that exists in time, but out of time. Film actors who are unafraid of the camera (not all of them are) seem suddenly to come alive. And the magnification of a close-up lens will also enable you to see detail that is too small for the naked eye to register from a distance. I first learnt this when working with Julie Christie on *The Gold Diggers*. It was my first taste of filming someone so experienced, with a face so widely known and loved. I discovered that she had a sure instinct for what 'reads' on camera. Only when I saw the rushes did I understand what she had been doing on the set, even though I had been standing next to the camera while we were shooting.

You can learn an enormous amount by taking photographs of your actor. Not just how they look through the lens but how they respond to it, and to you. You will also learn about how to direct whoever is operating the camera – as well as about the powerful effect that the person behind the camera can have on the actor – if you try shooting a scene yourself, at least once. Like many independent film-makers, I started out in my early short films by multi-tasking most of the crew roles. I loved operating the camera. Once my eye was glued to the viewfinder, the world of the film started to reveal itself to me. More recently, on *Rage*, I decided to operate the camera again. It was partly motivated by pragmatism (the lowest budget possible) and the subject-matter (a child filming interviews using a mobile phone). I was reminded how a thread, a kind of filament, seems to unite you with the actor across the lens as you move about him or her, searching for the angle, the right light or shadow, the place in which the actor's face will be most visible, most alive. You start to enter a zone in which you join in an unspoken duet of give-and-take, based on trust; the actor offering him- or herself to the frame. The exterior, visible self of the actor seems to hold a barely visible other: perhaps a character that has been subtly worked on, or a hidden quality of being. Sometimes you can seize the moment and catch the bare, surprising self that waits there to be seen. Every camera operator has had this experience. He or she becomes the 'eyes' of the film, the vital capturer of an elusive reality.

Your relationship with the director of photography (I prefer it when the DoP is also the operator) is one of the most crucial on a film. Not only do they offer up the cinematographic 'look' of the film, but they are also an essential mediator between you and the actor. For this to work, you have to attempt to see the film with the same eyes. When you share a vision, you effectively create the image together. Much of your time is spent, side by side, 'searching' for how to shoot a scene. As you do this you also generate an atmosphere of excitement on set. Everything seems to rotate around the camera, for good reason, for it is the portal through which all future viewers will enter the film. The eye of the DoP becomes the 'I' of the film and the eyes of the audience.

It takes time to understand how different qualities of light and different lenses can enhance or even destroy a performance. It's not so much a matter of technical expertise as a process of observation. When you choose a lens, or a distance from which to film an actor, a camera angle, or movement, you are working on several fronts at once. As director your decision about 'coverage' (how many ways to shoot the scene and from how many angles) will determine how you can edit it later, and this will be an extremely important and time-consuming preoccupation on set, especially if you are not taking for granted the standard 'long shot, medium shot, close-up' way of shooting a scene. 'Shot and reverse shot' as a way of shooting dialogue, for example, is just one way amongst many of structuring a scene, and your choices will determine the rhythm and visual 'language' of the finished film – what some directors think of as their 'signature'.

But each actor will also come alive in different frames. Some actors work expressively with their hands, or their posture. For others the nuance is in the face, and for them the close-up is where they will do their best work. So balancing formal and visual concerns with the best way to record a performance is a continuous dance of priorities, which ideally unifies in one aesthetic.

There seems to be a metaphysical aspect to framing as well. Where an actor sits in the composition of the shot can be a place of power or weakness: the centre of the action (not necessarily the centre of the frame) or on the periphery (again, not necessarily on the edge of the frame). And by framing the actor and his or her immediate environment you are also making the decision to exclude a great deal else. Framing the actor is bestowing importance. You are deciding on behalf of the audience where to look, whom to look at, and what to ignore.

This brings with it the question of point-of-view. Just who exactly is looking at the actor? Is it another character in the scene? Does the eye of the camera somehow represent the eyes of another person? Or is it more quasi-objective? All these questions and more will be in the director's mind when he or she chooses how and from where to point the camera at the actor. Light, shadow, composition, movement, and the eventual flow of the edit – how all the shots will cut together in continuity, even though you are shooting them in bits – become the cinematographic language that will hold the actor's performance and will guide the audience as to where and how to look.

22

The monitor (use and abuse)

Directors often fall into a trap whilst shooting of fixating on the monitor which shows and records the filming as it is happening. There are some valid reasons for this. Your naked eye may not be able to see the detail of the actor's work which the camera is capable of recording, nor will you be able to judge the framing or camera movement, especially when it is handheld. If you are to follow this while it is happening you may find that the framing or camera movement you had planned turns out to be wrong for the core of the scene. And you can find this out only through looking at the monitor, not by watching the actor with your naked eye. If you try to solve this by stopping after every take to watch playback, the crew and actors' energy will start to flag and the life will drop out of the scene.

Actors often need to feel your gaze in order to do their best work, especially if you have established a bond by looking at them in pre-production or rehearsal, a kind of 'golden thread' connecting you, which must then be transferred to the camera. So if you can set up a situation where you can follow a monitor with part of your attention and the actor with your naked eye, you're going to double your chances of getting the performance that you want.

Gazing at the monitor can become addictive – similar to the way in which people glance compulsively at their laptops, or mobile phones, even when in the middle of a conversation. This can feel insulting if you're on the receiving end. Incidentally, it's also a danger when you're in the editing room. You suddenly realise both you and the editor are blankly staring at random images flying past – when you are digitising some material, for example – instead of looking each other in the eye while discussing an idea, which is generally a much more productive way of communicating. So it is important to remember to remove your gaze from the monitor during a shoot if it has become compulsive. You still have to be aware of the framing, the lighting, and the camera moves, but if you forget to prioritise the actor during the take you will regret it later.

If you are shooting a scene from a distance, how you orchestrate giving feedback to the actors between takes becomes crucial. As a general rule, I have found it works best to move close enough to the actor to be able to give feedback without being overheard. If you need to give notes or corrections to camera crew or other departments immediately after a take, it is best to make sure you have first made eye-contact with the actor and given them some initial feedback, even if only a nod and smile. I try to keep my line of communication with the actor open, by explaining briefly what I need to do and why, before I disappear with my crew in a huddle around the monitor.

With David Toole between takes on *The Tango Lesson*

Some actors occasionally want to watch their takes on the monitor themselves. (Whilst visiting a set in Bollywood, for example, I was astonished to see that the stars routinely came to the monitor to check what they had just done.) For some directors this would be an impossible dynamic, and indeed it can be risky if actors start to modify their performance based on what they can see in the monitor. They may start directing themselves or adjusting an angle that they think doesn't look good, without understanding the work you intend to do to correct the lighting in post-production, or which part of the scene you intend to use. You may know which bits of a tricky or unsatisfactory take you can use in the cutting room but you may not want to – or even be able to – share this information with the actors. You may be making many intuitive calculations that you cannot analyse yourself. Some directors feel the monitor is their secret working tool and get very defensive about anyone else using it. However, if you are having trouble communicating something that isn't working – spacing or achieving an angle that catches the light, for example – sometimes inviting the actor to take a look at the monitor can be a quick and effective way of helping them to correct themselves, a form of auto-feedback.

I have found that the more confident I have become in my relationship with actors, the less defensive I have become about them looking at the material, at any stage in the process, including looking at the monitor on set. Interestingly, under these conditions of relaxed confidence, I have noticed that most actors have correspondingly little or no desire to watch themselves on the monitor.

23

Intimacy on film

Reading thought

There are many definitions of intimacy on film, but I have rarely found nudity or sex scenes to be the most important. What the camera can do is to observe and record other forms of intimacy: thought and experience – the nuance of feeling and interior life. This requires the actor to empathise with the character they are playing, to work with extremely subtle degrees of expression, and to track their own inner processes as closely as their outer ones.

The human need to be seen, to be heard, to look behind the mask at the truths that can only emerge in the one-on-one arena we call intimate relationships – or love – is at the core of the actor's work on film. Even when the role is that of a person in public life, it is the insights into the individual's inner life that make the story interesting to watch. And the actor needs to love his or her character, whether or not this person seems 'lovable' to the outside world. The quality of empathy that the actor is able to bring to the part will, in turn, help the audience to experience compassion for the character's struggles. Much of this aspect of the actor's work will remain hidden. It is a form of 'connective tissue' between the bones and muscles of the text and action. But the camera does 'read' this work, whether it is a fleeting feeling the actor conveys by experiencing it empathetically, or a sense of inner activity caused by the thoughts the actor is quietly tracking. This awareness – that the camera can somehow 'read thought' – is key to actors' work on screen.

Some scenes in a film will demand a great deal of an actor. They might need to enter a profound and raw psychological state in order to deliver difficult material. In this situation you need to walk onto that set and acknowledge, even if only with a flicker of the eye: 'I know what you're doing, I know what you're dealing with.'

Protecting the actor

On occasion, if I know that the actors are going into a very deep state, I have made an announcement to the crew (not necessarily in earshot of the actors) along the lines of: 'Today we're doing a scene where the actors are having to reach into a very particular part of themselves. There will be moments where we're banging around with lights and so on, but please be aware of their process, don't distract them from what they are trying to do.' The actors may or may not know that you are saying it, but either way they will feel protected and that will be felt as part of the bonding process with you, an outward manifestation of respect for their work. When an actor feels protected in this way and sees that you have demonstrated a respect for their inner process to the crew, then he or she is unlikely to need to 'act out'. There will be space and safety enough to express what needs expressing, and a protected space in which to channel emotion and stay focused.

Some actors, however, prefer a casual and unforced atmosphere on set when they are about to work on an emotionally demanding scene. A precious and over-protective atmosphere can make them feel self-conscious and patronised. They just want to get on with it. Again, it's a matter of observing what works for the individual.

Shooting sex

The time may come when you want to shoot a scene that is physically intimate in a sexual way. Even the most experienced actors usually carry an enormous amount of embarrassment about these scenes and may secretly dread doing them. It helps to encourage honesty about this. I have found that inordinate amounts of raucous, uncontrolled laughter – from all of us – are extremely helpful, before, during, and after the scene. The process becomes more human when the humans performing it are able to express to you (and each other) how they feel about doing it. This avoids the heavy, fake intensity that sometimes passes for sexual intimacy on screen. For although sexual feeling can be stimulated by looking at sexual behaviour, or simply gazing at the object of desire, this can become a form of alienated sexuality. Experiencing an erotic feeling is an interior experience, a form of deep connectedness, and can be evoked in multiple ways on screen, of which the least interesting may be watching people appear to be having sex. The scale of the image on a big screen and the knowledge that it is being acted (or the question: is it real?) can push the viewer away rather than drawing them in to this essentially private activity.

Body anxieties may emerge if there is any nudity in the scene, which you will need to deal with the same care and attention as any other anxiety. You do this first and foremost by making thoughtful, aware decisions about whether nudity is necessary, given the pervasive culture of exploitative use of the naked body in pornography and as a hook for selling anything and everything. If you have really examined the need for the scene and are clear that you are making choices with integrity, then a relaxed and irreverent attitude will help you make better directorial decisions about how to shoot what is, essentially, a form of highly charged choreography.

24

What to do with a diva
(what it means when an actor 'acts out')

I have learned over the years to recognise signs of apparent 'break-
down' in actors (i.e. tears, rage, etc.) as the necessary consequence
of an attempt to move beyond personal limits. By shedding the
defence mechanisms that contribute to rigidity or clichéd ways of
being and moving in performance, the root cause is challenged.
Just as an individual who habitually holds their shoulders up, when
gently released from this defensive muscular pattern, may well suddenly be flooded with feelings that the tension originally blocked
(people studying or teaching Alexander Technique will be familiar
with this), a performer – when coaxed out of familiar habits that
have helped them survive the stress and exposure of a life on stage
or in front of the camera – will suddenly feel naked, alone, confused, as if they are 'not doing anything'. I welcome these moments,
which are sometimes accompanied by tears. The work that follows
often has a beautiful clarity to it.

Self-doubt

I too sometimes have these moments during a shoot. I have shed
many tears in private when my way of doing things has been repeatedly challenged. It is not necessarily that I have been criticised by
others: on the contrary, the people around me may even have been
appreciative. But because I am aiming high and deep, I am a ruthlessly stern critic of my own work. The harsh words I whisper in
my own ear late at night or early in the morning are words I then
attempt to welcome, as a Zen student supposedly learns to welcome the blows of his master. Self-doubt and self-criticism seem

to be necessary, as the pain is a form of awakening in which it becomes possible to locate your deeper longings. Understanding your own doubts and self-criticisms as a form of self-worth (rather than self-disparagement) is an invaluable insight. It is also a guide to how to deal with actors' problems when they arise. For any outbursts that appear to be attacks on you or the production will have their roots in the actor's self-criticism and, at a deeper level, their desire to do better work.

'Tantrums' or other apparently infantile manifestations may have another cause. Actors occasionally experience abusive or manipulative behaviour at the hands of a director who believes provocation or exploitation will result in a 'real' performance. The only sure way of dealing with this legacy is to set a tone of safety, integrity and openness. This should provide the necessary contradiction to the previous experience but the actor may need to express some feelings about it in order to move on. You may also need to look to your own unaware behaviour of another kind. If you have treated an actor as an infant in some way – either by excessive mollycoddling in your attempt to 'take care' of them, or by not involving their creative powers and feeling of responsibility in the process – then you may achieve a mirror result. The actor will start to behave in a way that is consistent with the expectations you seem to have of them. 'Stars', in particular, are often treated with a caution that borders on a kind of contempt: as if they are incapable of being adult, responsible, professional human beings. (Some will react to this by becoming fiercely independent on set. Directorial intervention may even be experienced as an insult to their intelligence and capabilities.)

The flipside of celebrity-worship can be vicious attack. Many 'stars' will have had their personal lives torn to shreds in public. When people have gone through these kinds of experiences, what they crave is fundamental human respect and decency, at least in the workplace. But some well-known actors may also be tempted to use a safer space (the film set) as a place to let off steam, or even to make unconscious attempts to take revenge on what feels like a mean and invasive world. If you realise this is the cause of an actor's weird behaviour it will help you to feel and act with more compassion towards them.

But I have learnt to be wary of creating expectations that I can 'take anything'. True respect is not the same as phoney pandering to insulting or destructive behaviour. Above all, I have found that by and large what you give is what you will get.

When 'acting out' is really instinct

On occasion, apparent resistance – or what seems on the surface to be destructive behaviour – can be a sign of a deeper instinct on the part of the actor that something is wrong with the scene, the sequence, the character, or the action they are being asked to perform. The conditions of a shoot – the speed, the multiple preoccupations of the director, and so on – militate against this instinct being expressed in a calmer way. It may seem to the actor that no one is listening. I have on several occasions found that when an actor was apparently being obstructive – and the crew were getting impatient and angry – the scene was unbalanced or even unnecessary. I didn't find this out until the edit, when it suddenly became clear. Then I realised, with hindsight, that the actor had been right to be worried. Because he or she was at that moment necessarily working entirely intuitively, maybe out of reach of verbal reasoning, the lines of communication got twisted. It's worth stopping for a moment in these circumstances and checking if the problem lies not with the actor, but within the script.

25

Thinking ahead to the edit
(the part and the whole)

Everything you manage to capture during the shoot, often formless and rambling in its raw state, becomes simply material once you reach the cutting room. And all the decisions you made whilst shooting suddenly become painfully clear. You see the consequences of all your choices about an extraordinary number of details which add up, in the end, to the whole vision. You see how each detail relates – or fails to relate – to your original intentions. This applies to questions of location, set design, props, lights, colour, camera position or camera moves, costume, hair, down to the choice of lipstick, sunglasses, and so on – an infinity of choices you have made repeatedly, hour upon hour, during pre-production and the shoot. Every detail, every object, every colour, contains crucial information that an audience will later absorb and decode, often with extraordinary rapidity and sophistication.

This acute consciousness of what you really generated during the shoot also applies to each aspect of the actor's work: from each line of dialogue, to the total arc of their role in the film, the relationship with the other actors' work, and also the story and concept as a whole. Whilst shooting, therefore, you will always need to be thinking ahead to the edit, planning how the actors' performances will be cut together, which bits of takes you will use and which you will probably discard.

The best actors will also carry an awareness of the entire arc of the film, based on the script, but it is impossible for them to hold as much information as the director must do. And most actors will necessarily be obsessed by their own part if they are to occupy it with every cell of their body. This can on occasion appear somewhat self-centred, but in reality this is a quality to welcome, for it often reads on screen as conviction or authenticity: a density of presence. (Compare this with a director acting on screen – I've done this myself in *The Tango Lesson* – and you see someone whose attention is partly elsewhere, unable to stop themselves thinking about the whole, including a palpable awareness of a mass of technical and aesthetic questions.) In order to be fully present on screen the actor may need to appear 'selfish' – i.e. full of the self – on set.

It is the director's job, therefore, to keep track of how the actor's work will 'fit' in the total body of the film and guide the work in that direction. A virtuoso performance that overshadows the film may seem, at first sight, to make the actor look good, but in the end may make for a bad film, which, in turn, will not reflect well on the actor. In the heat of the moment in a shoot, it can be hard to put into words why one thing will work and not another. For example, there may be a moment that feels, from the actor's point of view, as if it needs to be frontal, close-up, intimate and intense, but you are choosing to shoot it from a distance, quietly, and more detached. It may be because you have calculated, consciously or unconsciously, that the scene that immediately follows it will be shot close, fast, and over the top, and you know you need contrasting material that will cut well to create an abrupt change of dynamic. The actor may not be too interested in this, even if you can express it: they are understandably just concerned with making their own scene work from their point of view.

There is also the question of when you have filmed enough takes of any given camera angle, or the scene as a whole. How do you judge when to stop and move on? Sometimes you may see a fleeting radiant moment in an otherwise dull take, but you sense how that will cut together with other moments from other takes and so you decide to move on to another set-up even when the actor wants to give it another go. These are the moments when you will rely on having built a level of trust with the actor. You may have to resort to a plain request, without explanation, to do it in a way that you know you can cut well, or is best for the picture as a whole, even if it feels wrong at the time for the actor.

At these moments you will be glad that you spent time earlier demonstrating your attentiveness to the actor's needs. He or she will know that you are asking for something that may 'feel' wrong, but that there must be a good reason for it. Without this level of trust you can end up either shooting something you know is unusable to humour the actor and jettisoning it later, or shooting it the way you need to, but alienating the actor and creating problems in the next scene you work on together. I have experienced both, which is why I repeatedly emphasise the importance of one-on-one preparation with each actor.

Robbie Ryan shooting the last scene of *Ginger & Rosa*

26

Blocking a scene

All the director's decisions about how a scene is shot, from which angles, and how the actors move through the scene, or remain static – in other words the physical map of how the scene unfolds in space and time – are aspects of the process known as 'blocking'. Blocking a scene can be surprisingly difficult and baffling, as the choices, once you start examining the scene and the location, can appear endless, inexhaustible and confusing. How do you begin?

You may have had the opportunity to rehearse the scene with the actors beforehand, but once you arrive at the actual location with a crew, many of your preconceptions will change. Filming a scene is not 'painting by numbers'. If you are fully alert and present to the unique shooting situations in which you find yourself, you will probably change your original concept, at least to some degree. A scene that seemed to demand someone talking whilst seated might suddenly seem much more interesting filmed restlessly on the move, for example. Or the weather, if it's an outdoor location, will suggest a completely different approach: sheltering from rain rather than walking in sunshine, or vice versa.

Here you find yourself in a delicate balance, for the camera crew needs enough information in advance to be able to light the scene, lay tracks, or whatever else is required. But if you make decisions before you have worked the scene through with the actors, then you will be asking them to slot into a predetermined shape, which may not work for them – or you – once you try it out in practice.

The usual solution to this problem is to invite the actors onto the set at some point before or even during their hair, make-up and costume preparations for the scene. You then walk through the scene with them, trying things out, until a shape for the scene has emerged that works in principle, for you and for them. The camera crew will be watching and thinking ahead about lighting issues, laying tracks for camera moves and so on, and the designer will be on hand in case it seems some unforeseen angle is likely that may need some additional work on the set.

Meanwhile, it's also a good opportunity to spot any danger points that have suddenly arisen now that the scene is becoming real. A weak link in the script, perhaps, a costume adjustment, or line of dialogue that is best dealt with immediately.

In practice, when you come to shoot the scene, you may need to revise the sketchy decisions you made when blocking it. But at least you have something to go on that will enable every crew member to get ready. And even an outline of a map of the action gives you something about which to make a judgement. The actors will feel rooted in the scene, and can in some sense 'own' the environment. And the scene is no longer an abstraction, it's a human choreography that you can refine and correct.

Storyboards

Storyboards are necessary if you are shooting a special-effects sequence, or doing a 'pickup' during the edit (a shot you discover is missing once you put a sequence together). Some directors also rely heavily on them for the shoot as a whole. I find that following a storyboard can blind you to more interesting solutions that arise once you study the real location and start working with a real person. The actor can come to resemble a cartoon character in a storyboard and if you treat them that way on set – just following a predetermined shape – an interesting performance is unlikely to emerge.

At its best, blocking a scene is a quite magical process of discovery in the moment when, for the first time, all the elements come together. If you can keep your nerve about the dangerously open-ended feeling of such a moment, rather than relying on storyboards to tell you what to do, you are more likely to achieve an uncalculated, live feeling with actors who are doing something not by rote, but because it has become necessary in a deeper sense.

One example of a last-minute live decision I have experienced was the 'maze' sequence in *Orlando*. The scene – which I had endlessly revised in the script and which somehow needed swiftly to communicate the passing of a hundred years – was set in a garden. But at the actual location it turned out there was a private maze belonging to the house. I eventually got permission to film in it, but only for a couple of hours. The original idea for a static time-lapse shot in a garden became a hand-held run through the maze – much more interesting than if I had stuck to a storyboarded scheme.

Tilda Swinton in the maze in *Orlando*

27

Shooting out of sequence (how to survive it)

It's extremely rare to be able to shoot a film in story sequence. If you are shooting on location and have several scenes in the same place at different moments in the story, for example, it will make sense to shoot them directly one after another, rather than move the crew and lighting equipment back and forth and lose time – your most precious commodity.

The jigsaw of the shooting schedule must take other factors into consideration as well: actor availability, grouping day and night shoots together in a rational way, or certain pieces of expensive equipment, or scenes which need additional crew. There are always multiple reasons why a strange shooting order (from the point of view of the story) seems to make sense from an organisational and production point of view.

Most actors and directors would love to be able to work in script order, allowing characters to develop organically and not having to calculate how they might look or feel at the end before you've had a chance to establish the steps in between. Some directors are able to insist on it and even leave the ending of the story open until they arrive there. But if this is not possible, then learning how to hold in your head the development of the story, the characters, the pace and timing of the performances and the camera's moves, is a crucial skill for a director. It becomes similar to a mental chess game: calculating moves well in advance, looking at the consequences of every action; and the reverse, working backward from possible future moves and dynamics to the present moment. This process applies equally to each actor, who will be jumping backwards and forwards in the life of the character, tracking the inner changes – which may be dramatic – and the physical consequences.

It helps to think of each actor's trajectory through the film as a map. You can plot the journey, together and separately, and need to keep track of the whole arc of that individual's journey in order to determine where he or she is, mentally, emotionally and physically, at any given moment. You may well need to discuss this out loud together, before you start each scene. When you are shooting a scene that takes place later in the story (before you have shot intermediate scenes) you need to remind yourselves what will have happened, not only the story events, but any subtle interior threads of feeling as well. Some actors may prefer to keep this part of their work private and focused as it takes great mental and emotional agility. But as director it is essential to stay extremely alert to the development of the story when it is being told out of order, to hold a feeling of consistent pace – the inherent 'musicality' of the film – or, likewise, of any deliberate changes of tone and pace as well.

Orlando was an extreme example of filming out of story-sequence and in three different countries – England, Russia and Uzbekistan – whilst also trying to catch four seasons in a ten-week shoot and cover four hundred years, credibly, in one human life-span. After this experience, some other forms of juggling with time and space during a shoot seemed relatively simple. In *Yes*, for example, we needed to stitch together angles of the same scene, supposedly in the same street, which for logistical and legal reasons had to be shot in two different countries (Cuba and the Dominican Republic). It worked out fine, to the degree that I even started to forget this schizophrenic shooting experience once we put the angles together in the cutting room.

The principle is one of holding true to your intention. If you don't maintain the thread, the hidden architecture of the story, you will discover your mistakes later when you edit the scenes that you shot out of sequence. If you do keep hold of the thread, shooting out of sequence is not necessarily a disaster, but the greatest challenge will be maintaining emotional consistency: the time-line of human development and change carried by the actor.

Shooting *Orlando* on the ice in St Petersburg, February 1992

Shooting *Orlando* in the desert in Uzbekistan, April 1992

Part Three

Post-production

28

The edit (the great teacher)

It is in the cutting room that you will learn what you have done. Not just the consequences of your shooting choices – how many set-ups, from how many angles and how the whole jigsaw fits together – but also what the actors really did and how you helped or even hindered them in the process.

Many productions organise an editor to work in parallel with the shoot so that there is already an assembly of the film by the time the director starts work in the cutting room. There are certain advantages to this: an editor can give feedback during the shoot about material that doesn't seem to be working when looked at objectively, away from the intense atmosphere of the set; or can identify some missing links that can be swiftly remedied while the cast, crew and locations are still available. The editor may also value the time alone with the material before the director steps in with other ideas.

I prefer to work differently. I like to be in the cutting room from day one, studying and shaping the material and finding its rhythm together with the editor. Even more importantly, I like to look at every single take of every performance, including the fragments of aborted takes. By the end of an edit I will have studied each take of each actor many times over.

Studying the work in such detail is an extraordinarily educative process. Not only do you learn about how you spent your time and energy on every visual decision, whether design or camera work, but you also find out which actors improve in a series of takes and which ones delivered their best at the beginning and then started to repeat themselves – the spark had gone. You ask yourself: why didn't I notice? Michael Powell famously aimed at only two takes.

Everyone, cast and crew, knew they had to be ready or the chance would be gone. A rhythm was established and respected and people paced themselves accordingly.

So you sit in the cutting room and wonder at some of your decisions which were patently wrong. You puzzle: perhaps you went on and on, take after take, because your attention was elsewhere: the camera move wasn't working as you had hoped, for example, and you were trying out alternatives. Or, conversely, you see a wonderful performance ruined by a bad light, or a label sticking out of the back of a shirt. These are moments when you were right to have insisted on another take. In this way you learn the importance of attention to all detail, things that can enhance or distract from the core of a scene.

You also learn that performances that seemed hilarious on the set don't necessarily 'read' on camera: a vital insight that will guide future direction. And you learn about your mistakes with actors. Sometimes you catch a moment of your interaction – you see yourself talking (you thought it was a brilliant insight at the time) but the actor is glazing over as they listen to you droning on. Or you see a miraculous difference between two takes and you know you did something right and try to remember what it was.

Later, when the film has been put together for the first time, you often want to revise your first choices, the takes that seemed to work best on first viewing, as you find you had missed something the actor was doing, or not doing. I often look at each character's trajectory separately. One can quite swiftly make an assembly of an individual character's scenes or moments. You find where there are holes or inconsistencies. You learn where you (and the actor) managed to hold onto a character's development even when shot out of sequence, and where you jumped ahead by mistake. You also learn the importance of continuity, in all its senses, from shot to shot and from scene to scene. Not so much whether someone was holding their glass in their left or right hand – though this matters too – but questions of pace and emotional tone.

And you often find out, in the process, what the actor was really doing, or reaching for. Subtle, fine moments within a scene that you couldn't see at the time.

Your secret gift

Most actors have no idea how much you can help or hinder their work in the cutting room. Many have had the bewildering experience of turning up at the first-night screening and discovering scenes cut, running order changed, strange angles chosen, the magnificent take they remembered from the shoot now nowhere to be seen. It can be a difficult experience. Others might see a performance that emphasises qualities they scarcely remember – and a script that seems to have changed – but which is pleasing, nonetheless, and may wonder what happened in the cutting room.

It would be difficult for most actors to be present during an edit. They would have to endure watching their own embarrassing mistakes – the stuff that ends up on the cutting-room floor and from which they are protected. Or, conversely, a good performance in a scene which must be cut for the good of the film as a whole. An edit is a long process and most directors would find the idea of an actor's presence in the cutting room inhibiting to an impossible degree; they need to be able to examine the work ruthlessly, with a cool eye. Directors and editors often sit and curse the screen and can be scathing about the material. But most actors would learn a lot about how much they owe to a good editor and attentive director if they could see just how much care and help is given to their performance long after they have moved on to something else. It is your secret gift to them.

It's not just about choosing the actor's best takes or fragments of takes. You discover that you can sometimes give a performance an entirely different emphasis – almost like meeting a different character – not only by your choices of take and camera angle, but also by your in and out points within a take or scene.

On the simplest level, you can protect the actor by cutting out the moments when they don't look so good, or perform inconsistently. You can digitally change the actor's look by softening the skin-tone, or correcting a distracting shadow. You can note areas where vocal problems can be improved by what is known as ADR (Automated Dialogue Replacement), where you call the actor back to re-record some lines which are then fitted to the edited picture. You can substitute different takes when the performance suddenly feels wrong in the context of another actor's work in an adjacent scene. You can use music as a form of counterpoint to indicate subtext, and give clues to a contradictory inner life by subtly emphasising the actor's eye movements. You can use sound to change the emotional energy and timing of a sequence.

The combination of this detailed work on many levels can effect a quite magical metamorphosis. What you take away – edit out – gives an intensity and focus to what remains. Like a sculptor, you are finding the shape that is waiting to be discovered within the raw material. But the material has to have been given to you by the actor in the first place, even if only in fragments, or fleeting moments. You are utterly dependent on what he or she has managed to deliver during the shoot. You can protect, shape and enhance a performance quite dramatically, but you can't create it.

As a director, you live with the actor's work for a long time and you need to love it. The work in the cutting room, unlike the shoot, which goes so fast, is relatively long, slow and painstaking. By the end of the edit you will have watched the film – in pieces and as a whole – many hundreds of times.

So your relationship with the actor's work – all the consequences of your collaboration – continues long after they have left the set. You are invisibly (to them) continuing to work together and your capacity to enhance or break their performance is as great as your time and dedication will allow.

29

When the film comes out (you meet again)

When your film is finished – after several years, at least, of dedicated full-time work, if you are a writer/director – you will probably meet your lead actors again for festival premieres and then for the strange, confusing and sometimes depressing process known as publicity: the press junket.

The actors will suddenly find out what you have been doing since they last saw you. Perhaps you will just have screened the finished film for the first time with an audience and watched it with them under the stressful – and exciting – conditions of a glittering premiere. They may have worked on several other films in the meantime. They have moved on. But in some sense, you have not. You will have been watching and shaping their work in extraordinary detail in the cutting room, during the sound mix and in the grading. You will probably then have been selecting the best production stills, working on the poster, or the DVD 'extras' and so on, for many months on end. You've never stopped looking at their faces. So you may feel as if you were never apart. But when you meet again, it may seem like meeting strangers. The actors will be finding you again, too, and you will have changed in their eyes. You are no longer a director hunting for a performance, gazing at them in that special way. Instead, you will probably be feeling vulnerable about the film's reception.

Negotiating this change of dynamic, dealing with the differences in time and energy that you will, inevitably, have given to the film, managing to keep your own insecurities about the film's reception under some kind of control (especially if it is receiving a mixed critical reaction, as most films do), may unexpectedly prove to be more demanding than anything you have done on the film up to that point.

And precisely at the moment that you desperately need some praise and reassurance about the film, its voyage into the world begins and you may be exposed to criticism or indifference. The rest of the world will want you to start explaining, justifying, perhaps even reassuring them about it, especially if you have taken risks in form or subject-matter that seem unfamiliar to audiences or critics. This can be perplexing and disheartening. What was all this dedication for, if the result can be dismissed so easily? Even praise can feel like an assault, somehow missing the mark. The precision of your intention, the purity of motivation you may have strived for, may well go unnoticed. For most people it will be just another film, judged on a level playing-field with every other film that happens to have been made that year (or released that week). A yawning chasm opens between the intensity of your devotion and the film's reception, even when the critics are positive and the audience is appreciative.

Meanwhile, your actors may or may not like all your choices. They may be gratifyingly delighted, or surprised, by the final result. But they too will feel exposed at this moment. As the 'face' of the film, they will be expected to front it up, explain the story, talk about it intelligently, or gossip about its making. Here, again, you will feel the consequence of the extent to which you built a clear, trusting relationship during the working process. If you can field this potentially difficult situation, keep your solidarity with the actors in the face of the strains of both 'success' and 'failure', you will recoup the rewards of your struggle for integrity as a director, and even this very public stage of your relationship with them can be a source of private joy.

It helps to remember that you have made something together that is bigger and potentially more enduring than any of you. Any immediate reactions to the work – positive or negative – are inherently transitory and ultimately irrelevant. They may well change over time. But the moment of completion is significant. You and your actors stand, side by side, in the glare of the lights after the credits have rolled, finally beginning to comprehend what you were doing in the shoot all those months ago. The memory feels like a strange, powerful dream, a world you inhabited together, briefly, before it dissolved. It has now reappeared, and has become a film, an entity over which none of you now have any control. It belongs to the audience, who will devour it and may savour it or spit it out. But what really counts at this brutal moment of reckoning is that you have each given your all in a working process that can be playful, or agonising, but which, at its best, is a form of love.

On the red carpet at the *Rage* premiere in Berlin

30

Postscript: the barefoot film-making manifesto

Writers' manifestos are one way of clarifying beliefs. They can give energy and you can read more or less at a glance the pithy conclusions from thought processes and working practices that have developed over many years. I write them from time to time, mostly as private documents to cheer myself on. When I was preparing *Rage* (the ultimate low-budget actor-oriented film, consisting only of performances, filmed in close-up, against pure colour backgrounds) I wrote this manifesto – which I later posted as a blog on my website – as a way of clarifying my principles as a director. Most of the points in it are a distilled expression of background assumptions that lie behind some of the chapters in this book, though they apply to every area of the director's work, not just those involving actors.

So here it is:

- The best time to start is now (don't wait);
- Take responsibility for everything (it saves time);
- Don't blame anyone or anything (including yourself);
- Give up being a moviemaker victim (of circumstance, weather, lack of money, mean financiers, vicious critics, greedy distributors, indifferent public, etc.);
- You can't always choose what happens while you are making a film, but you can choose your point of view about what happens (creative perspective);
- Mistakes are your best teacher (so welcome them);
- Turn disaster to advantage (there will be many);
- Only work on something you believe in (life is too short to practise insincerity);

- Choose your team carefully and honour them (never speak negatively about your colleagues);
- Ban the word 'compromise' or the phrase 'it will do' (the disappointment in yourself will haunt you later);
- Be prepared to work harder than anyone you are employing;
- Be ruthless – be ready to throw away your favourite bits (you may well be attached to what is familiar rather than what is good);
- Aim beyond your limits and help others to go beyond theirs (the thrill of the learning curve);
- When in doubt, project yourself ten years into the future and look back – what will you be proud of having done? (indecision is a lack of the longer view or wider perspective);
- Practise no waste – psychic ecology – prevent brain pollution (don't add to the proliferation of junk);
- Be an anorak – keep your sense of wonder and enthusiasm (cynicism will kill your joy and motivation);
- Get some sleep when you can (you won't get much later).

With Judi Dench shooting *Rage* – 'barefoot film-making'

Part Four

The Interviews

Simon Abkarian

I first encountered Simon when he turned up for an audition in Paris for a small part as a gypsy in *The Man Who Cried*. When he entered the room I felt that his immediately powerful presence demanded a larger role, but the script was complete and the leading roles already cast. The scene in which he eventually appeared was cut from the film, though he had been magnificent. I never forgot him. When I wrote the key scene for *Yes* – which I decided to shoot as a short film to test out the risky idea of writing entirely in verse – I contacted him again. At the first read-through he started to weep when he hit the words 'my land', two small words that meant so much to him as an Armenian who had grown up in Beirut and then emigrated to France. I bitterly regret not having seen him when he played the lead in many of the Greek tragedies for Ariane Mnouchkine's French company, the 'Théâtre du Soleil'. The productions were legendary and Simon was reputedly extraordinarily charismatic on stage.

Simon's eventual performance in *Yes* was his first lead role in the cinema and his first role in English. His expressive use of language, his unique intonation and delivery, together with his attitude of total commitment, inspired me. He has subsequently starred in many French films and television series as well as directing Shakespeare in the theatre, and is now also writing his own plays, in his own inimitable, flowing and beautiful language.

We met for this conversation in his small apartment in Paris. When he uttered the first words, the lights suddenly went out. The interview was interrupted by several phone calls to electricians, but by the time one turned up, just as we had finished talking at his cosy kitchen table, the lights mysteriously went on again. He served cognac to the puzzled electrician, a fellow Armenian, and then we went out to supper.

Simon!

Yes!

[SP laughs] When you're offered a role, how important is the script and how important is the director to you in deciding whether to do it?

The ideal is that the director has written the script.

Why?

Because I think there is no one that can relate more closely to a vision than the one who produced it. But the director would be more important.

More than the script?

Yes.

Why?

Because a good director can turn something not that well written into something good, but a bad director, no matter how good the script is, just kills it. With no willing of killing it but just doesn't have the strength, the cultural knowledge or the language to make it good.

OK. Let's say there is a reasonable script but you have never met the director before. What are the qualities you're looking for in your first meeting? What clues are you going to get about whether this person will be a good director for you or not?

Probably as an actor and as a man, the quality of how he or she listens. Because the quality of the listening and the hearing is the quality of the exchange. When I talk and suddenly become intelligent it's because the person in front of me makes me intelligent by the way they listen. So that's a good sign. *[both laugh]*

So part of the criteria for you with this director is that you feel intelligent in his or her presence. What else?

I like also to talk with them about the practicality of building something together which is very concrete, and which takes time. Layers after layers and always done together. As an actor you know that you have to embrace the vision of the person who will direct the film to make him or her happy and fulfilled. For this, I like to rehearse.

So in the first meeting, if the director said to you, 'I want to rehearse,' that would be a factor in wanting to do it?

Of course, yes.

And if they said they didn't want to rehearse?

Then I know that I will have to work on my own, which is never, never good. And I mean work, because when I arrive on the set I don't want to worry about anything else than putting everything I have into the camera. I don't want to worry about how to play. The film industry, like all industries, is inhabited by the evil which we call haste. When the first AD is yelling, 'Quick, quick, quick. We're losing time,' you just want to kill the person because it's killing you before you play, before you act.

So one of the qualities that you're looking for in the director is some kind of mastery of time.

Yes.

Even when there isn't very much. To give the feeling of slowness.

Of course. To take time. We call it preparation. But what has become of preparation in Hollywood now? Preparation is how many pounds you gained or lost for the role. Or how you learned to drive this kind of car, or how you learned to dive with a parachute.

So what is your definition of real, meaningful preparation?

My definition of preparation is to have a complete, secret understanding between the director and me. To create a space that is absolutely palpable for both of us, intellectually and with feeling. It's a secret recipe. One gaze and I know what's happening and what he or she wants. There shouldn't be any hesitation in the galloping process. Details come out of good preparation. No good preparation; no details. No details; no great craft.

How do you ideally like to prepare with a director?

To talk. Then to act in a room somewhere. Then to talk again, then to act again. And sometimes simply to talk about literature, about politics.

So not necessarily to talk about the script at all?

No. Some directors think they direct actors by saying, 'He is sad.' To which I respond: 'Thank you very much, it was written in the scene.'

[SP laughs]

Or, 'Be careful because at that moment his wife left him and he is very, very upset.' 'Thank you again.' *[both laugh]* Because it comes back also to what I said about the script. The script is in itself a preparation to talk, to exchange thought. And this is the ideal. So when I talk to some directors about politics, without giving any attention to the acting process, it's fine with me because I know we have so many things to share ahead.

So it's building trust. Building a conversation.

Of course. Building a conversation and eventually a friendship.

Yes.

I was shocked when some actors said to me, 'You have to protect yourself from the director.'

Did they say that? Really?

Yeah. Protect from what? I mean you need to be able to be naked, in a way, in front of a director, if she is or he is worthy of that title. You say, 'OK this is my secret place that you can see and smell . . .' But on the other hand, some directors are not so cultivated. I'm not only talking about books but about life. They have nothing to tell you except, 'I want to make a movie. I have to make lots of people see this movie so I can do another movie.'

You've had this experience?

Yes, I've seen this obsessive worry about being loved, successful, money and fame. It takes you nowhere.

So that's the bad directors. What about the good ones?

They are free of the result, in a way. Free of the commercial result. They are always worried about the artistic or poetic and human result coming out of the craft of the film, of course. But they don't confuse fame and glory. Glory is for good directors. Fame is a flower that goes away. Glory stays for ever. Unfortunately sometimes it's after death. I'm encouraging my friends to give the crowns of glory to people when they're alive.

How much do you think that because you are yourself a director it changes how you relate to directors when you are acting?

When I have an interesting person in front of me it doesn't change a thing because I forget. I forget because I am drawn into and taken by the thought of the other. When I remember I am a director it is a bad sign.

But in another way I think I have a good sense of how to translate the direction and even go further. Sometimes I can help the director have a little more than he or she imagined.

How important is developing the look of the part – the clothes and so on – when you're in preparation? And do you like it if the director is closely involved in that part of the development?

Yes. Oh, yes.

Tell me about it.

I think there is a visual DNA to a character. I think a character should be recognisable in silhouette. The costume is your armour. It gives you the way you handle your body, the way you walk, the way you stand. You draw yourself in space, without words. Acting is not a fashion show. Acting is to be beautiful but not in a narcissistic way. Acting sometimes is to be dirty. You don't necessarily look the way you want to. The start of acting is not just what's happening inside, it is also what's happening outside. The colours, the cloth, the material, how it shines or not. All these things are important. And sometimes unfortunately when you ask for something more this way or that because of the needs of your character; they think that you are capricious.

What do you think is the root of these misconceptions about actors when they are apparently capricious?

Me, I love actors.

Me too, by the way.

I know you do. I think there is a little bit of 'racism' towards actors. People don't trust actors' instincts when they are building their characters. They think they want things out of vanity. And mostly this 'racism' is put on women not men.

You're talking specifically about actors' anxiety about their appearance?

Of course. But what I like about the work of acting is that you disappear. You are behind the character, you are like a puppeteer. When people tell me, 'I didn't recognise you,' it's a big compliment.

Do you think of yourself as building a character or, as you just called it, being a puppeteer? Or is the idea of character just a concept, a vehicle for communicating?

For me a character does not exist. I lend my voice and my body to a vision written by someone. I speak through words that provoke emotion and chemical reactions in my brain but I never forget myself. There is always awareness in every gesture, it's a craft. I try to make something invisible be visible. Something that you cannot hear, make it hearable. For me characters do not exist, writing exists. For me Hamlet does not exist. There are as many Hamlets as actors can play Hamlet. It is never finished.

What about the text? What's more important: the words you say or what is not said?

Ah yes. We live under the rule of talking. People think that the more fast you speak and with more and more words, the more you exist. You see it a lot on television. People are afraid of silences. They are afraid of the void. We have to fill things with noises. Some actors feel that the faster you say it, the less people will notice their intonations. I believe in the rules of contraries. If no silence, no speech. If no darkness, no light. If no stillness, no movement. And stillness is movement in itself, but if talking is flying we still have to land. I need to be quiet. I know that with you, I can be silent, because you know I'm trying to build something. You're not afraid.

What are you longing for from the director once you start to shoot?

To feel free of me. Not to worry about me any more. And desire. I want to see desire in the eyes of the director. Not to be desired because of my ego but to be desired as an object of value that is part of their process. And I weigh my words: an object of value that is part of a process for the director. I want to see in his eyes or her eyes . . . peace. Not worry. Because a director has their own loneliness that no one else can understand. And in this loneliness there are a lot of questions, a lot of doubts, a lot of worries. And when a director is elegant enough not to show it to the actors, not to share these worries and doubts for a single second with the actors . . . Yeah. *[sighs – voice breaks]* . . . this is when I love them.

So this brings up a lot of feeling for you?

Yeah. Because at that point you want to give everything, even what you don't have. But it is a rare blessing. There comes a point when you can also share some worries together. Some directors do it in a way that does not weigh on the actors. They understand the moment of madness an actor has with himself or herself. This moment of fright that we call *crainte*; apprehension. We are full of apprehension. There is a French actor called Louis Jouvet who once said a young actor said to him, 'I never have apprehension,' and he said, 'It will come with talent.'

[SP laughs]

I think it's important to have apprehension because it's vertiginous. Especially when the script is vertiginous. When the script is pulling you up and giving you the scale of your fall. If there is no vertigo there is no grace. There is no grace because the scene has to be balanced, the take has to be balanced, you have to be balanced and it's boring because everything is balanced. But on the other hand sometimes we have to practise balance to achieve grace.

How important is it for you to feel the physical eyes of the director on you at the moment of shooting? Or has the camera then become the eyes of the director?

The eyes of the director and the eyes of your acting partners make you a king or a beggar. If they believe in you, you don't have to work so hard to be believed. I never go to the monitor. I don't like that. Unless there is something the director wants me to see because there is some spacing that I'm not getting, which happens. But generally I prefer to talk after a take. Or not, because sometimes silence is full of meaning and sense. Some people are annoyed when they see the director in their line of vision. Me, I like it. I like to be close physically to the director.

What kind of feedback works for you and what are the kind of things you wish a director would never say?

No.

Never say the word no?

It's the worst word to hear. I don't like the word no and the other one I don't like is 'not bad' after a take. One damn director told me, 'Not bad, not bad, not bad.' I said, 'You're not bad too.' Yes or maybe is fine. The most cherished verb is when a director says, 'Imagine'. 'Imagine your father was . . .' and it comes back to the muscle of your imagination. We tend to forget that the actor has inside of him or her, a space of imagination. The director has one too and sometimes there is one between both. Some imaginations meet.

What's the difference for you between imagination and memory? Bringing memory of direct experience into the working process?

I have my secret life and distil my secret life into the script. When you play Greek tragedies for example, Orestes killed his mother but I never killed my mother. But you can invent a memory. Of course the taste of lemon is the taste of lemon – *voilà*. But sometimes I think it's important to live, to have many lives when you are an actor so you can feed yourself – not for memories to bring back into the film but to see how situations can pull different strings inside of you.

Does it ever help to share — where you're bringing direct personal experience, even if it's only allegorical — with the director? Or do you prefer to keep that as a secret?

It depends very much who the director is.

What makes the difference?

Again it's the space that is allowed to open between me and him or her. If I feel that space is not open I will not give even as much as the head of a needle and this will be a failure and a waste of time. Afterwards I will say, 'Well, I did my job.' But I don't want to do my job, I want to work.

So what does the director need to do or be in order to create a safe enough space that you have the desire to share?

First of all to take the time to talk. To talk also about themselves. As an actor you invent things because of the vision of the director. No vision, no invention. You don't create by yourself. You create because the space is given to you. If the space is given to me, I can invent things. If the space is not given to me, I can't invent shit. Nothing. So the most precious thing is when the director allows the actor to take the space and makes them the king or the queen of the space.

Do you think that's a consequence of a quality of attention from the director? Of course there is a time element too — but is it something indefinable? A quality of presence? Or is it something more concrete than that?

It's concrete. It's both. Let's say we try out costumes in the light. The cameraman, set designer, costume designer and director – suddenly all step back to watch you. You become the centre of something. The centre of interest for many people. And the important thing is not to make the actor feel absent in the decision-making. If the director says, 'How do you feel about it?' you feel good. Afterwards maybe you have to rearrange things. Once I was doing a film and the pants were too long and at the very last moment they put pins in the hems. I refused to go on. They said, 'We're losing the light.' I said, 'Fuck the light, I will not go on set with pins in my pants.' Because in the wide shot I will hide – because I am a good soldier, good actor – I will try to hide my feet and I will be worried about hiding the pins instead of doing my work. And because I am not always a good Christian, I refused.

Good for you. How aware are you of the lens?

I always know where it is. I always know where the camera is but I rarely ask how large the frame is. But I know the frame is a cage and we invent what we call freedom in that cage.

What in your experience is the difference between projecting a performance in a theatre and projecting – or is it projecting? – when you're performing for the cinema, for the camera?

I think on the stage you have to invent different kinds of measures in order to create an equivalent of the close-up shot. You can do it when you decide to lift only one finger, if you lean your head towards your finger – people will see only this finger. But if you look at people with your eyes – people look at your eyes. The cinema is different because someone else is measuring for you. When you are on stage you take your own measures with the public but also with emotion and your voice. Sometimes you go into a theatre and because you do not have the right acoustic you are over-talking, when the moment in question should be whispered. So then they put microphones which alter your voice in another way. In cinema I think the microphone may be more important than the camera.

More than the camera?

It's as important because it is also the gift of the measure of what you deliver from inside. With the camera, because it captures everything, we actors tend to be scared of, 'Wow, this is going to be too much, maybe I am doing too much.' And then nothing happens. It's not alive.

So what's the secret of coming alive for the camera in your view?

The secret of coming alive? Knowing the measures, knowing the distances and you need to agree with the idea of failure.

Risking.

Of risking. Nothing comes alive without that. And again I will come back to the director and then the acting partners. They bring you alive. They bring you a reflection of your work, it's not the combo – how you say in English?

The monitor.

It's not the monitor. It's again and again about the eyes of the director for me.

Do you feel that your own sense of when a take is good or not is reliable, or do you rely on the objective look from the director to know when you've hit it?

Director. Always. I mean when I hit it, I know something happened. I know that it was smooth, it was right, it was hot, it was cold at the same time – I know.

But?

But it always comes back to the director, always, always.

What about a happy shoot: a necessity or a happy bonus?

Happiness. It's a necessity that has become hazardous.

[SP laughs]

I met an actress the other day. She said, 'I'm doing this film.' Obviously she was not happy to do it and she said to me, 'Well, you know, one cannot always do masterpieces.' And I said to her, 'One should at least try once.'

[SP laughs]

Happiness is the same. And I come back again to the pressure of money. The more money we have on a set the less happy we can be. Because there is so much pressure, so many demands. The material conditions weigh on whether it's going to be a happy shoot or not. I'm not saying one should be poor. I'm saying one shouldn't be under the pressure of money. But you can do good films with very unhappy conditions. And there are very bad people who are great artists. So *voilá*.

What does presence mean to you?

It's the basis of being an actor.

Talk about it.

Some people say, 'Oh, you have a great presence.' And I say, 'If I were not present I would be absent.' The least that someone should be is present within the frame or within the room or within the eye of the imagination of the director or the public. Presence is also how you arrive in a room. My family are people who practise that a lot. When we arrive, we arrive somewhere. We never go through the small door. We arrive through the big door. So you have to invent the big door to have presence. You never bend down inside. You never beg inside.

You remain hungry and thirsty but you remain who you are. It has nothing to do with pride; it has to do with being there.

How do you think you can be best helped to go beyond your own limits or habits? What are the conditions that allow you to go further?

What allows me to go further is to be given time.

Whilst shooting? Before?

Both. Time is the thing. Time is the thing.

Do you think that sense of time also comes out of your long experience in the theatre, especially with Ariane Mnouchkine? There is generally a great deal more time for preparation and therefore you know what that can do?

Yes, yes, yes. The thing is that film people sometimes say, 'I don't want them to rehearse too much because I want their spontaneity.' To be an actor is not a spontaneous thing. We are the contrary. It's an artifice. It's an unnatural craft, acting. It's a recreation of life or a reflection of life, a proposition of what is reality but it's not realism.

So then what is truth for you as an actor if it is not about serving realism?

I don't know what truth is. But I think in a way that it goes through the filter of imagination and then it's a proposal of what Hamlet is at that moment or what this film is at that moment in your life. I think truth is also being free of needing to be loved. To take the risk of being unloved.

What happens when you watch yourself in the finished film?

The first time I watched myself, I was shocked by the sound of my voice. I take notes now. I watch myself as a foreign person, as an alien, let's say.

And do you sometimes see — when you watch yourself — the mistakes the director made? Or you wish, 'Why didn't they get me to do x, y or z?'

Yeah. Sometimes I see that. I think, 'Why did he/she let us go in this direction?' But it's not necessarily about me, because I'm like a sponge, I cannot refuse direction. My work is to take. My work is to say yes. I cannot say no to a proposal. But sometimes you have to educate the eye of the director. You have to educate the mind of the director. You have to educate the way of talking of the director. And this is very tiring.

Would you rather that a director who knows something is wrong but can't find an elegant way to express it nevertheless just fumbles around and tries to say something even if it isn't comfortable? Would you prefer that rather than they remain silent?

I prefer to be put on track. Yes, of course. I am not always there to be pleased. I prefer roughness and cruelty if necessary to get back on track.

Because that's something that many starting-out directors worry about. They're thinking about so many things. They know intuitively something's wrong but they can't figure out what it is. They don't know how to express it precisely so they end up not expressing it at all.

But Sally, we come back to the fundamental of forgetting that we do cinema to watch the actors. You have to talk to actors in a different way every time and every day. And every actor has his own language. You have to invent a language, if necessary.

Exactly.

I remember you talking with me and the next day was always different. I remember you talking to Joan and that was different. It was like a ballet. And sometimes directors don't know this. They didn't learn. They learn how to manipulate the camera, they know the lens, they know the light. But sometimes they forget –

– to communicate.

To communicate. But this is the main part of the job.

What about the after stuff? All the publicity and all of that? How much does that impact on the work, and in good ways or bad ways?

I discovered that lately. The last day of shooting – the film is not finished. It has to go to the cutting room, then *étalonnage*, the music, the sound mix and then it has to go public. I understand now that the film is not finished until the last interview is done with the last journalist. Because you continue to carry in your mind what you have done. Some actors don't do these interviews because they didn't really do the film. They just took the money and ran. 'I can't talk about this film.' Why not? It's good sometimes to try to understand the value of your work, to try to formulate.

So talking about the work doesn't destroy the work?

No.

Just as talking in rehearsal doesn't destroy your vitality.

No, no, no.

That's another illusion that some directors have.

Well of course if you ask an actor to run from A to B again and again and afterwards he gets cramps – OK, that's the limit. We all have our limits. But we are not only creators, we are also re-creators. We must be able to do many shows, many takes if the director needs us to, in order to fulfil the vision.

Is there a metaphysical dimension to the actor/director relationship?

I think for me what is important with the director is when he or she takes the time to make the actor feel unique. I'm not talking about praise, I'm talking about taking intimate moments to talk about the work, that are shared only between these two people. To have a secret conversation that no one else can understand and no one else must hear. This can only happen with the will of the director to invite, because if you do not invite the actor, the actor will not come. You have to make the invitation and say, 'Come, let us create a very intimate and maybe sacred space that only you and I can celebrate.' That's what I look for, and when this happens, I feel my muscles, I feel my wings, I feel that I'm the greatest hero, ever, that will achieve incredible tasks for the vision of my director. And it's very simple to do. It's just human intelligence. It's to have one thousand eyes and one thousand ears and with one goal: to invite your actors into the space where you make them feel special.

You know, you should count friends on one hand. They are rare. My father used to say if everyone were a knight we would have no one to protect. Not everyone can be a knight and not everyone can be a great director. OK, sometimes directors can make films which make millions. But Coca-Cola makes millions of bottles; it's shit nonetheless. So I'm not talking about the amount you sell, I'm talking about the quality and why there are some directors that everybody longs to work with. I know there are a lot of actors who long to work with you – I'm one of them. And it has to do with your vision and your intelligence in creating these kinds of spaces. Everyone I know has a memory of the moment they shared with you. The space of all possibilities. And that makes you feel an actor. A human being and an actor. So it's rare, Sally. Like I was saying to my friend: at least we have to try once to make a masterpiece.

Riz Ahmed

When Riz Ahmed auditioned for the role of Vijay in *Rage* I was struck by his wit, quickfire intelligence and huge, expressive eyes. When we came to shoot he brought a heart-breaking quality of vulnerability to the role, that of a young man who is delivering pizzas but aspires to become a movie star. We filmed a sequence of Bollywood poses – a kind of voguing – that had me shaking with appreciative laughter. The sequence wasn't used in the end, but it gave me a glimpse of another aspect of Riz's versatile range, humour and insight.

By the time, five years later, that Riz came round to my studio in

East London to talk, he had amassed an impressive number of roles as an actor and had an active life as a musician and DJ. We were immediately deep into conversation – Riz talking in a torrent of words – before I could switch on my recording devices. The subject was the lure of America for him as an actor, which he was trying to resist. 'Blue-sky thinking' is how he named the attraction, compared to the omnipresent invisible ceiling in the UK. At the same time he valued the creative and cultural ferment of London. A deep thread of meaning for Riz is where he, and others like him, who have complex cultural roots, really fit in. The question of identity – always a live issue for actors who explore identities for a living – for him is amplified in its intensity.

Before I switched on, we were talking about –

England and America. Every time I go to New York I feel like, 'Wow, it's so similar to London.' But American cities are much more segregated in terms of class and race. Our legacy in the UK of post-Second World War social housing, cheek-by-jowl mansions and working class estates; love that. Great. But maybe now it's just decorative. The Bengalis here in East London, for example, live quite separate lives. They overlap geographically with the rest of the population, but they share space in parallel. In America they don't even share space a lot of the time. I find that a bit suicidal. I think there used to be a feeling in the UK that we're all in it together; we have much more a sense of 'society' than in the States. New York is quite a transient place. People don't tend to have kids there and put down roots. They leave Manhattan at thirty-five, forty because it's just too intense. The adrenaline burst of *[clicks fingers]* 'live for yourself and pursue your dream' is heightened in New York. And it's appealing. Over here it's diluted with something else, which also has value, which is 'you're part of something bigger.' But are we part of anything? The government is dismantling all those things, like the National Health Service, that brought us together.

How does all that affect your work?

Our creative industries don't survive on free-market models, because we're a smaller market, right? And there's less philanthropy than in America. So the arts are subsidised by institutions that have gate-keepers. Institutions are by definition impervious to change. So you've got this quite conservative nucleus with a cultural periphery. And people on the peripheries don't see any hope of climbing those walls, so they think, 'OK fuck you, I'm going to go off and do something punky and interesting.' And that's how we make Punk or Dub Step or Drum and Bass or Garage or some of the edgy films that people end up loving in the States. Our cultural periphery is really innovative because the cultural nucleus is so conservative. But is Dub Step going to get playlisted on Radio One? No, not until the Americans go, 'Oooh we love that, we'll have that.' Once it's rubber-stamped by them then it comes back to us. I've been lucky with films like *Shifty* (2008), *Four Lions* (2010), *Ill Manors* (2012). Super-low-budget films that have to varying degrees become cult classics. I'm proud of that. Everyone in our cultural nucleus has admired them but they don't quite know what to do with them. Whereas in America – people in LA, scriptwriters – I can't believe the stuff they've seen. Tiny films that my mates have made.

They're good absorbers. Do you think as an actor – we'll come on to whether you define yourself primarily as an actor or not – that you need to think beyond national and cultural boundaries in any case? Do you feel you're working in an international medium?

A lot of actors that I meet tend to have a fragile, shifting or chameleonic sense of self. Tom Hardy said something to me once, in one of his infamous rants to flag, poetry and bile – very intense guy – he said, 'I think that actors start off having no sense of self and what you want to get to is a universal sense of self.' A lot of actors I've met have been insider-outsiders who feel as though they live on the threshold of a room they haven't been welcomed into. Mongrelised identities are a common thread for us. It's something that has been a defining feature of my life and I think that forces you to take these labels with a pinch of salt. It also makes you want to kick against it and shed those labels.

Like the label of being an actor for example?

I mean even more specific than that.

Being a British actor?

Being British or working-class or middle-class or a black guy. I've had a more mixed-up life than that. I want to escape the labels that are put on me. I think that's something that's driven me into acting.

Do you think that acting itself develops a fluid sense of self, because you're embodying so many selves along the way?

It's a chicken and egg thing. I'm not sure whether people who become actors have already grown up in a way that cultivates a fluid sense of self. Or whether you like the idea of acting, and then at some point, as you develop the craft, you become a liquid, spongy thing. I suspect it's a bit of both.

Nevertheless, do you define yourself as an actor?

I am eager not to be defined as anything. No, I think I act. I do acting.

That's good. So it's a verb, not a noun?

I think so. If you define yourself as anything solid then you're trapped. No actor wants to lock themselves into a role for life. We like playing different people. Actors who become well known as brands and names in and of themselves find it hard to do the acting because they've become the noun. The verb becomes out of reach.

How do you think music relates to the doing of acting?

I think it keeps me feeling the insider-outsider status that I grew up with along class and cultural lines. It drove me to want to act and I think it gives me a different way of appreciating, looking at things, having different life experiences. Doing music means that I don't ever fully become an actor. I'm able to do these little guerrilla raids and then get out again. Even if that's a fiction in my head.

For those that don't know, how would you define your class and cultural background?

Well, I struggle to. But to give you the facts: my parents moved to London in the mid-1970s, their families are ancestrally from North India via Karachi in Pakistan. I was born and raised in Wembley. So it's an Indian heritage but also a Pakistani heritage and a London heritage. Inasmuch as I'll settle for any of these reductive labels I'll call myself a Londoner first and foremost. I guess you would say I'm from an 'upper working-class' family. Not comfortable middle-class by any stretch of the imagination. My parents didn't work in factories, they had university educations, but not in the UK. They're not cultural insiders. We've never had money. The Conservative government used to subsidise places at private schools for high-achieving kids. So I was bussed to school, an hour and a half from where I lived, every day. I encountered a different setting, class-wise. But still not particularly establishment. It was more aspirational. I met a lot of nouveau riche kids from Jewish, Asian or Gujarati families. Then sons of diplomats with double-barrelled surnames. Then I went to Oxford and that was the big culture shock. That's where I encountered the English middle-class culture properly. It was still something alien to me. I was in a different world and feeling very much like an outsider. I found a space I could make my own through music. I started throwing these music events – hip-hop, drum-and-bass events – and it became a magnet for other outsiders within the university. So those are some of the fault-lines that I've grown up along.

That fluid understanding of the nebulous – but nevertheless clearly defined – territory we call 'cultural identity' has given you a great armoury, right?

Big time. Yeah. I think when you're a teenager it's super-confusing – but everybody needs something to be confused about when they're a teenager – I'm lucky I was confused about something that became an asset later on, I guess.

That's a good way of putting it. So having said all that, when you receive a script, what do you hope for in the role, in the writing?

I don't want a script to be obvious. I don't want to invest in well-trodden tropes and be shackled to them. If something allows itself to be shaped by some of those dominant contours of story-telling, I want it to stretch them. I want to feel, 'I've never seen that kind of character portrayed in this size of movie before.' Innovation, the attempt to stretch culture in some way.

Why is innovation important to you?

It's progress. Maybe I'm deluded. But stretching the frontiers of our cultural space and our creative space is exploratory. Liberating. You know, we can go to new places together. But also, why do you always want to do the same old shit?

When you talk about cultural space, is that a concept or something that's palpable and concrete for you?

It's palpable and concrete in the sense of, 'OK, I'm going to have a look at what's on at the cinema this weekend.' That's a microcosm of our cultural space. But also there's the bigger cultural space you feel you're part of, that's intangible but in the ether, in the conversations amongst friends, in newspapers or whatever.

What about the role, specifically?

I'm still in that relatively immature stage as an actor, where I want to try to keep doing new things. I read this interview with Vincent Cassell who said that when he was starting out as an actor he was always trying to go to extremes and find roles that were as far away from him as possible. Then at a certain point you embrace who you are and you say, 'Well, I can't run away from it.' I'm still in the stage where I don't want to keep repeating myself. That's unhelpful and unhealthy to some extent, because I'm imposing a meta-level of analysis of a role rather than, 'Can I relate to this person, can I get into this person's head, is this a story I want to tell?' There's something else in me that's stepping out and saying, 'Here I am, the defined entity, Riz the actor that's watching this,' rather than just letting the role talk to me. I always want to do something different.

Is that because you get offered similar parts?

That's an interesting question. The parts that I'm offered haven't been particularly similar. But some of the terrain on which those stories take place has been. I'm a non-white actor in the twenty-first century, working in a Western country. But the film industry is becoming more and more global, so you're not really just working in the West. *The Reluctant Fundamentalist* (2012) was made with Qatari money, a New York Indian director, filmed in Istanbul, the States and India. Those boundaries are really evaporating. You look at someone like Gael García Bernal – where does he belong? I think he's an inspiring figure in that sense. But to go back to your question, I think there are more global stories being told which have to be colour-blind. But there's a sub-set of stories that engage with ethnic-minority actors as ethnicised entities rather than just as people, liberated from those ethnic markers. That's a gift and a curse really. I've done ten films or so. Four of them have been directly engaged in the post-9/11 narrative. I'm proud of them because they haven't reinforced stereotypes or caricatures, and I think that one of the higher callings of art is to cultivate empathy where we might not think it deserves to be. But I don't know if I would be tripping over myself to do another project in that universe. I think the global centre of gravity is shifting eastwards. There's still a delusion on the part of a lot of Western creatives to deal with this melanin-heavy 'other' as a peripheral entity. But that doesn't reflect where and how cheques are signed these days and where the creative engines are. I'm around a mix of growing pains between that way of thinking and a more democratic culture-world.

So, you've got a script which may or may not reflect some of these desires that you're talking about, or your vision of what a script could be. It's time to meet the director. What do you hope for in a director?

You want to be able to trust them. That's the main thing straight away when you first meet them. You're putting yourself in someone's hands. You're saying, 'Will I feel comfortable and confident, going to potentially quite vulnerable emotional places, for this person, with this person? Would they be able to guide me to those places? Not necessarily with gentleness and pastoral care but in a way that I feel is not exploitative for me or for an audience. Can I put myself in this person's hands? Can I trust them to be on top of the big picture?' On some level you're looking for the perfect parent, so that all that other stuff is taken care of so you can just . . .

. . . so you can play.

[laughs] Yeah, exactly.

What does embodiment mean to you as an actor?

I can feel it sometimes. I'm getting better at knowing how to set the right conditions for it to happen more.

What are those conditions?

I think it's about getting away from your conscious mind. Most good artistic creations happen on the level of the subconscious. So what I do more and more is give myself to a process of osmosis. Just immersing myself in the interests, loves, fears, world-views of this person I'm trying to be. Thinking about the kinds of things they think about. So for instance in *The Reluctant Fundamentalist* I'm playing a finance whizz. Finance terrifies me, I'm not good at maths. So I spent months subscribing to the *FT*, taking stock-brokerage lessons online, reading economics books. And could I do that job right now? No, I couldn't. Am I closer to being in a place where I might be able to? Yes. But walking around all day with a maths thought in your head makes you walk differently to walking around all day with a hip-hop question in your head. Trying to think about how I should walk from the outside in, I find troublesome and a red herring. In terms of embodiment it's more about thinking, 'What does this person do in their spare time?' For a while you feel like a complete fraud. It's like you're inviting this guest to come over who repeatedly doesn't come, but you keep making dinner every night and one day the guest turns up.

[laughs] That's lovely.

So you just keep cooking. *[laughs]*

[laughs] What's the difference between preparation and rehearsal for you?

Preparation is quite an internal thing. It's the world of scrapbooks. Where I like to get to – before taking on a role – is bingeing on basketball or maths. Or making music playlists – always. I find that really important. What music do they listen to? Music tastes make connections with identity markers. I want to get to a stage of preparation where everything I see starts becoming a part of that. So I'll be on a park bench and someone will be walking their dog and I'll be like, 'My character's just like that dog. Look at the way it's so loyal but it's on a leash.' You just get to that place where everything you see is like, 'Yes, yes.' Does a process of osmosis take place to the point where you are walking like that person or you are like that dog? I don't know.

Do you like to do that preparation with the director or alone?

Alone.

By definition?

No, no. I like there to be dialogue. In an ideal world you have a thought and you email the director and they email you and pat you on the back and say, 'Yeah, good, keep going.' And then they fling something else at you which is better than anything you would have thought of. And you're kind of suspicious of it because you're doing this very private thing and then you look at it and it's like, 'Oh yeah, wow.' And that is part of your osmosis. I love there to be things flung back and forth but I think a lot of it is about spending time walking around trying to cultivate a way of seeing.

Privately, from the inside out.

Yeah, exactly. Inside out is a good phrase. But rehearsal is when you bring your half-baked pudding to that dinner table and it's always very exposing – because rehearsal is tangible rather than this private seed you're trying to cultivate – it feels out of sync with where you're trying to get to. I never feel ready to rehearse. But it's crucial because whenever I don't rehearse I feel so sad I didn't get that chance.

And you end up rehearsing on camera, right?

Every time. Yeah.

So what do you need from the director at the point of rehearsal?

I don't want them to impose too heavily their version of the character or a way of doing the scene. Of course you want them to end up imposing their vision of the film and of your character, but you don't want it to feel like that. It has to feel organic. They have to bring it out of you like an amazing politician or diplomat or parent that you're confiding in. *[both laugh]*

And so I guess you want them to ask you the right questions. Notes are very powerful things – and at the point of rehearsal, you're not quite ready for them as you're still in the middle of this preparation process. So because anything the director says is potent and powerful it's best if they distil down those notes to the most seemingly unintrusive, nurturing, helpful things possible, realising that anything they say at that point echoes in the actor's spirit. You want them to be quite gentle. But you don't want to feel like they don't have a clue about how they want it to be, either. You want to feel like, 'Well they know where we're going, even though I don't,' and that goes straight back to the trust that this person is going to steer the ship, confidently, in the right direction.

So to emanate confidence and leadership but –

– to be open and gentle.

What about the director's eyes? Being watched.

In rehearsal?

And in the shoot.

I suppose the ideal mixture is someone who's got your back on a checking kind of level. Making sure you're not taking their ship off course. Hopefully by this point we know where we want to go together. It's either been explicitly stated or through rehearsals. And so they're keeping you on track, they're watching, they're checking but not judging. Just having a 'loving curiosity'. That phrase – I've started meditating this year and so much of what they talk about is how to cultivate good practice. I just wish we had meditated at drama school. It's about being present in the moment and approaching the moment with a loving curiosity. I guess that's what I want from a director's eyes.

Text or subtext? Which is more important to you? What's said or not said?

I think what's said is the tip of the iceberg and is the key to everything beneath it. When I learn lines, I try not to learn them directly. I record all the cues and I keep playing them and I won't say my line until I manage to arrive at it by a thought process that ends up at that line. For example someone says, 'I hate you' and I have to say, 'I love you.' If I just say, 'Well, I love you' then I'm a fraud. But if I know that they're bad at expressing themselves and they're trying to express a strong feeling towards me and I know what they need to hear . . . So the cues are much more important to me than my lines.

The thoughts in between that lead to the genuine impulse to speak, the need to speak.

Yes, that's exactly it.

I track those thoughts with people. Do you ever do that with directors?

I've never done that, but I'd love to. It would be very interesting. But most film directors are making films with no time, no money: they're overworked and over-stressed. There just isn't enough time given to this. When you hear that a theatre director is doing a film you feel excited because they know how to do this work. Many young directors, no one's ever spoken to them about it.

That's what this book's for, amongst other things. On the last film I got the lead actors to talk through the whole script from memory but with none of the spoken text. Just saying, 'What do I think and feel in this scene but can't say?' By the time we came to shoot, they were rock-solid.

That's perfect.

How important is the look to you? You've talked about some aspects of working from the outside, but what about clothes, hair, make-up, all that stuff?

I think it's the icing on your half-baked pudding.

[SP laughs]

It allows you to invest in the illusion that the journey is finished, you've arrived. It's like a crowning of the character when you put on the clothes. You look in the mirror, just for a moment, and feel like, 'Ah I've travelled there, I've got to this place.' Of course you never really find the character as much as you like, until about three weeks into the shoot. But I feel it's quite ceremonial, going into a costume fitting.

Nice way of putting it. So you arrive on the shoot. What do you need, want, hope for from the director under the warfare-like conditions of shooting?

You want to be protected from the mayhem. You need a safe space or a quiet space to be able to do your thing. But you also want a vibe that feels open enough that if you don't need to be in a private mode, you can interact with people. What I really want on a film set is the sense of play – yeah. It is that. Openness, friendliness, you can do your own thing and there's no judgement. Basically good vibes. Even if we're trying to get bad vibes, in which case we'll nurture those. And the tone is set right at the top. If the director's having a shit day, the runner who is bringing you your tea is moody and stressed and then you feel like an arsehole because that runner is being pulled in ten different directions by the third, who's being pulled in ten different directions by the first and all because the director's had a bad day. Then you feel a weight or a pressure because all actors are acutely socially aware, slightly anxious, insecure, over-analytical people. So then it's your job to vibe up this runner. You can't have this runner running around spreading bad vibes.

[SP laughs]

I've done films where my focus becomes vibe management on set.

[SP bursts out laughing]

Genuinely. It's about, 'Wow, I can feel these horrible vibes between these people and I've got to talk to them.' We have to try and get to a place, collectively, of play and not of bullying or fighting. We're all up against it. It's very hierarchical; it's like a military operation. That is what making films is like, but it's better if there's a way that we can be merrily marching off the cliff together, rather than people being dragged by their hair. If I come on set and I feel like there's a strong playful leader then that vibe just permeates everywhere. I'm not just imagining it, it's true.

   And you don't want the director ever to say, 'Do it like you did in the audition.' It's useful if people ask in rehearsals, 'What do you like on set? Do you like to be on your own and doing your own thing, or not?' Because so much of the first week on set is about, 'How am I going to survive in this war zone?' It's negotiating space for yourself and knowing who can be relied upon to communicate. Like needing to know when we're moving on to the next scene. 'I've been sat here thinking about my dead mum for an hour and a half and you're coming in here to tell me we're doing that scene at the end of the day.'

[SP laughs]

'I've been crying here for an hour and a half and now we're doing the scene where we merrily skip through the fields.' Communication. I got there in the end.

You've already mentioned what kind of feedback helps and what kind of feedback hinders.

Inside-out feedback helps. Outside-in feedback hinders.

So for example – 'Don't lift your arm like that' – useless?

If you're a genius then you can find a way of giving someone a reason why not to lift their arm like that. Then that's really helpful.

You need reasons.

Exactly.

What about the director staring at the monitor or standing by the camera watching you – is that meaningful for you?

No. I don't care where they stand but I feel like if we do a take and then there's silence, other conversations happening, and then we're going again, you need reasons. Why are we going again? What was good, what was bad? And not even 'Well done.' Just give someone a new reason or a more refined version of the old reason that they didn't nail before. Communication is the big thing. If the overall vibe is one of focused play, clearly heading in a direction together, then the ideal currency is clear and continuous communication.

Where do you find reality or truth in performance?

You mean when you're on set and the situation is as real as it can be for you but there's a seven-foot dude standing over your shoulder?

What does it mean to be real when you're in a pretend situation? Including people looking at you with cameras.

I think the closest you get to knowing that it's there and something went well is when you weren't thinking at all. When time passes quickly rather than slowly. If you're thinking, 'This is going well,' then it's not.

That means you're too detached and the focus is too much on the outside?

Exactly. The shit happens when it's out of your control. That's when it feels really real. Because I didn't think of putting my hands down like that, it just happened. How do you get there when there's a pretend situation going on? There's a dude standing over your shoulder, holding what looks like a stuffed animal on a pole, right?

The boom operator.

There are two ways of dealing with that reality. One is a level of complete comfort with it until it's not of interest any more. It's not exposing. That's about the vibe of open playfulness with all these people and with the whole environment. It's good to be introduced to people instead of, 'OK, welcome to your first day on set, have a seat.' Next thing, I'm stood there: 'I don't know what the DP's name is, who is this dude with the furry animal?' So it's either about having a level of familiarity with all those distractions so they're not of interest any more or the other extreme is to try really hard to seal them out of your little tunnel of existence. You only exist in your little trailer and you try and maintain your narrow focus. You'll come on set and you will try by force of will to make this person or that person disappear. I think that's not good because you're making them an object of effort.

New media and the Internet. Do you think it's having an impact on films and on how you perform?

Massively, yeah. I think that quick cutting, shrinking attention-spans and the constant over-stimulation of multiple different screens at any given time leads to faster-paced film-making.

What about the language of performance?

I think the bar is raised in terms of trying to get to a place . . . well, get past performance. Getting to genuine truthful interactions because of the culture of confessional, non-performative performance. With YouTube and blogging and all that, people can access passionate truth in close-up at a click of a button, a billion times, at any given time of day.

That's what Rage *was about.*

Exactly. We can't help but define ourselves in relation to that as film-makers, because it's the dominant consumption of the moving image. So we're either going to subvert that or go with it and say, 'We're going to take on that language of storytelling.' Like – 'Oh, we're just filming this, you're watching the real thing. Found footage.'

*What about money and how we measure value in such a profit-
driven industry? How do you relate to the economic structures of film-
making? I don't just mean how much you get paid.*

You feel it on a film. So many people around the world are trying to
make films that when you do a film that sits on top of that money
pyramid, that human heap, you feel it. It sometimes gets in the way
when there's lots of money involved. You feel the waste, you feel the
extra bodies, you feel the extra fuss, the noise, the time that's able
to be burned and wasted, the energy that you're trying to keep up
doing a scene for two days rather than twenty minutes. It increases
the distance between what you're doing and reality, the bubble that
you are inevitably in. The walls of that bubble can become like thick
titanium walls. Big time. But if that money is spent wisely – and
somehow, amazingly some people do this – you create an alternative
reality. And that's exciting. But when the money just erects big gilded
walls between you and real life – I think that's counterproductive.
Some of the work that I'm proudest of – and I feel I've given my best
performances in – has been the opposite of that. Where the reality
can't help but bleed into and under the fingernails of everything
we're doing, because we can't pay for those walls.

But in terms of the overall economic structure, I feel what we
need to focus on is diversifying the different kinds of exhibitors
– the French do something like that – rather than putting all our
money into production where lots of films get made but don't get
shown, because of the bottlenecking when it gets to exhibition.
You don't have much diversity in the different cinema chains and
multiplexes. Small cinemas are pushed to the brink and they die
out. What I would like to see is subsidies made available for independent cinemas that will show independent or homegrown films.
There's a big bifurcation taking place between films that get shown
in cinemas and films that don't. But actually you know what?
Maybe that's not such a bad thing. Why prop up cinemas? Maybe
they're a dying breed. With some films there's an opening weekend

which is the be-all and end-all and then there's films where the opening weekend is just the little trailer for the real life of the film, which is people's pride of place on their DVD shelves.

Or on the Internet. So we're talking about a moment of profound transition. But do you still hold an image in your head of cinema as the monumental form?

Inside a theatre?

Well, that's a good question. Is it just to do with the physical architecture of the space of projection?

The shared experience within the cinema? I think there's been a redistribution of that cultural capital.

[SP laughs]

I think it's different experiences competing for the same space, with a shrinking time and attention-span. But then that's why it's monumentally important that cinema does something different to the TV movie, the soap opera, the web series or the confessional YouTube blog.

What do you think that cinema can uniquely do? Feature films —the classic form.

Ezra Pound said something like, 'Poetry is language at its most charged.' I think cinema has to be the moving image at its most charged and emotionally potent, to try to draw you into a world. Maybe it's slightly outdated in its approach but it's asking you to stop your life, sit with other people in a dark room, and come into this other world. Whereas I might just dip in and out of this Vlog. But when I'm watching TV I'm also being drawn into a different world. I suppose there's something a bit novelistic about that. The

HBO series – and I don't think there's any bad thing in this – draw you in. They're highly charged. But the idea of film, of trying to do it in an hour and a half, is like a poem, isn't it? It's trying to do it over four stanzas, not over the course of a novel.

If cinema is the moving image at its most charged – then what is an actor within that?

Increasingly someone wearing a motion-capture suit. *[both laugh]*

But seriously, what is acting or 'being-ness' at its most charged? What quality of performance are you aiming at?

Internally what you're aiming at is to get beyond conscious thought and be. And for the experience of the audience, I think what you're hoping for is that the purity of that person's 'in-the-moment-ness' brings you as a watcher into their moment, into their virtual reality.

Is there a spiritual dimension for you in that?

Yeah, hugely.

Tell me about it.

It's all about trying to be in the moment, trying to transcend your ego. That's what the vocation is about, the act of acting. And that's what the spiritual pursuits of meditation or other devotional practices are about. Trying to get past your conscious thought and to be in the moment and yet not 'be' in a way that is isolated from your surroundings but is completely tied into and responsive to your surroundings, be they props or the person opposite you. So in that sense it's very spiritual at its purest level. It's a kind of synchronicity of thought, feeling and behaviour. But so much of what is in your mind when you're meditating can be, 'Shit, I wore the wrong underwear today.' And so much of when you're an actor can be about, 'Fucking hell man, XYZ bullshit stress has been dropped on my plate. What's up with the vibe from this actor? And the press are coming down to talk today and hang on, what the fuck? They cut my lines.' Meditation is about the act of sitting still, but you can get so caught up in petty bullshit. You're trying to be right there but every distraction is magnified. That's why acting is perfect for trying to get to a place of somewhere special and spiritual. But it's also a perfect recipe for going in the completely opposite direction.

The monkey on your back. And how does the spiritual vocation – which people rarely talk about in this area – jive with the cult of celebrity that parasitically feeds off the industry?

They are opposites. One is about reinforcing, adorning the ego and the act itself is about shedding it.

So how do you navigate that contradiction?

I think it's one reason for why it gets harder and harder for people to act. The best performances we see in cinema are always complete newcomers.

Do you think so?

I think so. It's raw.

How do you think you can achieve that rawness when you are already known?

How I deal with it is, I try and let it give me confidence. When I leave here and walk back to Old Street station, someone might stop me and say, 'I'm a fan' or, 'I liked you in this film or that film.' I try not to walk away from that interaction with the thought, 'Oh I'm that guy that's known. I'm that entity in that person's head.' I try and relate that positive energy that they give me not to me, but to a thing I did. It's something that happened in a space between what I was doing and what they were watching. Do you see what I mean?

I do.

But it's particularly hard when it's people saying something negative. A lot of actors are very hard on themselves. Every single day I'm on set, I go home knowing that I failed. I'm not that fun to be around off set. On set, I can be fun, if we're in the right state of play. But when I go home, I'm just so down. I wake up in the middle of the night, open up the script again . . . that's why when people say, 'You fucked up' or, 'You were shit', I go, 'I knew it! That's what I was thinking every day.'

Self-doubt is an incredibly important engine. Somebody called it divine discontent. It's good to welcome it because it means you're setting the bar very high. It's good even though it feels very difficult. But at the same time, one needs ballast against the cultural discouragement at large.

Yeah. I guess the main thing is – like any kind of performance – it's not about you. It's about this thing that you are a channel for. So if I'm rapping on stage, it's not about me, it's about how I can put these transient feelings and thoughts into words. I've got to try and serve them. Similarly, as an actor, I've got to try and serve the character who is trying to serve the thought that has just been triggered by their environment. Problems arise when it's about you. And that's why the parasitic celebrity obsession is nuts. It's exactly the opposite of trying to transcend your ego. But the crazy thing is that playing the game of this profit-driven economic model may well allow you to make more forays into the spiritual space.

JOAN ALLEN

Joan's fine, subtle work in films such as *The Crucible* (1996) is greatly admired by other actors. I first met her in New York City when I was searching for the right woman to play 'She' in *Yes*. I went to a small apartment she was temporarily camping in; it was a transition moment in her life. She read some of the scenes to me. The verse (all in iambic pentameter) suddenly sounded like ordinary speech, which thrilled me. Joan's theatre background gave her common ground with Simon Abkarian, who I had already cast. I called him in Paris and we put him on the speakerphone. They read a scene together and even under those unpromising conditions, the tender understanding of each other was movingly evident.

Joan worked harder and in a more meticulous way than almost anyone else I had met. She took copious notes in every one of our meetings. It seemed as if she was devouring every word, every moment. I loved her hunger, which was entirely appropriate for the role of a woman in another kind of life transition. Her willingness to reflect on her identity as an American woman who – in the story – falls in love with a Middle Eastern man, and the courage with which she entered states of both ecstasy and grief, was exemplary.

We talked on Skype for this interview. She was sitting on a porch in her mother's house in Illinois where she was visiting for a few days. I was in London and she could see, behind me, the room we had worked in together so intensely. I wanted to hug her, not having seen her for so many years, but made do with reaching out towards the screen. Our hands touched, somewhere in the ether.

What do you hope for when you're sent a script?

I think the thing that I hope for the most is to want to turn the page. I want to know what happens next. I want to feel like I'm being taken on a ride. I want to be engaged.

Is it the script as a whole, or does it depend on the particular role that's being presented to you?

It does depend on the role as well. But work has been rather slow in recent years, both for personal reasons and also I think because of my age, in this business. The independent film world is also much more of a struggle these days, unfortunately. But there are a lot more venues now, with streaming and so on, and it's exciting that there are different opportunities for exposure. Sometimes I love that and sometimes I find that there's too much thrown at the wall. *[laughs]* It's overload. I look for something that I feel could potentially stretch me a bit. I think Catherine Deneuve said, 'I look for the role that I know has to be in the film and will not end up on the cutting-room floor.'

[SP laughs]

Integral to the story. I want to be a piece of the action. So if I get something that is peripheral . . . I got a script from a friend recently, Sally. It was an interesting topic but the character was just tacked on, spouting exposition and ideology. I thought, 'I'm not part of the fun. I'm not part of the issue. I'm not part of the game.' And that tends to make me go, 'Thank you, but I'd rather see the movie than do that part.'

Which is more important for you, the script or the director?

They are really neck and neck. The director is very important for me. I would never want to work with a director that was a bully or used harsh scare tactics, thinking that was the way to get good work out of people. I never responded well to that even when I was a child. I always learned better from the patient teacher. It's the same with the director who makes you feel completely loved, then you feel you can do anything. I think the director's job is to make you feel safe so that you can stick your neck out and maybe do a take that's really abominable, but it's OK because you're at least taking a chance. And sometimes you don't know what's right unless you do some things that are wrong. If I had a question about a director – particularly about his level of compassion – I don't think I would necessarily do it, even if I loved the script.

Let's say you've read the script and you like it, the role is pivotal, but you've never met the director before. When you go to meet that director for the first time, what clues are you looking for that will indicate what the process might be?

The clues that I'm looking for the most are based on the director's humanity. What is he or she like as a person? What vibration do I get, sitting in some restaurant we've appointed to meet over coffee, when we say hello to each other? Do I like sitting at the table with that person? Do I feel an ease in conversation? Do I feel that this person is on my side; that he loves actors? Or she? *[laughs]* That was terrible that I just said 'He'! But those are the things that I look for. I worked with a relatively inexperienced director recently, in a very big part. And I found I had to lead the way a bit. He's more of a writer, so blocking, for instance, was just like *[laughs]* 'I don't know!' But I felt very kindly towards him and I could see that he felt that way towards me, so I felt that we could work together. I trusted his taste. I felt: he's intelligent, he will know a good take when he sees one. And as for the other pieces – I'm rather seasoned myself, having done this for thirty years, and it felt good to be able to go, 'I have some experience and maybe I can help him a little bit.' At the end of the day I just want to know – and feel that I can trust – that what he sees on the monitor is the best performance that we could possibly do. Though it's never perfect, it can always be improved.

What do you wish all directors understood about actors?

I wished they understood how difficult it is. Many directors do understand that – and you certainly are one of them – but not all of them do. The bareness, the vulnerability, the difficulty of exposing yourself. It ties into the things I said to you earlier about being compassionate towards actors: patient and not too critical. Although some people may need that. I've met actors who don't feel they perform well in anything unless someone is standing over them like a drill sergeant, cracking the whip. So it really is my own personal desire for kindness and an ability to understand and to relish the collaboration.

Do you think that you need to love the person you're playing?

That's a very interesting question. I don't think you always need to love them but you have to be intrigued, somehow. I'm about to embark on a play. I'm going back to my old stomping ground in Chicago where I learned everything. It's an unusual play and I love the director. She's very much like you: wildly creative. I want to go to work and be with her every day – regardless of how it turns out. I remember Ang Lee once said, when they asked him about how he chose his films – because he does such a pastiche of different styles and genres of storytelling – 'I choose the ones that I'm not sure I can do.' And I feel a little bit like that on this one, Sally. I'm going into it like it could be anything. And I guess maybe at this age I'm a little more comfortable, because life has thrown so many strange and difficult things in my direction in the past few years, that I can say, 'Let's give it a whirl.' It's that corny saying, 'It's not the destination, it's the journey.'

You've mentioned age twice. [both laugh] I have a feeling you might have something to say about this.

I consider myself very fortunate. I don't have a need to work back to back. And the older I get . . . I've acted now for . . . well I'm fifty-six and I started forty years ago. I don't want to have to pretend all the time any more. I recently heard Elaine Stritch – who has a wonderful body of work, and recently retired – saying, 'I'm tired of pretending. I want to wake up in the morning and be in the reality of who I am.' I have a bit of that. I don't want to always be pretending. I want to live and cook. I was always scared of cooking, I felt that it was a very vulnerable thing to do, to make something for someone else to sit and eat. I've gotten much braver about that. So I work about as much as I want to. And I've saved my money. I don't have to work to keep the roof over my head and food on my table. I've lived very frugally my whole life. But happily. I now live in the same one-bedroom apartment in New York City I walked into in 1983. Partly because there's a gorgeous terrace that I cannot give up! But I do not need houses with multiple bedrooms and cars and extravagant clothing. I prefer a quiet walk or an intimate talk with a friend, or to throw a ball for my dog. Those have always been the things that have made me the happiest.

You've obviously got an extremely positive and creative attitude to the challenges that actors, particularly female actors, face as they get older. With what's written for them, and so on. Let's be honest about this to each other.

You've made me think of something, Sally. I was very disappointed at last year's Oscars when I looked at the actresses that were nominated. I thought that there was nothing great that was written for a woman last year. There are so few interesting roles, nothing out there that is really challenging. I did this film on Georgia O'Keefe a few years ago and we could not sell it as a feature film. We ended up doing it for the Lifetime network. And because of their restraints about profanity – she had quite a spicy, interesting life – we had to damp all that down in order to meet the approval of the network. We compromised because the film wouldn't have been made otherwise. But I was disappointed that we couldn't really tell her story.

So the lack of interesting roles is not just about the lack of writing but the way that the networks and financing are controlled.

Yes.

What do you think a character is? Is a character also you? Where do you end and the character begins? What is that process?

I think there's quite a bit of myself in there. How I gesture is Joan. Every human being gestures in their own way and breathes in their own way. So how do you begin? When I prepare for a role I know that though I gesture like Joan, my body has to become someone else who doesn't move in that way, doesn't quite breathe that way. I feel you can make small modifications in your muscle memory. Clothing helps a lot, what shoes you are wearing. You hold yourself differently depending on your attire. Sometimes I say to myself, 'Don't think about this too much or you'll drive yourself crazy.' I worked with actors in an ensemble for many, many years and saw how they bent into multiple roles. And yet there was something of them in almost everything.

You're referring to your Steppenwolf years, in Chicago.

Yes.

How important is working from the outside in for you? Working on hair, make-up, as well as the clothes?

I would say it's about fifty–fifty for me. I think when I was younger – and didn't understand acting as well as I do now, and still had a way to go – I think I always thought it was an internal process. And as I've done it more and more, I found that it's more important to me to ask: what am I wearing? What are my shoes? Are her nails painted? Does she shave under her arms or is she a person who doesn't do that? What kind of reading glasses does she wear?

How closely do you link your own life experiences to the emotional space that the character needs to go through? How much do you consciously graft those together?

I do draw parallels between what a character is going through and things that I've gone through. Particularly if I have an emotional scene. If I need to cry I will sometimes take myself away and think about the sad moments of my own life. Sometimes I can do it just by thinking about what the character must be feeling at that moment. But if you do something over and over again, that vein can collapse a little bit. And so I will think about experiences in my life, or pieces of music that move me, or a poem that strikes me.

How much do you like to involve the director in all these aspects of preparation? The look and also the world inside, the emotional resonance and so on. Or are many of these things essentially private?

Some of them are private. What I do like to do is work very closely with the director on the intention of the story. Because for me the story is the king of any piece and we're just cogs that fit into the greater purpose of – hopefully – telling a story that people are interested in watching and taking in. So I like to ask the director, 'What do you think this really means? What do you think is going on at this moment?' I just finished a project and I liked calling the director on my weekends as I was preparing for the next week's work. 'OK, this is coming up. What do you think is really going on here?' I wanted to make sure we were on the same page when we got to the set because this last film – very much like when we shot *Yes* – was a low-budget film. There's no time to waste, you need to be prepared. And *Yes* trained me very well for this. I remember you saying, 'The less money you have, the more prepared you must be, so that you're not wasting a second of time when you're on set.' And that has stayed in my head. This was a three-million-dollar budget and I was in virtually every scene. I thought, 'I must be prepared. They can't change the schedule, they can't add days. I don't want to put them in a position of forcing them to do that because that would be selfish and inconsiderate of me.' So I like being clear about my intention, going into work. How I get there once I'm on set – I don't always want to talk about that. This last thing that I worked on – it was a Stephen King film – I'm married to a man and find out after twenty-five years of marriage that he's a serial killer. *[laughs]* It was really difficult to imagine what that would feel like: the betrayal, the horror, the fear. I had to be really, really on edge. The director would say, 'Action' and I wasn't always quite ready. I would say, 'Give me a minute.' Some actors are very good at snap, snap, snap, you know. One minute they're there talking to the crew and then they're in it. And I'm somewhere in between. I'm not someone who needs to stay in character the whole time. I don't go home and you have to call me by the character name, but I do have to be in a zone when I'm working, which is usually solitary. Then the director and I can maybe discuss it after the take and say yes, or no.

That brings us to rehearsal. With Yes *we had very intense rehearsals. Not all films have . . . sometimes there is no rehearsal. Tell me what you feel about rehearsal for films.*

It depends on the film. I don't like to over-rehearse because I like a bit of spontaneity. *Yes* was very specific because of the poetry. It was perfect to rehearse the way we did. With some films I don't want to rehearse quite that much. With this recent film I was more interested in having discussions with the director about content and intention.

That's another aspect of rehearsal, of course. You don't have to rehearse how you're going to do it, but why.

Yes. I don't want to do the scenes too much but I would like to understand them very well.

What do you think are the key differences between working in the theatre and working on film?

In terms of character and approach, they don't really differ. You study the character, you understand – hopefully – the story and how the character fits in it. I don't see that much difference in terms of approach. It's a different physical demand. It's a different kind of focus. It took me a long time to get used to film-making because I had done so much theatre. For the first four or five years, I didn't understand how you could focus with all the chaos: people grab-bing you and combing your hair, or straightening your collar. And the precision of film-making, because it's really a science. There's a lens and a focal point and they have to take the tape measure to make sure you're in focus; there's a precision that has to be achieved in addition to the emotional content. It's a synthesis of science and art, in a way. Once I got it I found it quite exciting. People used to condemn Marlon Brando for walking away from the theatre. He said something like, 'In the movies if you can have heart-breaking emotion whilst knowing that if you turn your head a half of an inch you're going to be out of the light, who's to say that's not a significant acting achievement?' I've always thought about that. I like to work with the camera operator. It's like a dance. I find it exciting, a lovely collaboration. I tend to fall in love with the camera department. And I'm very moved by the focus-puller and dolly-grip. I would *so* not want to be a focus-puller on a film. It gives me goosebumps just thinking about it. *[laughs]* It seems so difficult.

What do you find that you really need from the director at the moment of shooting? Do you like the director to be watching you? Does it make a difference to you if the director is over in a corner, looking at a monitor?

I've actually gotten quite used to the monitor now. Sometimes it's better for the director to be by the camera once in a while, but it's very rare. I've gotten so used to not seeing the director. But I so want to please the director. I admit that about myself. I want to please the director.

Is that bad?

[laughs] Well, some actors really want to please themselves. Some say, 'Don't do what that director says because he may use it in the

film and you won't like it. If he's telling you to go in the opposite direction and you don't feel that that's right, don't do it, so he doesn't have the option to put that in.' I could never do that. I'm not that duplicitous.

Thank God!

But actors do do that, Sally. I've heard them say, 'He gave me a direction and I don't like it so I just won't do it.' Sometimes I think I might be a little too willing and just go, 'Oh yes, yes. I'll do that.' But I would rather do it my way than the other way. I don't think I could be the other way. It's just not in my nature. I like seeing the director's face once the take is over. I want to walk right back to the chair and look at his or her face and go, 'Again?' That's really when I want to see their face.

So the director's facial expression is as important as anything they might say?

Yes. Absolutely. Communication is apparently seventy per cent body language, twenty per cent voice and ten per cent the words. And so I really want to see the reaction. I can tell immediately with body language and expression.

What kinds of feedback are useful and what kind of feedback is horrendous?

[laughs] I don't like hearing, 'That was terrible' or, 'Ewww.' I don't really like hearing the negatives. I don't mind doing it again but I feel it can be communicated in a way that makes you feel like you're still capable. You know, that you're not a complete loser. Then you can get up on the horse and try it again. So anything that is too blatantly negative, I have to shake off. I would rather hear comments that are put in a positive light.

Does there seem to be a correspondence between how you feel about a given take and the director's view? How much do you trust your subjective sense? Or do you rely on the director to be the most objective mirror?

I tend to rely on the director. But I've found most often that we feel the same way. Once in a while I'm surprised that they feel like they want to move on when I'm not quite sure that I hit it. And I do question my own take sometimes. But I find that we are usually in agreement. I feel I was in the zone and he or she feels good about it too.

You've used the phrase 'in the zone' a couple of times. Can you define what that means to you?

I think it means to be totally present in the moment, not thinking too hard. I like to get myself into what I feel is the correct emotional tone before going into the scene. Is this person happy at this point? Are they sad, are they scared? So to me getting in the zone is getting that feeling inside. Once I've achieved that feeling then I just have to stay in the moment and carry through with the words. So 'in the zone' to me is getting in the right emotional place before action is called. And then hopefully that is powerful enough that it carries me through the scene so I don't have to think about it all that much.

So it's not a conscious state, it's more like accessing an unconscious state?

Well, it's certainly a conscious process of trying to find it. Because I have to think, 'She's very scared right now,' and then keep myself on edge. A person moves differently when they're scared than when they're sad. I just get myself into that place and then maybe the unconscious part of it kicks in.

Well, maybe the word 'unconscious' isn't correct anyway. I can
remember with great clarity watching you go into a 'zone' when we
were shooting. You've talked about the science of film-making, but
you also had an extremely precise way of working with your states,
in parallel with the other technical things you have to be aware of.
There's a lot of agility required.

Well, yes. Acting takes a lot of technique like any art-form. You
have to have your tool-bag of technique because you can't wait for
hours or days for the inspiration to hit you. You have to have those
different techniques that you can pull from. And then the more
ephemeral side works in tandem with those tools.

What about the afterwards? The film is complete. First of all,
what's it like for you leaving a film where you've had these intense
collaborations?

It depends on the film. *Yes* was so special. Really I've had very few bad
experiences on films but that one was magnificent. I felt high from
it. Everything about it. You, Simon, the poetry, the character that
you were allowing me to play, a sensuality that I hadn't been given
the opportunity to explore. I don't usually get that attached. I just
finished a film a few weeks ago and it feels like it was about five years
ago. I don't make deep friendships with many people on my films.
My friends tend to be non-actors. I have this intense experience and
then it's over. I'm rather used to it. I understand the nature of this
work and that it does have an ending. Most often I'm ready for it.

And then months later you get to see the film. The director meanwhile
has of course been watching you day-in, day-out. You turn up to
the premiere and suddenly get to watch the film and see yourself on
screen. How is that moment of completion for you?

Well, the first time, I'm a bit dislocated from it. I'm often thinking
about what we were doing on the day that the scene was shot. All of

that is playing in my mind. 'Oh that was the day that it rained and it was such a muddy mess. And the hair-person twisted her ankle.' It takes the second viewing for me to watch it a little more objectively. Is this story succeeding or not? I'm always curious to see how it turns out. But I don't watch them again afterwards. I haven't seen *Yes* since we watched it so many times throughout the film-festival circuit. Maybe it's because I want to keep moving forward. When I'm in the process of making films, I feel, 'This will turn out the way it's going to turn out and all I can do is the best job that I can possibly do every day.' And then it's up to the film gods. Because everyone tries to make the best film possible and there's a certain mysterious process to it that some succeed and some don't. Everyone sets out with the intention to make a great film.

What's the experience like for you of the press junkets, the critics, the gap between the process of making something and then what happens when it becomes something for the world?

I guess I feel that junkets are a necessity. I don't rail against them because we do make things to be seen and people need to hear about them in order for them to be seen. So I feel a willingness to participate in that process. Would I rather be doing something else with my time? Yes. But I understand needing to put the word out and be part of that process. I see that as a very temporary phase of the process of getting the film out. I feel it's workmanlike. This is part of your job and don't whine about it. It won't be for ever and then you'll move on to the next thing.

The other face of that is your relationship to your feeling of purpose.

For me it is the primal need for story. People need stories and they have done for hundreds of thousands of years. When I question this crazy business that I'm in, I ask: does it help? Am I making a difference at all in this short life that I have? I don't want to monumentalise it, but I always go back to the need for story. I am addicted to public radio in New York. I almost never turn on my television but there's a wonderful programme called *This American Life*. Ira Glass picks a theme and tells people across the country stories about things that they've lived through. I can't get enough of it. I want to hear how people live so differently, the good things and the catastrophes that happen to them, how they manage to get through them. I am very drawn to the triumph of the human spirit. I love reading depressing memoirs of people who prevail over really bad circumstances. And I guess I tie that into my work. If I can tell a story – any kind of story – I don't think it has to be serious, it can be frivolous. There's room for entertainment and there's room to have a scary experience too.

If you didn't care what anyone else might think about it, what would you say is really the core of your passion about your work?

I don't know if I'll ever understand that. I knew from a very young age that I was drawn to doing this. I didn't even know what it was, because I grew up in this area where there weren't plays or acting classes. I don't know where the desire came from. Part of me feels – and this might be true of quite a few actors – that there are things they feel they can say with the safety-net of the story rather than in real life. I know I felt that when I was young. 'Wow, I can scream and cry and do all these crazy things that I just don't feel I can do in life.' So initially for me it was like a release. I think there was also a genetic piece to it. I think I was born that way or it was in my birth order or in the dynamic of my family. All these unique creatures with all these different components that come into play that make us up. It was just there, Sally, I don't know how else to depict it.

Something of a mystery?

Yes. Something of a mystery. I don't quite understand it myself.

ANNETTE BENING

Annette's reputation precedes her as an intelligent, principled woman whose acting choices reflect an ability to work with integrity on a broad cinematic canvas. She is widely admired by her peers as well as by the general public. When we met to discuss Bella, the role I was offering her in *Ginger & Rosa*, in the lobby of the Chateau Marmont hotel in Los Angeles, in the year following her great success in *The Kids are Alright* (2010). I was utterly charmed by her warm yet astringent manner and by her willingness to consider what was clearly a relatively small – albeit pivotal –

Tilda Swinton in *Orlando*

Tilda Swinton in *Orlando*

Tilda Swinton and Billy Zane in *Orlando*

Johnny Depp in *The Man Who Cried*

Cate Blanchett in *The Man Who Cried*

In *Rage* . . . Judi Dench

Eddie Izzard

David Oyelowo

Jude Law

Riz Ahmed

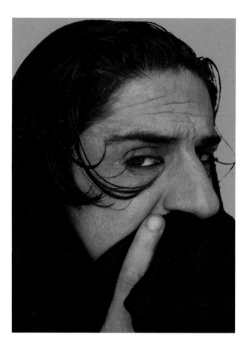

Simon Abkarian

Lily Cole

Steve Buscemi

Simon Abkarian and Joan Allen in *Yes*

Joan Allen and Sam Neill in *Yes*

Alessandro Nivola and Christina Hendricks in *Ginger & Rosa*

Alice Englert and Elle Fanning in *Ginger & Rosa*

With Elle Fanning on the set of *Ginger & Rosa*

part. Right from the start it was the vision of the script as a whole that interested her. She talked as animatedly about the other roles as she did about her own.

A year or so later she was a vividly engaged participant in rehearsals in London, and had researched Bella's poetic roots with a sharp intuition. She had picked out a poem by Denise Levertov, 'The Secret', that had also inspired me. She imbued her role, as an acerbic, intelligent anchor in the turbulent seas of the story, with all the qualities I had hoped for. We met once again in the Chateau Marmont for this interview when the film was finished, this time in a room upstairs. She admired the kitchenette, perhaps fantasising about a simpler life in a smaller space. The conversation lasted twice as long as I had estimated and the light faded outside the hotel until her face was illuminated only by the flashing billboards on Sunset Boulevard.

What are the factors that make you decide to accept a role?

It's the script itself, to begin with, and then it's the director, because movies are a director's medium. It's enjoyable to throw yourself behind someone and say, 'OK, what's your vision?' In plays it doesn't work that way. In plays you're the last one standing and everyone else, including the director, eventually goes away. In film it's the director's prerogative to focus the story, it's ultimately the director's sensibility and of course it's the director's choices in the end when you've moved on to other things and he's still sitting there, poring over you, editing your performance. So if I feel a connection to a director, that's a privilege. When I started, of course, I was going out on auditions and I would take pretty much anything I could get, with some exceptions, but now that I'm in the position that I'm in . . . it's different. I love to meet directors and yet I also often feel very awkward. A director's 'vision' can be very hard for them to articulate. And they shouldn't necessarily have to be good at it because it doesn't matter in the end. If the script doesn't seem like it's very cohesive then of course you can talk about that, but if that's not really the issue then it's just meeting them and feeling if there's a connection.

When you have that first meeting with a director what are the qualities you're looking for?

Oh . . . I guess passion, that's the most important thing. And then that's not even totally fair because sometimes people don't project that kind of image even though they're incredibly passionate. But I guess it's some kind of intuitive connection that I want to feel, because I tend to throw myself in. It's like falling in love, right? You can't decide to fall in love. You sometimes would like to be able to, but you don't feel it in your gut. That's the same thing with the work. You want to fall in love with it and you don't. On the other hand sometimes you fall in love with something and yet there's a part of you that knows that it may never come together.

I was lucky because I made a couple of movies, right when I started, which had no commercial life. And having never made any before I did not know what that second chapter might be like, so it really was just about the process. And then later, I had the other experience when something comes out and it's either critically well received or not. Now I know that for me the most satisfying part is the doing of it. After the movie is made and you're showing it, people's opinion of it, or their indifference . . . *[laughs]* Yeah, that's the hard part.

So let's reel back a minute. Do you ever meet a director before you read a script or is the script always the first port of entry?

Oh, that's a good question. I must have done but most people want you to read the script first.

The way that you answered the first question it seemed the director was slightly more important than the script in determining whether or not you would go with a role.

If a script isn't there then I know that there's only so much I can do, so not really. You know you're riding the wave of the narrative and no matter what you do, no matter how successful, convincing, moving, involving or interesting a moment-to-moment perform-ance can be, if the narrative itself doesn't support you then there's nothing, you're helpless.

So what do you look for in a script?

I guess I love to be entertained and we are in the entertainment business. I hate earnest things. I really hate that. *[SP laughs]* I look for something surprising and unique. Or it might be that it's based on a famous book that I know and that I'm dying for it to be great because I love the book . . . just involving. Involving.

What about the role and its relation to the whole?

If the role doesn't appeal to me, then it would be a real disservice to the film-maker to accept it, to do something that I don't feel a connection to. But if someone is graciously asking me to do some-thing . . . I recently had dinner with someone. I didn't really know him but I had seen his work and he said, 'I have this thing I want you to do.' I said, well, send it to me and then . . . I didn't feel any connection. I tried to say graciously that I don't feel any connection to this, but it's hard not to hurt someone's feelings. But I couldn't do it. And then if I do feel the connection, I get so involved and excited about it that it makes no sense, it's like a love affair, like *crazy*, irrational, God! And of course in my life I can't always work that way, because I've got children. There are lots of things that I would do, but choose not to because I've got that responsibility. Sometimes it just doesn't work to try to do both. But that's OK.

Pragmatic. It's interesting that you call it 'falling in love'. I sometimes call it 'falling in work'.

Well, isn't that great, though? I feel so lucky to have that, that the hard work is a joy. When you love working and you have fun working hard, oh my God! I see that in my kids sometimes and I think there's nothing that makes me happier than watching them so busy. They're loving it and then I feel, 'I know you're OK, you can make a life.'

OK, so you've met the director, you've read the script, you're resonating with both. How do you like to prepare?

There's very little nuts-and-bolts preparation to do. Much better to put it aside and let it stew and germinate inside and read the story and talk to the director. If it's a period film then I love the research. Historical novels are great to read because often they give you more of a sensory and emotional take on the period. But I also read non-fiction, look at paintings, photographs and listen to music. Music is really, really helpful. Sometimes I just play music in my head, imaginatively, when I'm working because that will get me into a certain place. Then there's meeting people who have had similar experiences to the story. I've had some of my most amazing life experiences in those sojourns, where you're out investigating a particular scenario, meeting someone who might have gone through something like your character. Often the encounter has a whole different meaning for the two of you than actually serving the movie. It becomes a kind of catharsis for the person you're speaking with if there's a certain amount of trust involved. Thinking about the intimacy of the work that we do . . . It's such a privilege. It's so unusual and it's also kind of crazy, kind of nuts. We work so closely together when we work on these movies. There's a level of intimacy that we leap into that transcends all the other normal cultural societal barriers. And that's why we love it.

It cuts through to the essence of things.

Yes. But the preparation is also very private.

Interesting. Why?

I think that most actors that I know and have a particular respect for don't talk about it a lot. That's why it's awkward when you're doing interviews. You don't want to be unfriendly or unhelpful. But a lot of it is so personal that it's almost like walking around in your underwear or something. And in the end it doesn't really matter. I mean to you, the director, or the audience, and nor should it. We use the most ridiculous kinds of things as stimulation. It doesn't matter how ridiculous it is if it works. Of course movies are so different from plays, when you're doing it over and over and over, so you're looking for a particular stimulus that will work in many different moods and on different days of the week for however long you play. Whereas in a film it's a day or two for a particular set of moments, and then for the role it's maybe two or three months. The level of immersion is what you're looking for. So preparing is really fun because you're not having to do it yet. *[SP laughs]* When you're preparing you're just in your imagination and no one's saying 'hmm'. That's why rehearsal's so great. You're just *free*! And it's not like it's yet there, frozen in time on film.

So that leads into the next question, about rehearsal.

I love to rehearse.

Why?

Because you're just feeling out the area you're going to be inhabiting and getting to know the other people. That's so much of it: sharing stories, sharing each other. The magical alchemy of that particular group, that little family of people. And it's not about going for the 'moments'. That's why some people don't like to rehearse, but you're not doing that at all! You're finding your common language, your vocabulary, and a lot of that is completely unspoken. Especially with issues of romance – God! It's fun to watch, too, in rehearsal, to absorb and listen. Watch how people discuss things and watch the director and how they like to draw people out and on what level they really engage the actors in trying to refine the work. Because you're always trying to refine, you're always trying to make something better, until the last take. You're always thinking: do I need this, do I need that? Can I lose this? Can I not lose that? Generally speaking in movies, one ends up saying 'Can I not say this?' versus 'Can I say more?'

Subtracting and distilling.

Yes. It's the beginning of the adrenalin and the beginning of the whole, trying to create something new. And it's the same feeling I had when I first started working, if not intensified. The love has just grown and deepened. Maybe it's because I'm older and I've had more life experience and can see that real life is so much more complicated. *[laughs]* To me, going to do a movie is like a vacation now. It's like, 'Oh God, it's so much fun! We're all pretending! Yay! This is easy.' It's not easy really, but you know what I'm saying. It's a joy.

What do you hope for from a director in rehearsal, as opposed to when you are shooting?

Questions, watching, encouragement. You also get a real sense of their taste, their sensibility, how they observe. In the theatre everybody is so verbose but really good movie directors often just listen. They really listen more than anything. They're fabulous audiences, they're terribly interested in what you're doing, they're approving of you. You want their approval, you want their good opinion and then of course you have to learn how not to be seeking that. Good directors know how not to interfere. I remember one of the actors

who worked with Ingmar Bergman many times was asked, 'So
what was it about Bergman that was so great?' and the actor said,
'He knew where to put the camera.' Bergman didn't really say a lot.
He didn't say, 'Go over to the window and then turn the lamp on'
and that kind of stuff. He would just sit back but he knew where
to put the camera to see what he wanted to see, and how to avoid
and eliminate what he didn't need. But that's not always true; I've
worked with people who were much more specific and niggling
and bossy about . . . 'No no no, you have to close the curtain and
then turn.' That kind of thing. And they're right. It is better. Sometimes it comes across as very lifelike. But in fact they've been on top
of people, dictating people's behaviour.

How aware are you of when the director's gaze is truly on you?

It makes a *huge* difference.

Can you describe it?

It's opposite to the fucking video monitor where everybody's gone
in the other room. There's something deeply symbiotic and connected between you and the director in the moment of making
something and their level of immersion is reflecting of yours and
yours is reflecting of theirs and you're both in the moment. I'm
thinking about a picture I made with Milos Forman when I first
started and he was always by the camera. I mean literally, his head
was always next to the camera. It never bothered me. I loved it. He
was right there in your sightline. Because he was investing in every
moment as much as everyone else in the scene was and he had
incredibly helpful things to say. He was with us. I practically had
never made another movie. Colin Firth was in that picture, but we
were unknown actors and Milos was incredibly involved and specific about all of his direction and he was so right in his ideas. And
he would act it out as well, which became a way to communicate

with him. I would say, 'OK, show me,' and then he would act it out. And we would tease him because he acted it out in such a way that had we done it, he would have screamed at us, because it was so over the top. *[SP laughs]* But it was an illustration.

Like a cartoon version of what he wanted.

Yes. And then you have to try to internalise it and make it real. In some ways that's better than a person saying, 'Now you know when he says that to you, you've never heard that before and so I need to see that expression on your face when you suddenly get the idea because . . .' Blah blah blah. You know.

Too much blah blah blah.

Too much is terrible. Mike Nichols really taught me a lot about that. It's like, 'Could you say it faster?' or, 'This can take more time, you can be slower there.' That kind of stuff is very effective.

Simple, direct.

Right. And of course if something's not working, you know it too. Maybe you're shooting something that's three quarters into the picture and it's the second day of filming and you're supposed to be upset about things that have happened earlier in the story. And maybe it isn't very convincing. So there you are and the two of you are trying to figure out how to make it convincing. And you're feeling frustrated because you're the actor and you want to make it happen, and they're feeling frustrated because they also want the same thing but there isn't a lot of time. Those moments can be very frustrating. I feel an enormous responsibility. And it's scary.

Do you think that you always know when something is working or not working? In other words, how much do you trust your subjectivity and how much do you rely on the director's opinion?

The director's subjectivity means a lot to me because I've placed myself in their hands. Generally if they say, 'Yeah that's good, we're on the right track,' then I believe it. I sometimes know that I can do something better – meaning more simply – or I feel I could do something in a different way and need to be able to try without describing it. And I also know that my own subjectivity is incredibly unreliable. I've seen enough of myself to know that and I can be very critical of myself.

In the moment of shooting?

I try not to do that too much because then you're just in a state.

Then are you referring to when you see the finished film?

Actually I am referring to when I'm doing it. I can be very critical but I've learned over the years just how deeply self-defeating that is. Trying to wrestle that demon is a lot of what acting is about. Because the demon is always there. The voice inside that says you're inadequate or boring or phoney or whatever.

The demon of doubt and self-criticism.

Which of course you also have to have. It's necessary. But then when I watch myself in the finished film I can sometimes enjoy it. Very much. I watch myself and I think, 'Ahhh that was really quite good. I was moved by it.' But I'm often very critical and I try to spare other people from that part of myself.

How can the director best help with the demon of doubt and self-criticism?

That's a good question. I'm kind of questioning whether or not there is a lot they can do . . . I think that the reason that certain directors get such great performances out of people is that they create an enormous amount of joy and trust. You feel known by them. You feel they're seeing you, seeing what you're doing. They understand the delicacy of what's really going on inside, how fragile and exposed you feel. You have to walk this line of being able to be on time, be relatively good-natured and do the work, and at the same time, lose control, which of course is the whole objective. You have to step completely out of reality into this imaginative set of circumstances. It's pretend but you have to absorb yourself into that fiction in every fibre of your being. So the director appreciating all that is helpful. But I think it's great when you don't feel like you have to depend on the director at all. And I certainly encourage actors to work that way. It makes directors much more happy when you come in and just start doing it. And then they can say, 'Oh I see, now how about a little more of that and a little less of this' . . . So they have something to work with . . . Putty, you're putty in their hands. You can't go in and expect them to tell you what to do, it's a disaster. Just go in and do something.

Offer something up. Do you think of a role as a character different from your self or as a set of experiences that you enter into?

Oh, I think both. When I went to acting school, I got this notion that this isn't me, this is someone else. Also because I was working on the stage, you don't have to look at yourself. You never have to face your own expressions. You don't have to face how you sound. Then when I started doing movies, suddenly you have to face yourself and how you look when thinking this or that or when you are upset. So you realise the camera sees something and you have to submit to that. The camera is going to do a lot of the work for you, and you don't have control over it. I used to think maybe that I did. But in fact the camera still said something else whether or not I chose to say it. So you think, 'Well fuck it,' the camera is going to do what it wants to do. Then it becomes more the circumstances and the character. Maybe there's a region the person comes from that sounds different to how you sound and you have to try and imitate that. Or if you want to be someone who's physically different from you and that leads you to something that serves the story, then that can be very helpful. But if it's phoney of course, then it's nothing. In the end it's whatever gets you there.

So it's a route. It's not the goal, it's the way.

Hopefully you're surprising yourself. And that's the thing that's the hardest to do because I think a healthy psyche says, 'Don't put yourself in a precarious situation where you might lose control or look foolish.' But of course as an actor you have to be prepared to look foolish. And then the psyche says, 'Why would you want to look foolish?' And there's a certain amount of health in that because if you didn't have that ability, you wouldn't be able to tell the difference between fiction and non-fiction. Right? You can sometimes see it when an actor is using a movie to display their own inability to distinguish between fiction and what is real. And the movie serves their need to display this, like . . .

. . . a therapeutic vehicle?

Yes. And certainly if they're cast correctly then that can serve the movie. But you feel it.

How about appearance? How much attention do you like to put on clothes, hair and make-up?

It really depends on the project. Sometimes you begin to associate the feeling of the character with all the stuff around you. Shoes are really important, especially in the theatre, because you're standing up and walking around most of the time. *[SP laughs]* And rehearsal in the right shoes is very important. Because it's all about walk and rhythm. But in movies half the time you're sitting or in a close-up so who cares.

It can be really helpful, when you put on the wig or the corset or the glasses. And then on the other hand, sometimes stripping everything away is also really liberating, not having any of that to depend on, again only if it serves the story. But all of those things can be a great path, a great helper. Having things in your hands. A certain handkerchief that you are holding. It's huge: costume and hair and all of that. And it's really a joy. But again it has to serve the story and if it does then it makes an enormous difference.

Is it significant to you how much attention a director puts on appearance, the outside of things?

Some of the directors that are popping into my head don't deal with that. They're very good but that's not where they're focused. It's between you and the designer. And that can work fine. On the other hand some directors are passionately involved with every detail. 'No that's not the right watch. Or that ring.' And of course when you're getting down to shooting, it's all details. You're like that and it can make an enormous difference.

So can that be reassuring when you know the director is taking care of appearance issues or can it feel like a distraction?

It can be very helpful because it feels like they're thinking about it so I don't have to.

Freeing.

That's helpful. Once I've gotten into the shoot. Before that, I need to be able to be a part of it and helping in making those decisions. This feels right, that doesn't feel right. And there's so much to be taken from designers. So much inspiration to be found in their thoughts and their instincts. 'This is the sweater that was at the bottom of the closet that you never usually wear, but you are wearing today.' Those kinds of things that if you said to anyone else would sound mad. But to an imaginative mind, when you're trying to cook something up, it can be very helpful. But once I'm shooting, it's all about the moment, the look on the other person's face.

What do you most need from a director at the actual moment of shooting?

I don't expect a lot from them at that moment, I want to know that they're going to capture it. I want to know that if something happens, they're ready for it. That they have all of the machines going so that the thing that's working doesn't get lost. And what is crucial is their level of immersion. Their level of care. Because it has to be insane. *[SP laughs]* Right? It has to be the most important thing, whatever it is that you're doing. And that's why of course it makes no sense and why we are all a little bit crazy. Because it isn't actually happening, everything is made up. But you have to care about it so much. I don't think I've ever seen a director who was blasé. But if I sense that that's the kind of project it might be I don't do it. I feel as though the director is as vulnerable as I am. They are orchestrating everything and yet they cannot make something happen on someone's face and ultimately in movies that's what it's about. You can shoot something of great beauty but if you think about great moments in movies, it's usually somebody's face. And that person might not even be talking. If a director can help you feel that what you are doing is enough and you don't have to worry . . . that helps a lot.

Is there anything on the set that helps and anything specifically that hinders you feeling you're getting to your best performance?

People talking too much.

In general? Or the director?

The director. By the time we shoot I've thought about it all so much. Generally I like to try to do something first, because I don't know quite what it is yet. And if somebody is talking to me too much before I'm doing that unknown thing then I can't . . . In other words I want to try and get out of my own intellect as much as possible. And work from a place of not knowing. Of course you can't totally do that but you're looking for that surprising thing and someone's talking to you then you're engaging your intellect immediately. And for me sensory, physical things can be enormously helpful. Like you feel as if you're about to throw up. Something really visceral, something not intellectual at all. Not, 'Oh you know your mother died twenty-five years ago, remember how that . . .' What I'm actually going through I can't describe, because if I described it, it kind of takes it away. I don't know if that makes any sense.

Total sense. So too much talking is a distraction and too much analytical or intellectual engagement takes you away from your instincts. The director needs to create a space where your instincts can run. Are there other things that you know from experience can hinder you getting where you need to go?

What I've observed with other movie actors that I respect is that you have to be able to do your work under any circumstances. And that's where you can separate the people who are really great, because there's always something going on. It's either the wrong time, you were supposed to do it at nine o'clock and you're doing it at noon or you did it already, which is just the worst. *[laughs]* I don't even want to say it –

– say it –

– because then it might happen. A scene haunts you in a way. You're doing the movie because of that scene. You know where it can go. You are terrified but you do it. Oh thank God it's over, you've done it and then it's on the call sheet three weeks later. It's like a nightmare. You're like, 'Is this real, is this actually happening? What? It was too dark?' It's one of those things that happen. So you learn how to just simmer all the time and that's where you have to remain . . .

How important do you think it is for the shoot to be a happy experience? Is there a correlation between that and the end result?

I don't know. Isn't that fascinating? I've had very happy experiences that turned out excellent, I've had unhappy experiences that turned out excellent. I've had kind of unhappy tense experiences that have turned out horribly. I don't know how that works. I know that I do not like to work in an unhappy, tense, acrimonious atmosphere. And I think it's probably safe to say there are times that I put that first and I maybe shouldn't have.

Having a good time?

Yeah, and I should have had an argument with someone but because of my personality I haven't and I'm not proud of that. But I've probably done that in the past where I'm seeing something that isn't right and I think, 'Shit, that isn't right – do I say something?' Or – and this is very rare – I've been pushed in a direction that I don't feel right about –

– and you'll keep the peace.

And I keep the peace. But less so now. *[both laugh]* After turning fifty you get so much more liberated. You say to yourself, 'Well you know what, I don't care if you don't like this. I'm going to say it anyway.' It's a horrible moment when you have to say, 'I'm sorry but I don't think this is right, it feels awkward to me.' I also know more now when there's a problem in the writing. Whereas before I would be hesitant, now I can say, 'I think we need to work on this, the reason we're having trouble with it is the writing.'

Is that something that you would have preferred to deal with in rehearsal?

Yeah.

Nevertheless sometimes it comes out later.

Yeah, it's fascinating when you get up and you start doing it you find that a scene that you thought was a certain kind of scene is totally different and it needs to be. I also know that I'm not always right too. Sometimes I don't want to say something because I'm not quite sure but I'll see it afterwards and think, 'Oh yeah that was a problem and it's still a problem,' and then other times I'll think, 'Well I thought that was a problem and it wasn't.' So it's very hard to generalise about it. I like to get along and have a good time, even if it's very difficult, dark subject-matter. Generally speaking, I don't think acrimony helps. But what I've noticed too is that sometimes the so-called difficult person on the set, the diva or the divo, the drama-maker who seems to be bringing their own personal issues into a work situation – they're often not the actors. And often not even the director. It might be a designer or cinematographer or someone else bringing in unhappiness or neuroses or just garbage.

In those circumstances how do you wish that the director will deal with it?

Sometimes they're helpless just like the rest of us. *[laughter]* Depending on what the person's job is and whether or not that person must be there. And then other things happen. People start having affairs and it's like, 'Oh my God.' That can be disastrous. Sometimes there's nothing the poor director can do.

You were talking earlier about the script and silences and speaking or not speaking. What do you think is more important in a script? What somebody says or what they don't say?

Do I have to make a choice?

No. [laughs]

Thank God. *[laughs]* I'm thinking of some of the great Hepburn roles, when everyone was talking so fast in movies. All of that was so delightful and about articulation, words and diction. When I first worked on movies, I would approach a screenplay like I would approach a play. I would go back to the screenplay in order to re-investigate and re-invigorate. When you're working on a play you can read it and read it and you find, 'Oh there's that and there's this . . .' But a screenplay is different. What I began to learn is that the only moment that matters is when the camera's rolling, and that the script is just this funny blueprint. The shape of the story is important, but once you're into the shooting then a lot of it is just what happens when, as you say, you're not saying anything. So it's a funny balance between the two, but in the end it's more of a visual medium. I saw a movie last night for instance, and if I sit here and think about the moments I remember in the movie? Nobody's talking.

So the script is the architecture of the unsaid. How aware are you of the camera and the lens while you're shooting?

I've grown to love and appreciate the experience of working in front of a camera and you're calling this 'Naked . . .' ?

Naked Cinema.

Well with the camera you are aware of the nakedness of your experience. The fact that you are naked. Then you either keep doing it or you stop and walk away and say, 'OK, no one has a gun to my head here. I don't have to be an actor. No one's forcing me to be in front of the camera. I'm choosing it.' So then you start to say, 'I'm inviting you in and I want to try to do something that's truthful and involving and could mean something to somebody else someday.' So I've begun to understand how it's good for me to know – to a degree – where the camera is and what the lens is and how close it is. If you're seeing more, that's good for me to know and if you're seeing less then that's also really good for me to know.

Do you have a visceral feeling about it, a sort of link with it, an energetic thread with it? Can you describe what that feels like?

I don't know if I can describe it. It's also a link with the camera operator too and that's a curious thing, a really fun and interesting part of making movies. I'm thinking about a particular camera operator and his intuitive sense, his ability to capture what was happening. And like Robbie (Ryan), who did a lot of running around with the camera and you were telling him what to look at but also trusting him to sometimes grab something. Then it's an enjoyable sort of dance, a really wonderful symbiotic conflagration of people working together. That's why we do it and why we don't just sit in rooms alone. It's fun to try and make something together and know that you couldn't have done it without the others. It's funny . . . when I do movies, invariably I come into the room and there's all these people and I think, 'Oh I thought it was just the two of us sitting in a room talking.' *[SP laughs]* And then I realise – oh yes, it's a movie.

But back to the eyes of the camera for a moment and the eyes of the director. In rehearsal you have just the eyes of the director and then in a shooting situation, you've also got the lens and the camera operator behind the lens. You talked about how you don't like it when the director's somewhere over there . . .

No it's much more fun when they're close.

So the eyes of the director are still important to you even when the eye of the camera is crucial.

Yes, in catching all the specifics of the moment and knowing the difference between one take and another. Again you go back to subjectivity. Sometimes I thought back and I was sure that one take was better and that I would *die* if they didn't use it, and then found out it was the other one that was fine.

A director has that experience too by the way. Absolutely convinced that that was the best take and then in the cutting room . . .
What does presence mean to you?

My experience is so much more satisfying if I feel that my own level of presence is as total as possible. With the camera seeing it.

So how do you fill out that sense of presence?

I don't know. I guess if I feel I have a real intuitive connection with the people around me, then that's the focus or the inspiration. But sometimes it's quite a lonely feeling on set because everyone else is working. Then everybody else, except for the camera operators and the people who are recording the sound, stop working when you work and it can be kind of embarrassing. There are times that you feel so exposed, especially if you feel that you're not finding something. Everyone's looking at you and you feel, 'Why the hell am I doing this? Why aren't I on the other side like all of those people? Why am I choosing to be the one that everyone is focused on?'

What do you wish more directors really understood about the actor's process?

I've been really spoiled because I've worked with so many good people. I think that most directors just love actors, they just love them and you really have to be loved to do good work. You just have to be. If there's a kind of hostility . . . *[laughs]* I'm thinking of a director, of a play I was in. There's a moment in the play where I'm supposed to burst into tears. It's not like a slow welling up. So there was this moment in the play where I was supposed to do that and we were in previews and we got to the moment and just couldn't do it. And I didn't do a fake version of it, which probably would have been a better idea. *[SP laughs]* And I remember afterwards the director was giving notes and she said, 'Oh Annette, what happened? You just didn't do it.' And I had nothing to say for myself. So for as long as I was in the play I would open my eyes in the morning and think I have to do that at about nine p.m., and if it was a two-show day then it would be around three and nine. *[SP laughs]* You have to learn to live with that or you go nuts. But sometimes you don't know what you're going to do and you don't want to know what you're going to do. I've been so lucky to have mostly worked with people who are sensitive to how vulnerable you feel.

So the film's done. You sit and you watch it. How do you feel about watching yourself on the screen?

I'm generally very critical. So if I can, I try to watch it by myself because then I don't bother anybody else with my self-criticism. And I know that sometimes it takes me seeing it a couple of times before I can begin to see past things that bother me. I'm not always that way. I've also watched things and understood that they were good. But I've learned that I am critical of myself and that sometimes, it can be really painful.

What are you critical of?

I think I could do it better. There are times that in fact that's the case, and I know that's the case. In the moment of shooting maybe I didn't know it, but generally it's something prosaic that just presents itself, such as being simpler. The more time goes by the less I remember what was actually happening when we were shooting, so then I can immerse myself in the movie much more. I don't know how it is when you guys do it, directors, I really don't, but as an actor you're thinking, 'Oh yeah that was the day my kid was sick, and she threw up on me and then I went to work and I was really tired,' or, 'That was the day something romantic happened.' You know all kinds of associations that have nothing to do with the movie. Your brain is giving you those as you watch it. But as time goes by there are fewer of those. But it's hard to feel satisfied.

A good thing probably. For the learning curve. And what about the 'after' experience – the final product and its trajectory into the world? How is that for you as an actor?

I have a lot of ambivalence about it. In a way I'm very happy to be done shooting but the media machine is now so gigantic. Even since I've been doing pictures it has grown so astronomically. But it makes the process of rehearsing and making the movie even more precious because you know that that's really the crux of it. And then if it has a life and people enjoy it, that's wonderful. I love when people see things and find them interesting or moving, if it resonates in some way. I've had so many interesting encounters with people, throughout the years, who have talked to me about something in a movie that affected them because of the closeness to their own experiences. That's what we want, right? When we go to see something, any form of art, we want it to speak so directly that it's like, 'Ahhh thank you! God, I've never been able to get at that, whatever that thing was, and now you said it! I see it! Oh God, it's not just me. We're in this together, we're connected.' Fiction can be truer than anything else. And that experience is incredibly gratifying. I've been pulled aside by people so many times and they're telling me their life experience, something very precious, and they're telling me all about it because of something they've seen me do on a screen which was just happening on a set somewhere. So that is really a thrill. And of course movies really live on. I'm as much an audience member as I am a participant, so I feel as passionate about going and seeing things as I do about being a performer.

What about fame and celebrity? How does it affect your working relationships and your life?

I've had a certain amount of fame. What would I be like if I was fifty-four not having had that? Of course, you have no idea. But I was lucky because I didn't do movies until I was almost thirty so I was a grown-up for a while before I was recognised in any way. It's a mixed bag.

What's the mix?

Well, the best thing about it is that when you take your children to Disneyland, you get a private person who takes you around and you get to cut in front of the line. That's what I've figured out. *[SP laughs]* Of all the good things, that's the best thing by far. Other than that, you want to work with people who do wonderful things, people that you admire, and they're calling you up. That's really fantastic. But in a way as an actor it works against you, because you want to be able to disappear and be able to be believed in a totally different circumstance, which is difficult if someone associates you with a certain kind of story or character. But I feel pretty lucky, I've been able to kind of dash around and do different things and I don't feel too pigeonholed at all. And if you want to avoid being photographed and chased around, you can, most of the time. There are certain circumstances that you can't control. I have four children and when it affects them in an adverse way it's just enraging. I could kill. But it doesn't get to that point very often.

We're now in a culture which uses fame and celebrity to sell things. It's very much accepted, whereas when I started it was frowned on, you know, selling a handbag or selling a perfume, all that kind of stuff. There used to be a notion that as an actor you were there to serve material. You were there to disappear. You were appearing but your 'self' was secondary to whatever you were trying to present. But that is really not the case now. That is considered old-fashioned. It's perfectly fine now for everyone to be selling everything. Does it compromise our ability to suspend disbelief? I don't know. That's the question. But that's what you want, right? You're trying to convince people you're not the famous person they might have some idea about, that you're someone else in a story in London in 1960, or somebody from a different socio-economic status or whatever. I really have an idealistic notion about acting.

Which is?

Stella Adler was never my teacher but I have read her books and she says that actors really should be monks in a way, we should be so dedicated to what we're doing that we are willing to make sacrifices. Now of course if you only did that then you probably wouldn't have a very good life. And I couldn't live like that. I have responsibilities and I'm very grateful for them because in a way they have grounded me and helped me to tolerate being a creative person. As an actor you have to be able to tolerate a lot of discomfort, a lot of uncertainty. Not just professionally but when you're actually working. You have to face a lot of doubt, like any creative person, you have to face your demons, your insecurities, your vanity. You have to face the ugly parts of life that you're trying to dramatise. You have to be able to face all of that and be able to tolerate it, not get rid of it. Tolerate it.

Bear witness.

That's a better way of putting it. I guess as I get older fame and celebrity becomes less of a problem. Because people aren't chasing you around as much. But any actor has to face themselves and you can't continue in the profession if you can't face yourself. And sometimes you don't want to but there's no way of getting around that. And being photographed and going on shows and talking and all that stuff, I've learned to do to a degree. And I think: Should I? Shouldn't I? How much should I do? How much do I want to do? Oh dear. So it's a lot of choices and you have to find your own personal balance and what you can tolerate. And again no one is making you do it. If you want to walk away from the profession you can.

Nevertheless it's a vocation?

What do you mean?

It's not something you can take or leave, like a career. It's something that you're giving yourself up to completely.

Yes. Absolutely. It chooses you. No question. You do it because you have to. One of the professors in my college, when people would ask him, 'Should I pursue this or shouldn't I?' would say, 'Only if you have to.' And if you have to then you have to, no one can talk you out of it, no one can make you do it and no one can make you stop doing it. And when you are in that arena then you just thank God! Because you're working in a world of passion, doing something that you really want to do. Sometimes it's satisfying and sometimes it's not and sometimes it's glorious and sometimes it's not but at least you know that you're trying to figure something out. I feel really grateful for that and I wish that for everybody. To find the thing that you must do. Then you can tolerate life, you can tolerate the parts that are painful and difficult and the parts that happen to all of us irrespective of our vocations.

STEVE BUSCEMI

When Steve Buscemi walked through the door of the tiny apartment I was renting from time to time on the Lower East Side in New York City, during the development of *Rage*, he looked pale and haggard. He had recently returned from India where he had picked up a stomach bug, but I also wondered if he was unconsciously morphing into Frank, the thin, traumatised war photographer he was to play. He read his monologues aloud to me, entrancing me with his delivery, the reticent understatement I associate with the best American screen actors. I was also impressed by his honesty when some detail didn't quite seem to work and the careful, modest way he expressed this to me. Filming him in the small studio we hired in Harlem was an education in quiet professionalism, good humour, and immaculate timing. The camera loved his lived-in face, familiar from his roles in so many films by the Coen brothers and Jim Jarmusch, amongst others.

He found a moment in his busy shooting schedule for the new series of *Boardwalk Empire* to speak on the phone for this interview. Hearing the unique timbre of his voice as he quietly answered my questions from his home in Brooklyn made it feel as if he wasn't so far away from me in London. Even without seeing his face, I could feel his presence and sense the warmth and lightness overlaying the intensity of his focus.

When you're sent a script, what are you hoping to find? What's going to attract you to do it?

I guess that's changed over the years but I think that now what I'm really hoping is that the whole script is really, really good. That the story works and that all the characters work.

So it's not just about your own role and character.

No. I think in the beginning you would be literally counting your lines: 'Oh I have this nice bit, oh and I have this.' Now when I'm asked to do something that's not a lead, maybe it's even just a cameo, what's important is that the character that I play affects the story or the other main characters in some way. Or sometimes it's just a matter of who's making the movie. I feel: 'Oh I would really like to work with these people.' But the script has to be there. I have to be able to relate to it. That's where it all starts.

Is there an order of importance between the script and the director? Which is more important to you in deciding to accept?

Boy, that's a good question. I guess I would really have to intensely dislike a script or feel that I'm not right for the part, if it comes with a wonderful director that I've been wanting to work with. There are some directors that I feel like, whatever it is, it's going to be worth it. Even if I have doubts about the script or I have doubt about my playing the character.

So if you like the director's work, it becomes an act of trust.

Absolutely, yeah.

In that first meeting with the director, if you haven't already worked with them before, what clues are you looking for?

Well, I guess part of it is just to see if we get along, we can relate in any way, or if there's an easiness.

An easiness?

Something that feels like we will be able to work together, or that this will be fun or interesting. I'm just looking to see if we'll get along and if I'll be inspired or moved. And if the director is curious about what I have to bring to it. I guess I'm looking for a sense of play. A lot of effort goes into this work and it really helps if it's fun and you feel like you're all in this together. I really do like working with directors. There's a lot that I bring to the table but I also feel I'm a better actor when I have a director that can focus me or challenge me or take risks with me.

Do you like to rehearse for a film?

I do. Sometimes you end up rehearsing on camera, there's just not time to rehearse beforehand. But there are a few occasions where we do rehearse. I'm thinking of two films in particular – one was Jim Jarmusch's *Mystery Train* (1989). We shot the whole film in

Memphis and Jim had us rehearse in New York. Not only reading the script. He would think up other situations that our characters could be in and he had us improvise. I think it was very helpful for him because some of those improvisations – maybe just one little thing, one little discovery – he would then add to the scene or the character. But I think for us as actors it was also really helpful to get to know each other and to feel what being in this character was like, being able to make up your own story line. Another time we rehearsed was on *Reservoir Dogs* (1992). Quentin [Tarantino] had a two-week rehearsal period before we started filming. He insisted on that, it was in the budget. Again, that was really helpful because by the time we got to the set, there wasn't a whole lot of talking about the scene. Actors do tend to want to talk. *[laughs]*

Yes. Of course.

And I think, especially on a low-budget film where the director doesn't have a lot of time and there's a lot of stuff to be covered in one day, then a rehearsal period is good to let these questions come up. Not only to rehearse the lines but also to talk about the characters as much as each individual actor wants to. Some actors don't like to. They don't like to rehearse. Right now I'm doing *Boardwalk Empire* and there's not a lot of time. Basically the rehearsal is about blocking the scene and then we just have to start shooting. There are some moments to ask quick questions and that's necessary. It may feel like you're taking a lot of time but if you don't ask those questions, everything just takes even longer because you begin the scene and you realise, 'Something's wrong. Something doesn't feel right.' Those first few takes that we do on camera are sort of a rehearsal as well. I feel like I start to warm up after I do it a few times and feel the rhythm. I'm one of those actors who really likes to know their lines before I get there. I find that gives me more freedom to experiment with what I'm doing rather than just *[laughs]* trying to remember the next line.

What about other aspects of preparation, for example working on the look? How important is that to you and how much do you like the director to be involved in finding that look with you?

I think the look is really important but it's not the first thing that I'm consciously aware of. When I read a script and study this character that I'm maybe going to play, I'm sure an image forms in my head but it's not specific about how that character looks.

So it's not a visual image?

That's just not the way that my mind works. But I've always found that when I work with a costume designer and the director on the look it informs the character so much. An example is on *Fargo* (1996). I didn't really imagine that my character would wear corduroy pants and turtleneck sweaters when I first read it. I've played some other similar characters when you wear a cheap leather jacket or a polyester shirt. When the costume designer Mary Zophres came up with the idea and I put the clothes on I felt, 'Oh, that's who this guy is.' It helped me so much. I would just look in the mirror in my dressing-room, you know, along with my hair and I had a moustache – just this whole look – and I was like, 'OK, I think I know who this is now.'

When you mention polyester and a cheap leather jacket, what I immediately get is the tactile feeling of what those clothes were like as much as how they look.

That's interesting. I find that with what I'm doing now on *Boardwalk*. I can barely dress myself, I mean I literally have a dresser come in and button my collar. The suspenders are tight and the material is heavy and you really get this feeling . . . but sometimes on set, I catch a glimpse of myself in a reflection and I think, 'Oh there he is.'

[SP laughs]

I don't have to do much. There he is. Looking like the part just does so much. In those clothes I have to stand a certain way or else it's uncomfortable. You really have to fill these clothes, it almost forces you to act in a certain way.

It's interesting that even when you're talking about appearance, you're somehow talking about it from the inside out. The experience of how it feels. I'm wondering if there are other ways of working from the inside out for you in the preparatory process?

I guess it is a combination of interior and exterior preparation. I do feel the physicality of the character is important but for me it does start on the inside. It always starts with me. Whatever character I'm playing is me. It's a version of me. Who would I be or what would I sound like if I were this person? Some characters are easier than others to put myself into. Other times it just requires a little more work. Sometimes I don't know where I fit into this character so it becomes more external. I remember once playing a doctor. I guess I'm more used to playing either working-class guys or a criminal element. *[laughs]* I've also played artistic guys but for some reason playing a professional, a doctor – one time I played a lawyer – there was a block in my head. I found it hard to imagine myself doing this. I've had a similar challenge on *Boardwalk Empire*, playing a guy who runs things, you know, a boss. A man who is really well respected and who is in charge. I remember when I read the script, I just loved the character and I was hoping I could play him, but I never believed that I was going to be cast. This character is so well written, all the characters are, it's been a real challenge to me, but it's been so much fun. That's where the fun in acting is – to be able to do something that you wouldn't be doing in your own life. I feel like I have been able to use that same process of putting myself into this character, but it requires a lot more thought than, 'How would

I speak if I was this guy?' I'm really depending on my director to give me different ways of thinking about it.

When you come to shoot, what kind of feedback works best from a director? And what doesn't work?

I like directors who listen. What doesn't work for me is when a scene is already blocked.

You mean when it's blocked before you arrive on set?

Yeah.

Oh God.

You know, the director and the DP have figured out a way to shoot it, either because it's visually interesting or maybe they don't have a lot of time *[laughs]* and so they've already figured out a way to get it done. Sometimes it really is a visual thing, when a director has their own way of telling the story. I like working with directors that have a strong visual sense. But I also like to participate in that process – *[laughs]*

Yes! [laughs]

– and sometimes it certainly gels, you know. 'Steve, if you wouldn't mind starting here and walking to there.' 'Yeah OK, that feels right.' And usually I try and keep an open mind as an actor. I think that's also from having directed myself. I know what a director goes through and what their thought-process is. I think actors can sometimes close down too much and convince themselves that, 'My character would never do that,' or, 'Why would I go from here to there? Why would I do this? This makes no sense.' And sometimes that's absolutely right and I think it's good to voice it but at the same time to try and see how the director sees it. Maybe there's a different truth looking through the camera. Maybe it does make sense. But if it's an intimate scene, for example, and for some reason the other actor and I are positioned too far apart then I'll say something, just so that it's noted. I'll say, 'Maybe it doesn't look this way through the camera but right now it feels like we're too far apart.' And usually it's addressed. There always seems to be a compromise that can be made. So I like directors that have a strong visual sense, have strong ideas but at the same time aren't locked into a certain way of doing things.

What about the physical eyes of the director? How do you feel when the director looks at the monitor during a take rather than directly at you?

I guess I've gotten so used to directors looking at the monitors that I don't really think about it. On the occasion when directors are in the room, I like it. As long as I don't see them.

They need to be out of your eye-line? Not next to the camera, for example?

I have a really hard time with people in my eye-line. They've gotten used to me now on set, so they'll clear a crew member or someone that is visiting so that I only see the actors that I'm supposed to and the crew members that are essential. I easily get distracted. But when a director is in the room, I have to say it does kind of change the energy.

In what way?

I feel like the director is the audience. I don't know if this is a good thing or a bad thing. There's always that question, when you're in a scene, about how conscious should you be that this is something that people will be watching. I think I'm very conscious of it on one level, but on another level you have to forget that. You somehow have to strike that balance. You can't be totally lost in what you're doing. With stage acting you have to be aware that there's an audience there: they have to hear you and they have to see you. But I think that it's the same with film too. You could be playing a scene one way and feel that you're giving enough but the director says, 'Your energy was a little bit low there.' And it's like, 'Oh, OK.' And just that little minor adjustment changes everything.

What are the key differences for you between your work as an actor on stage and for the camera, for the imaginary future audience?

On stage you're really feeling the audience's energy each night. That can be really helpful and it can also be distracting or misleading. There can be nights when you think you can feel the audience like, 'Oh, they're not into this. That line should have gotten a laugh.' And it maybe throws you off or you start to push a little bit. You may even think, 'Well, I'm not going to give my all for this audience.' *[laughs]* But I found out from watching plays and then meeting the actors afterwards that one of them might say, 'Oh my God, what a terrible show.' 'Oh really? Cause I thought it was great.' – *[SP laughs]* – 'I wasn't feeling what you were feeling.' And the same thing applies where I've done a show and people have come and said, 'This is so interesting.' And I'm like, 'Really, because I thought we had a terrible show tonight. You should have been here last night, the audience was great.' So sometimes you can feel it's off but that doesn't mean that it feels off to an audience.

Do you think that subjective/objective split applies equally to when you're shooting?

I think it's harder to gauge when you're doing a film or TV without an audience. In some ways the crew becomes your audience when you rehearse and sometimes I will use that. But I think the actor needs to forget about the audience and let the director be responsible.

Be the mirror. Is there a significant difference for you between working on television and film?

I'm really lucky with the show that I'm on now because we shoot it like a film. We spend a lot of time on the scenes and a lot of production value goes into it. I think I'm kind of spoiled. I have worked on TV in the past and other shows where you don't get a lot of time. You're just thrown in there, you do it the best you can, in a short amount of time, but you never quite feel satisfied. But I've had that experience on some films too. On a really low-budget film you don't have a lot of time. So I've learnt to work quickly and get used to the fact that I'm not going to get a lot of takes and that's OK.

So this constant lack of time doesn't have to be a tyranny?

I don't think so. I think we're mostly put under pressure by ourselves. There's usually more time than –

– than you think.

Sometimes it really helps to take that attitude in the beginning so that you don't run into problems later.

Do you think that a necessary part of a director's work is a mastery of time, so it feels as if there's enough time even when actually time is pretty short?

Yeah. You can tell sometimes if the director is not really present. I've had this experience as the director; I'm thinking of the next scene *[laughs]* but I'm still directing this scene. It shouldn't be so complicated but the next one is – and that's what I'm thinking about. Meanwhile the actors need help in this scene. I think it's always good when everybody is right there and present.

And as an actor do you think you can always feel it when a director is pretending to be present?

I don't know. I tend to pick up on things when I'm being told why we're doing something and I start to suspect, 'I think you're just saying that.' *[laughs]* 'Just pulling me along.' And I think actors can generally feel that.

You have incredible presence on screen, more than just embodying a character. But in the moment of shooting does the concept of presence mean anything to you?

It's something that I don't really think about. There's a certain mystery to acting that I like. There's a mystery to this whole thing of what happens on a set. It's magical when it works and I don't think there's a formula for it. But I think there are certain things that an actor and a director and a DoP and a crew can bring to it that creates an atmosphere where people can do their best work. But even with all of that there's something that's intangible. And I guess it's in the chemistry of everybody working together, that either makes it gel or it doesn't. And the mystery continues. It can feel like, 'Hey, we are really gelling,' and then you see the final product and you think, 'What happened? I thought that felt really good.' *[laughs]* I think the opposite can be true too, where there is tension. We certainly all know it, instances where there has been a lot of tension on set between an actor and a director or between two actors, then you see the end result and there's a magic there. *[laughs]* Then you say, 'All of that stuff that was happening is different now that I'm seeing it on screen.'

Which is something very similar to what I was about to ask you: whether happiness in the working experience is a bonus or a necessity.

I think it's a bonus. It's wonderful to get along with everybody but I've certainly had instances where it does get difficult for one reason or another. It may require a lot of extra work or a lot of attention to one actor. But if you're getting the desired result I guess the question is, 'Was it worth it?' *[laughs]* There's just a lot of different ways to work and it doesn't all have to be harmonious. Some directors like to create a bit of tension or keep actors in the dark. It all comes down to what the final outcome will be.

Because you're also a director yourself you know a great deal about the magic that can happen in the cutting room afterwards and in post-production –

Yeah, absolutely.

– to either help or indeed ruin somebody's performance. What insights have you gained in that area?

Well, as actors, we really have no control of how our performance is going to be shaped. *[both laugh]* And that's definitely what it is. It's being shaped. There are some actors where the performance is just there. Any way you cut it, it just works. Other performances are hard to find. You have to take things away to get to the gold, but it's there. Each way of working is valid. Some actors have to go through different processes to find that gold. And they should be allowed to do that. If that's their process then that's their process. A director should adjust. You don't want it to be at the expense of the other actors so there does have to be a balance. But some actors do require more attention or more experimentation to get there.

When the film comes out there's suddenly this interface with critics, with the press, with photoshoots and all the other razzmatazz. How do you find that impacts on the work or even really relates to it at all?

It is all a bit distracting. I understand why it's necessary. There's certainly a lot riding on it for people who have invested money. When reviews are positive you really feel like, 'Hey' *[laughs]* but at the same time you just can't put too much thought into it. I've learned over the years it's really the doing, the making of a film or a play . . . that's where the real satisfaction and joy comes. I used to put more importance on, 'Oh, I can't wait till this comes out. I can't wait to see what they . . .' and now I've learnt not to have too many expectations. We all want our work to be recognised and seen and responded to in a favourable way but to me that's not the most important thing.

Is there a devotional aspect to the work?

What do you mean?

The private passion some actors and directors feel about their work and can rarely talk about. It has nothing to do with success, celebrity or fame.

Well, I feel like it's a privilege. I have to remind myself of that when we're on set and we're going into the fourteenth or the fifteenth hour. *[laughs]* But it's harder when you're exhausted and everyone just wants to go home. But sometimes when I'm on set, in a scene, I remind myself, 'This is me, I'm doing exactly what I've dreamed of doing.' You know how rare is it to be able to make a living, doing something that you truly enjoy? So I remind myself, 'Boy I'm just lucky to be here doing this. Who cares that it's going to be a long day?' I try and be there and take in that moment and be grateful that this is what I'm doing. And so I guess, in that way, I'm devoted to being the best that I can. It does require devotion and commitment. Giving it your all.

JULIE CHRISTIE

I first saw Julie Christie when she was filming a night scene for *Billy Liar* (1963) on Hampstead Heath. I must have been about twelve or thirteen at the time and was entranced by what I saw. It wasn't just the towering white film lights casting their magic glow on the trees, and the busy crew scuttling about on mysterious errands, it was the glimpse of Julie sitting in a car waiting to go on set. Even through the window of the car where she sat huddled in the shadows with Tom Courtenay, I caught the radiance of her smile. Her face was as readable from a distance as it was on the big screen and as achingly familiar. There was an energy and beauty about her that represented every quality I aspired to as a shy, blushing adolescent.

Many years later I was preparing to make my first feature, a complex, collaborative and ambitious film without any discernible realistic narrative but lots of ideas and images that referenced the early history of silent cinema and its heroines. Julie's was the face we wanted – the only face – and in due course we approached her. She was open to, but puzzled by, the project. Perhaps what eventually attracted her to the idea was that we would be filming it in winter in Iceland and she would be paid the same as the lowliest member of the all-female crew. How could she resist something so obviously idealistic and impractical?

She was an absolute trooper under very difficult conditions. We nearly drowned in a raging torrent when our Jeep got stuck in a freezing river in Iceland, she was carried on a creaking wooden plinth through the City of London in the middle of the night, she was whisked off on horseback out of a crowded ballroom by her co-star, Colette Laffont, whose only previous cinematic experience had been in my earlier short film, *Thriller*.

Julie's political commitment, idealism, and lack of interest in the trappings of stardom make her a unique figure in the history of film-stars. We met in my studio in East London to talk, in a building we share – for we became close friends following our arduous mutual endeavour – and she exhibited her usual mix of modesty, rigour and puzzlement about the industry we both work in, an industry in which she has experienced the clamour of fame but rejected the very notion of celebrity.

What do you look for when you are sent a script?

I look for a good director, because then I've seen what I need to know. I don't always end up with a good director, by any means, and sometimes I do things with people I have great doubts about. But ideally, that's what I look for.

So the director is more important to you than the script?

Yes.

What quality do you look for – or hope for – in a director?

That they make good films that I would go and see.

So it's not a personal quality that you're looking for in a director but rather evidence of what they've done before?

Evidence . . . because I don't think you can tell from a meeting. You can meet people for hours and hours and think that they're very nice or they're clever but it doesn't really mean anything. Something magic happens when a person makes a film – that includes the relationship between the director and the actor – but many processes go into making a film: the script is one and the actor is one, but there are always others that are hidden, that make the whole thing come together. That's why I have to see the work.

What do you wish directors understood about actors?

You need to be terribly kind to them, *[laughs]* that's the main thing. But directors usually learn that one. I think that's number one on the director's list of how to direct. Constantly reassure your actor, even if it's a piece of shit. Then try to make them do it another way. It's so secret to me, how a director guides you into a good performance. It comes from what a director has in their head and I can't see what's in their head. I can't see what they can see when I'm working, either. Most directors watch a video monitor when shooting now, which I think is quite dangerous, because a monitor makes one zero in on things rather than really looking and seeing. I would have thought that when you watch a person acting and you see the scene progressing you could play with the feeling that you're getting and with what you're observing. You have more room to play with the scene than you do if you just watch it on that little screen.

So for you, it's important that a director is watching you with their naked eye watching you directly as you perform.

Not just watching me but watching the whole scene with their naked eye. I think it's got something to do with the playback monitor constricting the imagination.

Do you feel the eyes, the gaze of the director upon you . . . as something specific?

No . . . when I'm acting, I don't feel anything except what I'm doing in the moment.

Anything else you wish directors understood about actors?

I think most directors do understand actors because that's who they work with, but it isn't even to do with you being an actor, it's to do with you as an individual and whether or not they understand your mind. And it's not how they direct the acting but about being a good teacher. The wonderful gift a good teacher has is the ability to find out how the person that he or she is dealing with – in this case the actor – operates. You don't know how good teachers manage to teach you things that you have never learnt before. They somehow manage to fill that hole in your imagination and twist it to the angle they need. But of course not all directing is teaching. And teaching is also to do with letting go – letting the student or the actor fly. Not always telling them what to do. Although actually I find that most directors don't tell you very much. In fact they don't tell me enough – but then they're in a great hurry. They're always in a hurry.

What about rehearsals? Are they important?

I don't like rehearsing for film at all. I don't find it's a help. And I don't know why that's different from the theatre. Maybe it's because you're not actually rehearsing when you prepare for a film. When you rehearse for the theatre you go through lots of processes. You have maybe three weeks or more, if you're lucky. But it's solid work from morning till night. Solid discovery. A great complicated journey. And rehearsing for film can't be that. There isn't the time for it. That's what film is, it's spontaneous! It's a quick business. You do it at that moment for the camera, however much work you've done before on your own. I don't like to squander that thing you rely on – which is the immediate – in rehearsal.

Do you believe the camera can follow or read thought?

I think that the camera can create thought. And I think it can make all the difference in a performance and can make all the difference in the film as a whole.

What do you mean by the camera creating thought?

By being put in the right place, I mean if you're in a wide shot or a medium shot or a close-up, you're going to create a completely different meaning to the scene. You can have something that needed to be in close-up but is in a medium shot, which is therefore lost, or you can have something which is ugly and boring in a close-up and loses the magic it needed that it would have had in a wide shot.

And when you're filming are you aware of the different lenses?

No. *[laughs]*

Are you aware of the camera when you're working? What does it feel like to be looked at by the camera?

I'm unaware of it to the point where I'm actually quite skill-less *[laughs]* and people find it very hard to believe that I can do a whole scene with my back to the camera. *[both laugh]* It then becomes a joke.

Has it always been thus?

Yes it's always been thus.

So you actually are quite unselfconscious about the camera. You're genuinely not aware of the lens?

I'm not, no, no, no. I think I'm telling the truth. I really don't make that wonderful calculation that some actors make about where the lens is. That part of my brain is space.

OK, not so much a calculation about the camera but the feeling of it as an object – a shiny lens pointing at you?

No, they're always saying it to me. They're always telling me that 'the camera's here Julie, not there'.

It's fascinating because you would be one of the actors that people think of on screen as most able to absorb the lens . . .

No, not at all.

What are the most important aspects of preparation for you, once you have decided to play a part?

Learning the script and through learning the script, learning what it is you're being asked to do. What vision you're being asked to fulfil. You only get that by learning the script.

How important is the look for you? Hair and make-up, costume and so on?

Well it's very difficult to say because so much of it is mixed up with vanity and I'm not one of those actors. I'm also not a character actress. I'm not one of those actors who puts on the clothes and suddenly looks in the mirror and thinks they're somebody else – though I know a lot of people who do. *[laughs]*

Let's take period, for example. The look is not that important for me because I don't know what that particular person would wear at that particular time, I can't know. I can't know all the references, or the economics involved. So there I depend on the costume designer. If you don't like something – for example, you think it's unflattering and it's a part that requires you to look your best – then of course you have to work it out with the wardrobe mistress: maybe it needs to go in a bit there and go out a bit there, because you know yourself so well. I've been dressed up many times in ways that I think are idiotic . . . but if it pleases them then that's fine by me. This is all period costume I'm talking about.

Now with modern dress I participate a real lot! Then I do take character into account because I know what references I'm looking for and I do a lot of looking around. It's usually shopping now-adays. Once they would make the clothes and now they don't. So I spend a lot of pre-time trying to find exactly the right thing with a good costume designer. The result is less obvious. Costume design-ers are usually called good because they've done period film.

But your definition of a good costume designer as far as in helping or hindering your work . . .

Well, it would be someone who comes up with clothes and ideas which embody the character.

How much do you try and anchor the work, if at all, in your own direct personal experience?

I think every actor anchors work in their direct personal experience. I've got a belief that there are only about five different human emotions. For example you may have fear, or you may have a feeling of loss, that's a common one. And the loss you are portraying in a piece of work may be unimaginably huge and awful but even if your own personal loss (that you're comparing it to) would be considered by the outside world to be tiny, if to you it has been crucial in your life, I think you can draw on that totally different source. Maybe some wonderful actors can find the truth in an experience which they've never had in any way whatsoever. Maybe they're able to do that, but I can't.

So you work with your own experience quite consciously while you're preparing?

Yes.

Also in the moment of filming?

No, because it alters from the original moment of pinning it down when you're preparing, until eventually, it becomes the experience of that person who you're acting. It changes.

What is more important for you in a scene? What is said – i.e. the text that is written – or what is not said?

I know the right answer to that is probably what is not said.

There's no right answer.

Well I think it is the right answer. *[laughs]* I think it's the subtle, clever answer and I see it with lots of wonderful actors. But for me it's what is said, because very often I don't know where to go unless I've got the words to guide me into what is actually happening. I'm thinking of a good script and not just my lines, but also what the other person says. So many scripts which are not good have two people talking to each other who are not referring to each other at all, it's just empty dialogue. But a good script and a good actor working with you can help you discover things. In fact being in close proximity to a good actor to work with, saying a good script, can help you discover things you didn't know could be discovered.

So the text, the words you were given to say, become the signpost, the map?

They do. And sometimes you don't even need to think about it. I mean if you're doing a Pinter script – and I don't just mean his plays, I mean his very conservative film scripts – they do all the work for you. You don't need to think much, it's done. It's being the person, being the emotion, being exactly the right word or even the not-word. Well that's Pinter, but these scripts are very rare.

On the set when you're filming, what helps and what hinders?

Well I'm very easily distracted, although not by a film crew or a noise. I've worked with people who say, 'I can't work with that noise,' and I haven't even noticed it was there. That's to do with all our different attentions. That actor may be better at noticing something that is valuable for the film that I wouldn't even notice. The usual thing that people say distracts them is noise.

But you? You said you're easily distracted, but not by noise or by the crew.

I can get distracted by the other actor doing something.

What kind of thing might another actor do that would be distracting?

They might be coming up with their own word for something in the script, but if it doesn't make sense and it doesn't carry things through it is distracting. If they keep saying the wrong word, that can subconsciously affect your attention. Not consciously, because you know you've got to carry on whatever they do. I'm also very easily distracted by bad writing, which I can't make follow through. Yes, that distracts me very much if I can't find a through line.

So your rational analytical mind is quite busy when you're working.

Unfortunately, yes.

Is it unfortunate?

Yes, I think it is unfortunate, I would very much like it to be less so and to just go into a space where the words are there, you speak them, and you leave it up to fate to then bring out whatever you bring out.

But if you're speaking Pinter, the words speak you.

Yes, the words speak you. And once or twice you have other people besides Pinter who write so beautifully. To me it's the most wonderful thing to meet a script that honours the part and the character. An example could be the different humours of different people.

Humour as in wit?

Yes. If it is the writer's voice coming out of the characters, it doesn't work. But if it's exquisitely written there's a different version of humour for each character. That's rare and difficult at the best of times.

How important are the working relationships for you when making a film? The hidden world, the process during a shoot?

Well I've just made a film in Canada and the camera crew had me in awe. They worked so well, like camera crews should work, and

in very small spaces and under difficult conditions and very short
of time. And I was aware of this wonderful machine that's made
up of all these different parts and they were doing it so beautifully,
and as quickly as they possibly could. And absolutely right. I was
so aware of their skill and that comforted me. This particular crew
were particularly kind, as Canadians are renowned to be, and I felt
them to be with me. Very caring. And I think that makes a difference because it fills you with love. That's always a good way to feel.
I remember I made a lot of films, especially in the old days, where
they really couldn't care less. They did their job, a really skilful job,
and that in itself is fantastic. But it really was a wonderful feeling of
solidarity on this shoot.

*And have you had the experience where it was a fantastic experience
on the set but turned out not to be a very interesting film, or vice
versa – a very difficult experience on the set and yet it turned out to
be a very good result?*

I have observed that a film wasn't a very happy film, but I don't
necessarily expect a film to be good or happy. I work, on the whole,
with very good people and you hope that they have . . . you can
only call it a talent really, it's so magical and mystical. I know that
may sound like bullshit to some people. But you hope that each
film will be one that will work out. Because even the best director
in the world makes things that are failures in many ways, and I'm
not just talking about economic failures. In fact, I'm not talking
about economic success, ever. But I really don't expect things from
a film. If the director is somebody I admire then I know that he or
she will do the best that they could possibly do. You admire their
originality of thought and their intelligence and – yes, if they can
make a crew happy, that's a great gift too. I've seen directors that
are just out to make everybody happy and they work bloody hard
at it. I can't imagine how they do all the other stuff as well, but
it's marvellous! It's an absolutely wonderful thing to do because

film-making is such a tense business and the tension *[serious tone]* stays with the director. *[laughs]*

I've also known very happy shoots and I don't really care if they don't work . . . if you've had a happy experience that's just wonderful.

And vice versa? Have you been surprised by a tense experience turning into a good result?

I doubt it.

Circling around this question again. What do you long for from the director while you're working?

Intelligence.

Because it's their intelligence that gives you faith and confidence? Does that need to be an out-loud expression of the way the director is thinking? Analysing what you're doing rather than leaving things implied or hanging? Is it that? Is it about being verbal?

I love direction. I love it if they're not getting what they want, and then they find a way of directing me towards it. I love nothing more than that. If they can't do that – and some people can't communicate very well – it's not very nice.

So language skills and communication skills from the director are very important.

Yes, yes, yes. And that comes with intelligence.

Some people can waffle on and on, can't they?

But it's not about waffling, that's a different thing. Though indeed some people can waffle on like anything and you think, 'Oh just tell me what to do to make it what you want. Do you want less of that? Do you want more of that? Is that not at all where you want me to go? In which case say it for me!'

So you want directors to be more direct . . . to be simple and straightforward about what they want.

Oh yes! It feels like a secret society sometimes, with no one saying what they really think. From the worst-paid job to the highest there seems to be a kind of accepted rule, which is that you have to keep your mouth shut.

To you?

Well I'm the one who has experienced it. You need sympathy sometimes and you need to share the experience you've just had, if it's very puzzling or very upsetting . . . But nobody wants to talk, to be seen to be complaining.

It's very difficult to get a personal opinion from anyone – I think it's because everybody knows that if you join in with critiquing it might get back. But just sometimes somebody says, 'I agree, I've had that experience since we started,' and you think, 'Thank God! It's not just me!' But they take a risk when they do that, you know.

Talking about directness and plain speaking, do you think that directors are sometimes afraid to tell you what they want?

There's one thing about directors, which is probably a good thing and a learned thing. Historically learned. On the whole, though not always, they don't criticise what you've just done, thank God. They have to find a way – without criticising – of getting what they want. That's usually prefaced by, 'That was very good,' *[laughs]* 'Yes lovely work, hmm.' And then they either say something, which gives you a real clue like, 'Let's just do it again,' or . . . I've had 'quicker' a lot because I'm quite ponderous *[laughs]* and I find that very difficult but I'm intelligent enough to know what it means

– that the scene is dragging. Although I don't think 'quicker' is a good direction.

What would be a better way for a director to communicate, if they need the scene to speed up?

I don't know, because that's the director's job. But I get it in the end because I know jolly well what he's saying, however indirectly it is expressed.

But for example if the director said to you, 'I think the scene is dragging.' Would that be more helpful to you than 'quicker'?

Oh no! Not at all, because you're always doing your best, always. They have to find that magic key.

Do you feel vulnerable and exposed when you are working? Or does it not matter to you how you feel?

Well, I've changed over the years. I think I probably felt very vulnerable and exposed at first. Now I feel . . . I've got to a point where I don't feel vulnerable and exposed at all. Because I see that I'm surrounded by people who are all vulnerable and exposed, and they've got to do a very difficult job, even the people who get the caravans there and – if they have been given enough money – make sure that we have a tea bag or two. That idea makes me feel less vulnerable, that we're all in the same position. But if as an actor you do things like hold up shooting you know they're going to go back later at night or do more days and it's a very bad feeling. That's when you are aware that your responsibility is larger than just feeling vulnerable and exposed.

It's wonderful when you have an assistant director who never pressures anyone. Everyone is trying to make everyone else's life easier, if it's a good crew. We had a wonderful AD on the last crew who never ever mentioned time. Not once. And I've had so many films where people have come to the door, over and over again and looked at their watch and said, 'How are we doing? How are we doing?' And it just makes it so tense. But you're always doing the best you can.

What do you think is least understood about actors in the world at large? Can you generalise?

Probably their skill – their unbelievable skill. I mean the skill of a singer can be understood, but all those actors, not just the ones who are in the front, but the ones in the back. What they do is meant to be so natural and so real that it's easy to miss the extra-ordinary skill. That's what I think is most misunderstood. Also all this stuff about luvvies do this and luvvies do that, is an appall-ing misunderstanding. I think it's completely understandable that after doing this job you then need to express yourself ebulliently and extravagantly – which actors do – and be completely over-the-top and inappropriate. It's because you've been using all of your emotions in your work and you can't just turn them off like that.

What does fame feel like?

Fame, fame, fame. It gets muddled up with celebrity and success and all sorts of things. What it feels like is always being recognised and losing your anonymity, therefore being constantly vulnerable. It can take all your courage and it can render you a coward. It can also make some people forget that they're human beings and think they have become what it is that they're famous for. But in fact they're not this person with this make-up and this way of talking and this way of making jokes. If you're a great singer you don't go around singing in ordinary life, but actors can begin to identify with their roles and feel that they are only alive when they are in the papers or on television.

How do you personally separate a sense of self from the projections upon you because of your fame, because of being Julie Christie?

Well, I've always had a very strong sense of rejection of other people's perception.

Rejection?

Rejection of other people's projections. I don't think that means I have a very strong sense of myself. In fact, I think that's why I chose the word rejection because I think if I were stronger I wouldn't need to reject so much. Ultimately, what is the self and does it really matter if things are projected on you?

Are you aware of it as an issue nonetheless?

I'm very conscious about it. Very conscious of anger at the misconception of other people. Not just about me, I get very angry at other people putting their own, unintelligent readings on people. Actors and others may be much more intelligent than the people who write about them.

What do you think or feel when you see yourself on the screen? What are your preoccupations?

Well, I try not to look at myself on the screen. I've hardly ever seen a film through that I'm in. Although if I've got a very small part and only have to catch glimpses of myself then I've got time to see what the film is actually like. Which is fascinating. I often don't like to watch myself, because it takes me out of watching the film.

Why?

Because I become critical and self-loathing. I don't feel I've served the film, that's the awful thing. I know lots of actors feel like that.

How do you relate to the idea of being thought of as an icon?

I don't really know what that means. I think it's a bit rude actually. Because what it means, usually, is that you've been around an awfully long time. *[laughs]* And it's not correct. I agree with Lauren Bacall when she was doing a press conference with Nicole Kidman and someone called them two icons. And Lauren apparently erupted and said, 'She's too young to be an icon.' I don't think she said she herself was an icon but she was cross about what she saw as a deeply incorrect use of the word. And I agree with her. The word icon used to refer to people who were dead and who had accrued a certain sanctitude or awe. They had to be looked at from very far away to see that they were fabulous, as they had been thought to be. And none of us is old enough to be called icons. It's a silly thing to call living people iconic. I think it's part of a widespread debasing of language. We're so desperate for sensation and to feel something nowadays. It's all been taken away from us, everything has been made safe, and so we just love having our emotions aroused in indignation or criticism or shock or horror or anger. So much so, that the tabloid press has taken words such as terror and fear, the real great stuff that unfortunately an awful lot of the world is afflicted with – and used them for the tiniest little things. An icon is a word that is to do with history and if you snatch it away from history, you are giving a person a grandeur that really they don't have.

How do you explain charisma?

What a wonderful thing it is, isn't it? I love charisma but it's a very difficult thing to explain. There's an awful lot of magic and unexplainable things in the world and charisma may be one. Obviously it's a combination of genes and energy and some sort of physical presentation. I think energy has got a lot to do with it. It is that old cliché, someone who lights up a room. You may be talking to some people you adore and love but suddenly feel you would really like to be with that person over there that you don't know at all. That's charisma. I think charisma is a quality that makes everybody else feel better. Even if it's completely fraudulent.

You've mentioned magic and mystery a few times in the film-making process, in the acting process. Do you think making a film – acting in a film – is in the end a mysterious process that one can't analyse? Or do you think that ultimately it could be analysed?

No I don't think so. I think it's part magic and part skill. It's like ninety-nine per cent skill and seventy per cent magic! *[laughs]*

LILY COLE

When I met Lily to audition her for the role of Lettuce Leaf in *Rage*, her face was already familiar from her work in the world of fashion. Her height, huge eyes, apparently innocent presence and long red hair were distinctive and her professional experience was clearly appropriate for the part of a young model caught in the middle of a murder story. What I didn't know was how swiftly intelligent she was, and that she had a photographic memory. I handed her a long monologue that would have daunted the most experienced actor, but she read it through quietly to herself, then put it down and said 'OK'. She was virtually word-perfect. Working with her as she navigated the transition to an inner life, accessing and expressing deep feeling, was enjoyable and rewarding for me. She embraced direction enthusiastically and adapted to our stringent, low-budget shooting conditions immediately. Photographing her was, of course, a joy.

In the years since then she has completed a degree in art history as well as continuing to act. She has also been active in campaigns encouraging ethical practice in the fashion industry, is involved in running a bookshop, and leads an extremely busy life. We talked early one morning on Skype. Lily was sitting, wearing a T-shirt, in front of a grand piano in her apartment in London. I could hear sirens wailing, occasionally, in the background as we spoke.

Do you think of yourself primarily as an actor?

Er . . . No.

What do you think of yourself as?

I'd like to say artist but I think that sounds so pretentious.

No, it doesn't. It's just a word.

Anyway I consider myself a creative person and I am happiest when I'm being creative. And sometimes that's acting and sometimes that's other things.

How old were you when you started modelling? Was it fourteen?

Yep.

Did you ever think of modelling as a form of performance?

In a way. I had been acting previous to that; I started when I was, like, six. Just some mediocre, professional stuff. So I actually started acting first, in a funny way. When I was modelling, I never saw it as a substitute for acting. It didn't give me the emotional depth and push that I currently want to devote myself to. But at the same time there is a performative aspect to it. I would especially enjoy the more theatrical set-ups at couture shows, because of the surrealism of it. I was modelling in some very surreal experiences.

Talking of theatricality, do you think there's a connection between the catwalk and theatre in a minimalist kind of way? Or modelling and cinema? The lens and the lens? Do you see a link?

They are in the same family in the sense that they're closer than many jobs in the world. Like plumbing and architecture. *[both laugh]* And the demands of the camera and the audience are similar. But I think there are also fundamental differences. I wouldn't really compare them. I just recognise there are some similarities.

When you are in the acting part of your many selves, what do you look for in a script or in a role? What do you hope for?

It's an obscure combination of things that would excite me. I think first and foremost it's the director. Before I've even read the script, I have to trust the director, however great or mediocre the script is. It will only ever be as great or mediocre as the person who is at the helm of it. So my interest is working with directors I really admire. And then when it comes to reading the script itself, it's a combination of things: a character that I can see myself playing, or when I think the journey to play that character will be interesting or rewarding and push me in some way. If the story is engaging, that's always a bonus. And also who the other actors are. The people I will be collaborating with, potentially, on a project.

What are your criteria for what an interesting director is?

Good question. Well, it's entirely subjective isn't it?

So, what's your subjectivity?

Part of it comes from knowing their work previously. If they've made films that really work, then I would love to work with them. And usually that's a distinct vision, without necessarily being super 'arty' *per se*, in quotation marks, but that I can feel they're an artist, with a voice that will come through the film. And when I meet them, I can get a sense from their personality whether they've got an interesting mind, an interesting spirit, and an interesting heart that I want to be involved with for a few months, working together.

How crucial is that first meeting with a director for you? What are your antennae looking for?

I think the first impact is pretty crucial. You're always changing your opinion of what's important to you, but that first impact is often quite strong.

When I first meet an actor, we're sitting opposite each other talking, but I'm also looking for ephemeral substances that are going to give me clues about the journey that we might embark on together. What's that like from your side?

[long pause] It's hard to put into words.

It is.

It's just getting a sense of the person . . . *[laughs]* I like people that I can't quite get at first.

That's interesting.

So you definitely can't put that into words because that's the point; you can't put them into words. *[laughs]* So, somebody who makes me curious. And who I have good chemistry with. A sense of respect, that is mutual, and you can imagine yourselves being able to work together.

Immediate evidence of respect?

Yeah. But me being respectful and admiring of them, too.

Let's assume, then, that the script is interesting, you're interested in the director, there's this mutual respect and you're taking it on. What for you are the most important aspects of preparation?

I think being willing to go on an interior journey to be that character and not judge her. It's a very interior process for me.

In that interior process, what are the signposts that you're looking for? What's the work that you've found you need to do to access the interior landscape?

I think I just try and empathise. Try and find that character within myself and the parts in me that are empathic to their situation. I believe that a lot of our personality is a consequence of our experiences and culture, and that really I have the potential to be anything and anybody. As I believe does everybody else. Recently I played a saint and then I played a sadist, on two different projects back to back. *[SP laughs]* So I had to find the ability to empathise with both, however challenging it was. It's often more challenging – for me anyway – to embrace the darker side and not judge it. But I did it. *[laughs]*

Is it important for you to love the character even if they're, in quotes, 'not lovable'?

It's not, for me, about loving them, it's just about *being* them and not judging them.

Have you found that the preparatory interior work on the character is something you do alone, or that you like to do with the director?

It depends on the director. Some directors are very performance-oriented. The more performance-oriented, the better, for me. I appreciated working with you and your process so much, because you were so involved with the characters and the performance. But not all directors are like that. I've had other experiences where I turn up on set, and I haven't had one conversation about tone or character and I felt kind of stuck by myself. I prefer support from the director, as long as it's not limiting. As long as I still have the freedom to make choices. Actually, I've never experienced it as being limiting. I wish I could work more with directors who are really engaged in the actor/performance side because I want to grow as an actor and there's only so much I can do alone. It's a lot easier when you have people who are helping you in that journey, you know?

What about your work from the outside? Especially given your extensive experience of clothes. How important is your relationship with the look? The costume, the hair, the make-up . . .

I listen to the opinion of the director, the costume designer and the hair and make-up people, because that's their job. But I often give my opinion . . . I'm opinionated about what I feel is authentic to my character, because authenticity is what you strive for. So it has to be reflected in all elements. Having the experience of controlling the look helps me to enter the character. I used to find – when I was modelling – that being dressed as a certain persona, I could play to that persona for the day and have fun with it. I remember – it may only be a photograph – but in my mind I was imagining being this girl on top of a roof who's smoking a cigarette and wondering what tragedy is going on. You know, creating a little fantasy out of that role-play. It's only natural that how you dress informs how you act.

Absolutely. Every detail counts. Outside and inside. When I met you you'd already had an enormous amount of experience of working with your own image and being part of an image. And then, what I saw was you taking courageous steps into a relatively unexplored inner landscape. What was that transition like for you? From the outside to the inside?

I guess I didn't see it as clearly as you did, because inevitably, even though most of the emphasis was on the outside, there was a part of me always in an inner dialogue. So I didn't see it as such a drastic shift. But it was interesting doing your film before doing Terry [Gilliam]'s film because the approach was so different. Terry was a million elements, and horses and carriages, it was an extraordinary experience. And from an actor's perspective, it was an amazing learning experience. But it was a lot of attention outside of myself when it came to the days of shooting, whereas when we were filming, you stripped away all the set, you stripped away all the other actors, you stripped away any kind of effects until really all you had was the actor, the character. It was amazing to have these two experiences, side by side, which were quite polarised. I remember you said to me at the time, 'You don't know what a luxury this is, because you're new to this game, but it's a luxury to have this time and space to really work on performance.' And it really was. It was luxury.

What about text? There's spoken language and there's subtext: the gaps between the words and the words that are not spoken. Which are the most important way in for you?

Probably subtext.

Can you say more?

Very few characters in life are absolutely honest about everything going on within them. So a lot of what people bring to a moment is – I think – in subtext. I also particularly like films that don't rely necessarily on language. That have a sparse amount of words and the meaning comes through the silence. So then subtext is very important.

Let's talk about your relationship with the camera and with the lens. I've worked with many extraordinary actors but you're one of the most at ease with the presence of the camera. I could put a lens in your face and it's as if you could let it wash over you, be with you.

Interesting. When I was younger and someone got out a camera, I didn't know how to react. I'd sort of smile and feel self-conscious and then, as I worked with it so much through modelling, I wasn't scared of it any more, it was just there. *[laughs]* Now when I'm in a room and there's a camera filming me, it's so easy to be immediately self-conscious. I feel it's a go-to in our bodies and I really try my best to resist that.

To resist what?

To resist letting a camera make me feel self-conscious. To just accept it as you would a tree or a table, you know? But I think there's always going to be an element of self-consciousness, which can be a good thing too, because you can use that. There are some people who can completely forget it, but it's a very specific object.

Is the camera a mirror? Is it making you over-aware of how you look, or how you're being looked at, or what is it?

I think it depends who's behind it. If I really trust the person taking the pictures, or filming, then the camera becomes an extension of them and it doesn't bother me at all. I'm able to work with it and invite them in. If I don't trust the person . . . an extreme example is in a public space and you've got press, with cameras. Then you've got a completely different relationship to it because it has an aggressive quality. The camera itself is actually quite neutral. It's about the person behind it.

The camera operator . . . Go on. You look as if you were about to say something.

I was just going to continue that thought and say, as much as I accept – as you said – that I'm good with it, I think it does make me a tiny bit more self-conscious than I would be if there was no camera in the room.

Well, it is doing something.

Recording. And there's a certain judgement attached to that.

What's the judgement?

That people will see it.

So it's not the judgement of the people in the room, or the camera operator, it's the imaginary audience in the future.

Yeah, it's the future. It takes you outside the moment. It's like when someone writes an email – it's one thing to say something or think something that has an ephemeral quality to it and dissipates, and it's another thing to put it into concrete language. You've got to be really careful about what you say because you're going to be stuck with that for a while. So there's an element of that with cameras.

An acknowledgement of the fact that filming is a transitory process but has a permanent consequence.

Yeah. I don't care about that when it's just visuals, just static imagery. It's more about the spoken word. It applies to acting, in terms of judgement about your performance, but it's more so when you're being yourself on camera.

What does that mean, to be yourself on camera?

To not be playing a part.

Let's go back to what we were talking about earlier, the idea of the self. You said you could be anyone, potentially. The self is a construction, in some sense. So what does it mean to 'be yourself'?

The self that you've created as your identity. Me as Lily, you know. I'm not saying that makes it OK, but people do inevitably judge me in a way that they don't with a character. I can play and say things freely as a character.

Do you ever play Lily as a character?

Yeah, I play Lily as a character. But if Lily was a sadist you'd have different consequences. *[both laugh]*

One of the consequences of a degree of fame in the world is that there is a known entity with a name attached: Lily Cole. Which may or may not be the same as being you. Have you ever experienced yourself acting 'being you'? Being Lily Cole?

Yes, I do have a sense of that. When someone in the street says, 'Oh, that's Lily Cole,' I don't even associate myself with those words any more.

Like 'who's that?'

Not 'who's that?' but it means they don't really know me. They probably know parts of me, but there's obviously a lot of projection. I made a conscious choice to separate myself from that, the more I felt my name had become owned by other people.

Do you use a different private name?

My friends still call me Lily. But with a different understanding of my identity.

And using a different tone of voice, perhaps?

My friends will never call me Lily Cole. There's something impersonal about saying first and last names together.

You've come to the moment of the shoot. What do you feel you really need from the director at that point?

To feel supported and for them to believe in me. And then to be able to guide and push me.

How does the director need to show that they believe in you?

I don't think it's about showing. It's the truth of that relationship. You know if someone believes in you or not; it comes across in subtle comments and nuances.

What about the way that the director looks at you while shooting? Some directors look at the monitor, some directors stand by the camera. Does that make a difference to you?

No, not really. I'm not too aware of that. When I'm doing the scene, I try to be in the scene.

What about feedback? What's useful and what's not useful as different forms of feedback?

It's tricky. Humans – and actors, probably, in particular – are like these obscure instruments and you need to know how to play them. It's as if you are playing an emotional landscape; you press a button and it makes a certain sound. It's a very difficult art-form. I'm saying that from the director's perspective, concerning how they can get the best performance out of you. I don't think there's a concrete path. It's an alchemy in a way, the complexity of two humans inter-acting to try and find an emotional truth.

You will have found that different directors attempt to work their way into that alchemy in different ways.

Yes. I did a film at the end of last year and there was a line where the male actor had to say to me, 'I love you.' We did it once and then the director gave the actor, David, permission to take his time. Sometimes you need permission to take what seems like a robbery of everyone's time to deliver the line. 'Take *so* long,' he said. I can't remember the exact metaphor he used but it was like ice melting, or something. 'Make it painful, how long it takes to say those words and when you think you're ready to say it, take longer.' The scene ran for ages and we just had permission to wait and wait and wait. The director made that intuitive offer as guid-ance. And I remember when Terry was trying to get me to seem to be hurt, Andrew [Garfield] was giving me anger and I was getting angry back. I didn't know exactly what it was that Terry wanted, but he knew that I wasn't in quite the right dynamic yet. Then he said to Andrew, 'Don't look angrily at her; be hurt, be wounded by her.' So then Andrew played it to me that way and it broke me. So he got the emotional reaction he wanted by realising that – with me in particular – he had to go about it in a different way from how he expected. So it's that kind of funny dance I think.

Yes.

You look very thoughtful.

I am thoughtful.

What are you thinking?

I was remembering working with you and wondering whether I also needed to create a situation with a mirroring response.

I think it was more like empathy that he was trying to get from me. Andrew being hurt made me much more empathetic.

I was also thinking that the other director was creating the space and time for such a difficult line as 'I love you' to come from an authentic place. Finding a true impulse for that line is a very difficult thing to do. Let's talk about time itself, when filming. Are you aware of time as a pressure?

You get a sense of production getting stressed about time; they've got to shoot this many scenes by the end of that day. But I just roll with it, because the more time I have, the better, you know. So I just take what I'm given. *[laughs]* I don't like it when the process feels rushed. Which it often does.

Even a ten-minute shot doesn't have to be rushed. It's how one approaches time, isn't it, also?

Yup.

How has studying art history changed your view of the art of looking and being looked at?

I've done a little bit of thinking around this in terms of the object-ification of women and muses versus artists. But I think it's too easy to get intellectual about, and to complicate those things. It has informed my appreciation of art generally and the artistic spirit. And what I admire most in artists is when they break paradigms, whatever the medium is. I can see a potential for that with film in the same way that I think painters did a hundred years ago. It doesn't surprise me that some painters are great film-makers.

From the point of view of craftsmanship, portraiture and what it really means to 'look'?

Yes.

What's your relationship to your appearance? To being looked at?

I used to be really insecure. With modelling you get this weird combination of being put on a pedestal and then knocked down, too. You get so many conflicting ideas and messages that I think at some point I became a bit neutral towards all of it. Now I just am what I am. *[laughs]*

Let's talk about the pressures around appearance for female actors. Are you able to approach that with the same neutrality?

What do you mean?

The pressure to look a certain way.

Um . . .

That question seems to tire you.

[laughs] I don't really think about it too much.

OK. That's fine. I know that ethics are important to you. How did that come about?

I feel there's so much in the world that's . . . problematic. And when I say problematic, I mean things that people or the planet suffer from that aren't necessary. The consequences of structures that we created and we're all invested in. And so I thought it would be great if I took care. If I was to not care it would just feel like I was an arsehole. I feel we have a responsibility while we are alive. And the idea of people not suffering so much, being more united and the planet being protected, fills me with joy. So it's like a pursuit of joy, in a way. Or it's the pursuit of an idea that is joyful.

Have ethical issues come up for you on any of the films that you've been involved with?

In a practical sense or an internal sense?

In any sense. There are so many ethical issues in the film industry, particularly to do with money.

I think I've experienced that more with modelling, which is more overtly commercial, so I started looking at production chains. The consequences of manufacturing clothes are problematic a lot of the time. So, feeling complicit in that opens a big can of worms for me. I now do very little advertising and I try and research the companies I'm advertising for. So hopefully I represent ideas and values that I like. In film-making I haven't had so many problems. But even the environmental footprint of production is an issue and if I am in the position where I can ask that films be carbon-neutral, I would definitely do that. On quite a few of my films I have brought refillable plastic or metal bottles for water, to try and encourage us to stop the excessive amount of plastic water-bottle drinking. But other than the ecological footprint of film-making, I don't see it has the same ethical issues. I haven't looked at it in the same depth, but I don't think it has the same social impact that manufacturing clothes in factories does. I think you could argue it has ideological problems.

Such as?

Studio films repeating the same paradigms to big audiences. But as for the practical impact on workers' lives, I haven't seen the same possibility for problems as I did in the fashion landscape. And sometimes, in the big studio productions as well as in the more interesting, thought-provoking, quirky movies, there's space for really valuable work to come out. I don't really judge film-making in the same way at all. I'm quite political in thought but in practice I am actively non-political. When it comes to film and art-forms, I really don't like anything didactic or ideological. I would never want to apply that kind of thinking to film. If I ever did, it would only be to blow it up or poke holes in any sense of ideological conviction.

Because you believe that cinema works in a different way on the psyche?

No, because as Rumi said, 'There is a field beyond right and wrong and I will meet you there.' Within structures like business and fashion, I've worked to try and mitigate the crude, real suffering of factory workers, or a river that's polluted. Just crude reality that I think you can try and address when it comes to ideas of right and wrong. But I don't believe in ideologically proposing a belief system about right and wrong in general. So I don't like it when art and cinema are biased in that way. I prefer ambiguity.

One of the chapters in this book is about money, the true value of people's work in film and the idea of our work as a gift. Do you feel there's any true correlation between payment in money and what you can really give?

I think there's an element to it that's real. There is a monetary system in the world and we have to survive in it. I'm fortunate enough to have made some income from modelling and that's given me the freedom to make choices in film that are not dictated by money at all. But pretty much every actor on the planet – with a few exceptions – couldn't afford to work for free all the time. If we could, probably much of the world would be engaging in more artistic pursuits. Most of the films I've done I've been paid nothing, or next to nothing, and I do them because I want to. I don't know if gift is the right word – it's more a gift to myself to have that experience and to explore that character. Whatever I can give beyond that, great.

What about giftedness in the sense of talent? Do you believe in talent as an inherent gift?

Oh. I think gift is a beautiful word for talent. People are gifted with different things. It's easy for people to be egocentric about their talents, like, 'You're really smart' or, 'You're really good at this and that.' I read something about a monastery, somewhere quite obscure. And there was a line in it that said, 'What do you have that you have not been given?' or words to that effect. It makes you stop and think, 'Oh, yeah. I feel that I'm responsible for my mind and my soul and my body. But actually I've just been given all of this.' I feel the same about skills and talent. It's a really humbling way to understand the gifts that people are given and the ability to share those gifts.

How have new media and technology affected your idea of what performance is and what communication is?

I could be wrong, but I don't think it's had that big an effect yet on performance. There are some things, of course, like showing films online, as you did with *Rage*. And a friend of mine recently did a play, where I played a character from *A Midsummer Night's Dream*, and although it was happening here in London, I was in LA and San Francisco, tweeting. Things like that destabilise fixed ideas of distribution and performance, but I don't think it's really blown it up, at least from what I've seen. In terms of communication, I think it's had a huge impact. Social media is a phenomenon that has changed the landscape of social interaction in many ways and it's only in its infancy. It will be interesting to see how that moves in the coming years. Obviously privacy is becoming more of a rarity. It could be a good thing in a global dialogue that wasn't available before, so in some ways I think it has the potential to unite us more. It's a really interesting time in that way.

And has consequences for the notion of the individual and individual freedom. What does the word presence mean to you?

Just trying to be present, which is one of the hardest things to do. In the moment and not really thinking about the next thing or about the past.

How has celebrity affected your work?

I hate that word: celebrity.

Yes. It's a disgusting word. It's obscene! But nevertheless it's something you've got to deal with.

Inevitably it does affect my work because it changes what I'm offered. And then, as I said earlier, I've got a constructed persona that I distinguish myself from, for my own sanity. But it's given me the freedom to increasingly do the things I want to do. And I try – as much as possible – not to let it limit my ideas because of the bigger fear of judgement. There is also an expectation of a stereo-type that I really like to combat.

Is there a metaphysical or spiritual aspect to the work of acting for you?

Definitely, yeah. It's the main reason I do it.

Can you amplify?

Spiritual. I hate that word, because when you use it people have so many mixed connotations and ideas. My evolution as an artist, a person, a spiritual being – and hopefully everyone will understand that word – is the most important thing I can achieve in this life-time. A lot of that can come from the outside – doing different things, going to different places and having different relationships with people – but the relationship with myself and deconstructing or exploring that . . . it's such a gift to be able to do that as a job.

Would you say that affects your sense of purpose? Or is that a separate issue?

It's not really purpose-directed. It's just part of a journey.

And what about a sense of purpose?

I do have a sense of purpose. But I doubt having a sense of purpose, in general, because that seems antagonistic to the idea of being present. I think I've always been quite purposeful. I'm infected with it. *[laughs]* But I'm increasingly trying to deconstruct that and accept that maybe the purpose is in the present; it's not an end-goal.

JUDI DENCH

Working with someone as experienced and revered as Judi Dench can be unnerving. Although I had already met Judi over lunch to talk about *Rage* and had merrily discussed – amongst other things – the secret to maintaining her gamine haircut (clay! she exclaimed, the secret lies in clay!), and had found her to be entirely approachable, enthusiastic and willing, I was nevertheless anxious that I would have very little to give her as a director, other than the role I was offering.

Rage was going to consist entirely of monologues, which I intended to use in their entirety, with no internal cuts. It was both an enticing and challenging prospect for all the actors. Judi called me at one point to share her trepidation. 'Learning this is a nightmare. It's dreadful not to have anyone to play against,' she said. I reassured her that I would be behind the camera, attempting to embody the boy 'Michelangelo' and asking her questions. The shoot with Judi turned out to be joyful and hilarious. She was, of course, word-perfect. The only thing she had to learn was how to smoke a joint for one of her scenes and we brought in a young man to tutor her – she said this was a first.

We met for this interview in a basement room at the end of a warren of corridors beneath the National Theatre on the South Bank in London. Judi had revealed during the previous year that she had macular dxegeneration and was losing her sight. There was no sign of it when she confidently walked into the room. We discussed death for a few moments, as we had both recently lost people close to us. Then we began.

What do you hope for when you're sent a script for a film?

I hope it's going to be something that will immediately catch my imagination and I hope it will be something as different from the last thing I've done as possible.

Why is different important?

Because you do one thing and then you're seen by people who say, 'Ooh, I know a wonderful part for you,' and it'll be almost exactly the same kind of person. The last thing you want to do is to play the same character again.

What's more important to you: the script or the director?

First your imagination is caught by the script and the next thing you want to know is who's directing it. And the two things usually go hand-in-hand because the director and the script are so wedded.

If you get sent the script and it fires your imagination and then you hear who's doing it, it's grist to the mill. It makes you feel: yes, I'd like to have a go at this.

What if you don't know the director or the director's work already?

Well I think that's terrific, it's wonderful. If the director has asked you to do it and thinks that you might be right for it, then that's enough for me.

Even before you've met them?

Oh yes, yes, long before. It doesn't matter to me. A director has learnt ways of doing everything and therefore you're their putty. And if they've had the idea of doing it with you, that's the excitement of it.

That's an extraordinary degree of receptivity . . . to use a word like 'putty'.

Well that is what we are. You can make everything available that you know – and put forward what you think – but the final choice is in the director's hands. They say, 'How about a bit of that? Or how about . . .' – you know. Directing: getting all the horses over the line at the same time. And some horses don't want to run as fast as the others, I've found.

What about the first meeting with the director?

When Clint Eastwood asked me to do a film, I said yes, I flew out to California, I was called on to the set at nine o'clock in my wig and my clothes, I sat there and then just before we were about to start, I felt a hand on my shoulder. And that was Clint Eastwood.

[SP laughs] That was your first meeting?

Yes.

Incredible.

I'm *entirely* in a director's hands. Strange that you should ask about all this because only yesterday the director and the producer of something I'm going to do in September came down to see me and asked, 'How do you like to work?' I said, 'Not in all my years – fifty-nine years or whatever that I've been working – have I ever been asked by a director how I like to work. It's entirely your pre-rogative. I will do what you want me to do. Tell me and I'll try and do it as best I can.' Perhaps if a script was sent to me and I heard it was somebody who I didn't get on with then I would think twice about it. But then, if they've asked for me, I would think that it could be mended.

What do you wish more directors understood about actors?

Nothing. There's nothing at all that I wish directors understood. I'm just more concerned about them getting the right take, but I'm *totally* trusting of them. When the director says, 'Cut,' that's it. Then all I can do is hand it over and presume that they have got what they wanted.

Do you have a subjective sense of rightness, or do you rely on that view from the outside?

You mean rightness for that particular moment?

At any moment in the process of arriving at the final take. Do you trust your sense of 'I'm doing it the way I should be'? Or are you always in a dialogue?

I'm always in a dialogue with the director. Always. Then sometimes I want to say, 'Could I possibly try this?' I might have another idea, but ultimately, I *entirely* rely on the director saying, 'That's the one I want, now you've done it that way.' That's not to say that sometimes afterwards I've said, 'Are you *sure* that was . . . ?' I've just done a film with Stephen Frears and there was one moment in it which, in retrospect, I wondered about. He said, 'You asked me that at the time,' and I said, 'Well, I'm still asking it now,' and he said, 'No, I've looked at it and it's fine.' That's enough for me.

Trust?

Entirely!

Do you need to love a role?

No. When people say, 'Do you like this character?' I say, 'It's nothing to do with do you like – or not like – this character.' All people are shades of a colour. Therefore, there are some things that you may certainly not love about them, but it's not up to you to judge that, not from the inside. Other people can, perhaps.

What about an empathetic sense of them, even if you don't necessarily, in quotes, 'like them'?

If you mean *sympathetic* I don't think that's the business of an actor when you're inside the part. You don't sympathise with yourself. That's what other people do. I think what you try and put forward is a person with all their failures and unpleasantness and anything else that's relevant. That's not to say that when I see a film, I don't go, 'Oh, Christ! Why did I press that button and that button and that button?'

You mean when you see yourself?

Yes. Because in the theatre, *every* night you can press a different button and therefore it's always slightly shifting, whereas once it's in the can, it's there.

What is a character? Is it also you, or is it somebody else? And if so,
what are you in relation to this being that you're inhabiting?

You're the person who it's sieved through. Hopefully it's not you,
but we can only work from our own experience of the things that
have happened to us or the things that we have observed. You have
to have an enormous eye here *[gestures to her forehead]* and an enormous ear here, *[gestures to the side of her head]* because you've got
to be *ever* watchful and *ever* listening. So, all you can do is to use
what you have, or use what you've observed or what you're told.
When I played Iris Murdoch, I had no experience of somebody
with Alzheimer's, but Jim Broadbent's mother died of Alzheimer's
and so did Richard Eyre's, so I had a one-to-one source of knowledge that I was able to refer to. It's best, isn't it, when you're not
really recognisable in a part? When I did the film in India with
John Madden [*The Best Exotic Marigold Hotel* (2011)], I found that
really, really difficult. I said, 'John, I look just like me!' *[laughs]* I
said, 'It's very, very unnerving.' I want people *not* to be aware of
the actor behind the role. I don't like going and seeing a performance where you know that the actor thinks, 'This'll knock your
socks off.'

So a seamless transformation is best?

Well it never is seamless, but nevertheless, I just don't want it to be
recognisably me, because that's not what the story's about.

How much of that is also to do with appearance . . . clothes, make-
up, hair and so on?

All those things. It's wonderful if you can wear a wig, for example,
because on first sight, the audience doesn't go, 'Oh, it's Judi Dench.'
They suddenly see another person and only then they may think,
'Oh, is that Judi?'

In preparation, how much attention do you put on working from the outside in?

Because I trained as a theatre designer, I think a great deal about how the person looks and pay attention to that kind of detail first. Once that's done and we get it right, then I don't think about it at all.

But it comes first, in the sequence of events for you?

In the sequence of events I first like to draw the design. I've always drawn it on the script. Some idea of what she looks like, and then that reference goes. It's done. Then I have to start . . .

You're pointing at your gut.

Yes. I am.

So what's in the gut?

That is where the thing starts to take over. The thing has to grow inside you, so that you become a person who is as near the character as you, the director and your fellow actors think that person is.

And you are aware of it as a physical sensation, something filling up inside you?

It is something that starts from the inside. The only bit that I refer to on the outside is the design of whatever that person looks like. If I can get that out of the way then, yes, it seems to me to be something that just simply fills up and, hopefully, transforms into that person. By whatever method you choose.

Do you experience your work with the text as also rooted somewhere in your body?

Well, that's very difficult for me now, because I can't read any more so I have a terrible time. I have to sit down before, well before, and learn it, learn it, learn it. Then that's it. So at least it's part of me.

And once it's in you and you've learnt it . . .

Hopefully you're not going to forget it! Then it informs everything else.

This inside world . . . I was fascinated that when you talked, you gestured a lot at your body. And when you talked about looking, you gestured towards your forehead, not towards your eyes. Like sensing a third eye place.

Third eye place, yes. That's right, I think.

Emotional resonance. You said that what you do needs to be based on what you've experienced or what you've observed. How consciously do you root what's happening with the character in your own life experiences?

As a reference you mean?

Yes.

Well I don't think you do it consciously, but it's something you draw on. There's a great album you have inside where you have taken snapshots – without knowing a lot of the time – of many, many instances. For example, if a character is grieving about somebody, you refer, of course, to all the things about grief you know. But that need not necessarily be at *all* how that character would grieve. I'm continually asking myself, 'Would this person actually react in that way?' A way that I recognise in myself or in other people? Perhaps that person would react in an entirely different way. And then, of course, your director will tell you one way or another . . . hopefully.

Do you like to think about back-story, the person's history and memory?

Oh, I think that's essential. Essential. I had a whole family life for 'M': two grown-up girls at university, not that anybody knew about it, but *I* knew about it.

So, in a way, it's a secret knowledge?

Yes, secret knowledge . . . secret back-up! A kind of screen, you know, so that you are aware of a reference all the time.

Do you tend to do that by yourself or do you work with the director to find a back-story?

No, no, no. I do that *entirely* on my own. And don't tell anyone.

Would you ever want to?

No. I've not been asked and that's just the way I work.

The spoken word or the gaps in between the words – the feelings and thoughts, the things that are not said – which is more important?

Well, both are vitally important. But what you often see, especially with Shakespeare, are people who pause when the line is, in actual fact, telling you what they're thinking. You have to obey the way Shakespeare is written. If you have a line of iambic pentameter, then a half-line, then the iambic pentameter again, you *need* to know that there is a half-line missing and in that half-line there is obviously a reaction of some kind. If, on the other hand, you have an iambic pentameter, a half-line here, then a second half-line spoken by the next person, there's no room for a pause. He tells you *very* clearly to pause, or not. But I learnt about filming really late on. I knew nothing about it at all, and I've learnt from watching other actors. Kevin Spacey taught me a *huge* amount. I don't know that he ever knew, but he did. In film, if you have the actual thought in your head, that will be seen in your eyes.

I concur one hundred per cent with that.

One is often asked, 'What is the difference between theatre, television and film?' and I always say, 'Theatre: you go . . . *[smiles broadly]*, television: you will go . . . *[a smaller smile]*, and film: you'll go . . . *[an even smaller smile]* . . .' It's slices of cake! And I think it's true that the camera will pick up everything. And that is that! You work out the whole life of this character and then the next stage is exactly what their process of thought is throughout the script. Then, when you come to the front, you've very little to do because all that should be in there.

The mountain beneath the tip, I suppose?

Yes, it should be there! What shows is just the tip of the thing, but they should know what you're thinking.

What about the experience of working in the theatre, the experience of working in cinema . . . do you think they're the same art-form from an actor's point of view?

Yes, I think they're exactly the same art-form, it's just that one is of a different proportion than the other.

Just a question of proportion?

I think so. It is becoming another person in the most sophisticated way you possibly can. In the theatre, in order to get that to the man who's sitting up at the back of the gods, it has to be a different degree of projection. You could do the same performance on film, but it would have to be as if the binoculars were turned the other way.

Right. So that's not just a question of scale, it's almost like an energy reversal, from the way you're describing it.

Because on film it can be too much: it can be too big. It can be over-projected.

What about the relationship with the camera itself?

I don't think about it, nor now can I see it. Not long ago, in *Philomena* (2013), the film I've just done, I thought the camera was on me. But it wasn't on me at all! I just saw this thing that I thought was the camera on me and it wasn't!

Can you see me right now?

Not clearly. I can see your face. But from the door I would have difficulty . . . I know your outline.

Can you read my expression?

Yes, from here.

You can see that I am smiling?

Yes. In my own way, I can.

[SP laughs] Do you like to rehearse for films?

Sometimes, yes. I don't much like to have it jump on me.

It's like the hand on the shoulder – that Eastwood hand!

Everybody's talked to you about the way he works, I'm sure. He goes, 'In your own time' *[said in a low, gruff, Clint Eastwood tone of voice]* and then we do the scene, and he – very quietly – says, 'Stop.' You do two takes, then he says, 'Print it.' I'd say to him, 'Could we not do that again?' and he said, 'Why?' So I said, 'Well, I'd love to just have another go.' He said, 'OK, but don't think.' Half past four – wrap. Stop. Heaven. But I didn't know he was so right-wing. It put me off a bit when I found out, but it hasn't really put me off because he's absolutely, glitteringly wonderful.

Well that brings us to the question of feedback from the director. From your description, it's almost as if Clint Eastwood is creating a space with his presence, his attention and focus. What kind of feedback from a director have you found useful and what kind of feedback have you found horrendously un-useful?

I've worked a lot with Stephen Frears and he's got a quality of watching a bit like that *[imitates a wary posture]* and he's quite brusque, but then he has a way of letting you know if you're on the right track, without actually saying, 'That's it.' Do you know what I mean? I love that.

I'd love to know what you mean. Is it just a feeling, or an expression?

It's because I know him so well as a person. But on one of the Bond films I didn't hit it off at all with the director. He made me increasingly frightened and uncomfortable, and of course then, the lines started to go.

What was it he was doing that made you uncomfortable and frightened?

I just thought he didn't reckon me in the part. Perhaps I was rather forced on him. But surprisingly, he asked me to do another film for him at the end and I said, 'You have to be joking!'

So possibly not a good communicator?

No, I don't think so. I nearly ran him over in my car not too long ago. *[SP laughs]* By mistake.

Does it make any difference to you if the director watches you during a take or looks at the monitor?

Oh, I think it's much nicer if a director watches you during the take and doesn't look at the monitor.

Why?

Simply because it's a communicative thing. I don't mind if he looks at the monitor later. Not that I can see him of course, not that I can see whether he's looking at the camera or at me, but I think it's very nice if somebody watches. There's something – I don't know what it is, perhaps it's just the companionship. Also, you doubt whether what you've done has been caught on film. It might be more visible when watching than appears on the screen. Though it's probably the other way round.

Do you ever experience the director as the audience?

I want to do it for the director. That's why I'm there. And I have to go by exactly what they say. 'Yes, we've got it,' or, 'No, we haven't got it,' because when it comes to it I've not much judgement about it. In the theatre, the moment the director goes, I feel bereft. I feel like a child that's been left to walk on its own, having only just learnt to walk. I don't like that at all. So I *utterly* believe that I will be told by the director when we've got the scene.

Do you think happiness is in the process, on set, is a bonus or a necessity to produce a good film?

Well, it's the same as in a theatre company. I've just done a play called *Peter and Alice*, with the most *brilliant* six other people, just *brilliant*! It's like when we did *Comedy of Errors* with Trevor Nunn. There's no question, if you have that feeling in a company, although the audience probably wouldn't be able to tell you what it was, it's an extra dimension. I know it is. Whereas, if there is tension between people, an audience will pick up on that too. That may not necessarily be bad. A director may want that. It's not the way I personally want to work, but sometimes it happens. It's much more pleasant to work with people that you have a really good rapport with, than with people who you're not sure which way they're going to jump. You need all the confidence you can get, because it's too frightening.

You've mentioned the actor's fear a couple of times. What do you think the source of the fear is?

Oh, it's what Orson Welles or Tyrone Guthrie said: you go to the theatre and what makes it so wonderful is that it may be the night the man will fall off the wire. And that is it. Roy Kinnear – God, what a wonderful man he was – said, 'It's not when the audience goes out you need to worry, it's when the audience comes towards you.' I've always thought it and I've passed it on to everybody. Fear, oh yes. All the things that can happen. I once said to Johnny Mills, when we were in the wings, waiting to go on, 'What is stopping me walking on and turning to the audience and saying, "Why don't you fuck off home the lot of you?"' All we are doing is walking on to a stage and speaking words. It's tissue paper between me saying, 'It is always painful to part from people whom one has known for a very brief space of time. The absence of old friends is one you can endure with equanimity but even a momentary separation from one to whom one has just been introduced is almost unbearable,' and me turning and saying, 'I don't actually feel like doing this tonight, so why don't you fuck off?' Do you see what I mean? It's only discipline! It's tissue paper between one and the other. And I feel it *so* often. That's a kind of danger. And when I said that to John Mills, he said, 'There are about six people in this club, you are now one of them.' Sir Laurence was one and Ronnie Squire was another, who had said this same thing about the danger. If you're a dancer, you dance. If you're a singer, you sing. As an actor, that's all we do, so the difference between those two states is what you're frightened of.

And the same thing applies when there's a camera?

Not so much. That's only in the theatre, because the audience are right there. Film can be edited, but that can't be. The night you walk on and abuse everybody.

So what's the fear on a film set?

Oh, the fear on a film set for me is that I don't know enough about filming. That's a discipline I've had to learn and I know now much, much more, simply from watching good actors and being told by directors what to do. Wanting to get it right, that's another fear. And maybe there'll not be enough time. Take after take after take after take and you think: I've blown it.

When you do more takes do you find that cumulatively more alarming?

Yes, a bit.

So the Clint Eastwood, two-take method . . .

That was *really* alarming [SP laughs] because I only ever got round to first base there! I thought, 'I'm only just starting to try.' I haven't seen the film either.

So, it's not necessarily that less time is better, or more time to do it is better, it's something else about the relationship with time and the desire to get it right?

Yes, it is.

Do you always experience film-making as under enormous pressure of time?

No. Sometimes, but it's mostly a kind of anxiety with yourself. And always after I've seen a film I know what I should've done, or should have done more.

When you see it or when you just remember it?

When I see it. But I see so few.

I was going to ask, do you watch yourself?

Not often.

Why?

Oh, because. Actually I do know why. When we did The Scottish Play with Trevor Nunn and Ian McKellen, we televised it at the end of a long run. We all went to Trevor's house to watch it and I was sick with disappointment. I thought what we had been doing was much more than what I saw on the screen and that really shook me up.

Well, it probably was. Because television can be bald. It removes quality from a live performance.

And then of course you watch it a second time and it's no better. It's exactly the same. *[laughs]*

Theatre is so much an in-the-moment experience, you give out and then it's gone. Film you give out and it remains.

That's what irritates me. That it never moves, it's just there. It never changes.

And that's disturbing to you, the lack of change?

Because when I watch it I think, 'I know what I should have done. It would have been much better if I had done this or that,' but nevertheless that's what's there.

Does that mean that if you had the opportunity to look at what you were doing on the monitor, while you were shooting, you would be fine?

I know that good film actors do that. They go and see it and they're very much aware – but I can't do that.

Because?

Because I don't want to see it. *[laughs]* I don't want to see myself doing it. That's my own failing. I know if I did and could somehow bring myself to be able to analyse it . . .

Don't you think that that's the director's job – to be that kind of mirror? To be a living monitor?

I do. I do. And that's totally what I rely on. Totally. Stephen sometimes says, 'Do you want to go again?' and I pause and he says, 'Yes, let's go again.' And then I think, 'Oh yes, I see that.' But it's very nice of him to put it in my court. *[SP laughs]* It's wonderful to have a shorthand and to work with somebody so often that you understand their language.

Or their silences.

Or their silences. Or their vulnerability, or whatever.

What about shooting out of sequence?

That's very much for the director to keep an eye on and me to be extremely aware of.

*Back to the question of the afterwards. You finish the film, you see
it or don't see it. And then there's a process that seems to be a part
of film-making – publicity, press, photos and all that. What's your
relationship with that side of it?*

It's something you have to do. I find it unbelievably difficult.
When you have to sit for five minutes with each journalist . . . I
try and give a different answer to the same question as many times
as I possibly can. I feel sorry for the camera crew hearing it over
and over. And I think if I answer in the same way I will fall off the
chair. I don't think I'm cut out for that at all. I do it because I know
I *have* to do it. But I don't quite know why. I don't understand
why, when a film comes out, I've got to be there. I suppose it's to
sell the film.

Do you find it more difficult than doing the film itself?

Much, much more difficult. More difficult than learning the film
and shooting it. More difficult than learning a play and doing three
hours of performance every day.

Why do you think that is?

Because it's so boring! *[SP laughs]* Hearing yourself drone on.
Answering the same question again and again.

*I was once at a dinner and Willem Dafoe had just come out of a press
junket. He sat down opposite me, drooping, and said, 'I am so full of
self-loathing.' I remember that every time I do it . . . the feeling . . .*

Yes. Yes. It's got nothing to do with what we're doing or why we're
doing it. If it's film, it's there and you pick out what you want and
don't pick out what you don't want. Go if you want, don't go if you
don't want. Good luck. My job's done.

What about the genuine sense of purpose in what we're doing? Is it something that can be put into words?

What we do is to be in the incredibly lucky percentage of people who do a job we love and can make a living at it.

Do you think of it as a vocation?

No. I don't think of it as a vocation because I thought my vocation was to be a theatre designer. It was an unbelievably lucky chance that I went to see Michael Redgrave in *King Lear* at Stratford in the 1950s and saw this set, a completely open stage, which I had no concept of previously. All I had thought was: curtain comes up, you see a set. Curtain comes down for the interval and goes up again and there's another set. I had no idea of a huge, huge open stage with a set that just slightly revolved, which changed everything. Nobody brought anything on or took anything off. People just acted on it.

So minimalism appeals?

I know that less is more. I know it is. When you're young you think, 'Oh, come on.' When I played Ophelia at the Vic I tried every single thing to tell everybody I was mad. But I know now that all I needed to do was one small thing. But you don't have the courage to do that when you're young. You want to show every way you know.

Minimalism takes a lot of commitment.

And courage. Courage to do less. Because you think it won't be noticed. It's like somebody not crying. Someone crying is one thing but someone trying not to cry is quite another.

Do you think that there's a spiritual dimension to the work? Does that mean anything to you?

Yes, it does.

What does it mean to you?

When I was at the Vic, John Neville said to me, 'You must decide why you're doing this job and then you must always remember your decision.' He said, 'And don't ever tell anyone.' I'm a Quaker. I don't really want to put it into words – but when you go to a Quaker meeting everyone is just sitting. There is no other form. I think there is a relationship between that form and theatre. Somebody comes and sits in a theatre and you get ready and come onto the stage.

A meeting. I'm sorry to put that word into your mouth but it's what you were suggesting . . .

A meeting house is of course what Quakers go to. But I don't think there is a word for it. It's something to do with the interaction between people.

The space between?

Hmm.

OK, last question. What do you think presence is?

I don't know. You just know it when you watch. You know who has got it and you know who hasn't. Presence is a quality that is irresistible even when someone is doing absolutely nothing. Some people think presence is fidgety, but I think it's the complete opposite. When you're looking at a stage full of people and there is one still person you can't stop watching even though there might be a long speech going on somewhere else. It's a kind of magnetism. Or it's lack of show, lack of acting. It's something to do with just being a person.

Have you ever known those moments when you have presence? Can you recognise it from within?

No. I sometimes know when you can make an audience go very, very quiet. With Shakespeare of course it's his language. I don't know. I've never thought about it. An audience in the theatre will always tell you everything, whatever you're doing: tragedy or comedy. Audience. That's why the director has to be the audience and everything else. He or she has to have enormous antennae – like actors – in order to pick up everything. Yes, in a film you just have to totally rely on the director.

Thank you for talking to me.

Not at all. I've never put it into so many words, what it is that we try to do.

ALICE ENGLERT

I first met Alice when she was about four years old. I was sitting talking with her mother, Jane Campion, under the shade of an umbrella in the gardens of a hotel in the heat of late summer at the Venice Film Festival. Alice was dancing amongst the chairs and tables and wanted us both to stop talking and watch her.

Twelve years later, during the long hunt for a teenage girl to play the complex, contradictory role of Rosa – devout and sexually precocious, naive and knowing – I saw an audition on the Internet that she had done for another film. Her qualities were immediately apparent: a sure-footed presence, a seductive confidence and a volatile fragility. I sent her the script and we talked on the phone. 'I love Rosa,' she said unequivocally. It took a year before the film was ready to go and by then she had grown up a little more, but was still required to travel with a chaperone. Many people have asked about the connection with her mother, but it really was a coincidence in the casting process. Alice got the role of Rosa on her own merit.

We met for this interview in London, where Alice had decided to live, at least for a while, in an area not far from our locations for *Ginger & Rosa*. In the meantime she had worked on two movies in the US, including a lead role in *Beautiful Creatures* (2013), a big studio picture. We sat at the table in my studio, the same, familiar space in which we had rehearsed together.

What attracts you to a role, or to a script when you read it? What are the things that you're hoping to find?

I often find that I'm attracted to roles or stories that I feel slightly nervous about. For me, if I feel too comfortable about the story, or about the character, I have to search for something that makes me nervous. Why I like that is because it means I can't take the character for granted; they have that mysterious thing, the complexity that a human is. When I feel a tension with what I can do with it, and the tension of maybe making a mistake, it makes me alert, and that excites me. I like it when I feel provoked by a character.

Do you think that loving the character is also important? Or do you think that you come to love a character through working on her?

I do think it's really, really important to know that you can love the character. You may not love them at first, but you need to be able to put judgement aside. Even if we hate ourselves or hate the way we look, somehow, we're still here, we've got a life force that is taking care of us. So I think that when you play a character, you have to be able to lend yourself to their life force and there has to be a base of unconditional love that allows them to *live*, and then the whole complexity of being a person, and the strange stories that we tell, can grow and exist on top of that.

What do you hope for in a director when you first meet them?

I think maybe I have a slightly different perspective, or expectation, of a director than some actors I've met, because I grew up watching my mum work with actors, and seeing where they got on or where they didn't. For me it's not about getting on with the director, it's about being able to communicate and work together. So I find that I don't even think, 'Do I like them or do I not like them?'

What do you think instead?

Whether or not we are talking a similar language. I try and see whether they're stupid or not, to be honest, as well. What I really like is when a director can talk. Sometimes when I've met people who spoke in a juvenile manner . . . that's quite repellent.

You mean you they've spoken in a juvenile manner to you?

No, it's things like, to ask someone to 'do it sadder'. But then again I think that, even if I don't like them, if I *hear* what they want and understand it, and agree or don't agree, then that's really it for me. I think it's about communication. I like anybody that I can communicate with.

But also, for you, it's important that you can respect their intelligence?

Yeah, I have to be able to respect them. And be able to communicate and then I'll like them anyway.

What about the audition process? What are your thoughts and feelings about that?

I really like auditioning. But I don't like to leave an audition if I think that I have done badly. I don't stop until I've done something that's worth it, even if it's not perfect. And I feel quite at ease with the fact that I won't get everything. When I hear a 'no' it doesn't feel so personal. What I've found is that I just feel high before and after an audition. *[SP laughs]* I do! There's the famous complaint of Rita Hayworth who said you go to bed with Gilda, and you wake up with me. I think I'm more alive and I feel more articulate when I'm working than at any other time.

Let's assume you've got the role and you start preparation. What's the most important way in to the work for you? Through the outside? The look? Or through the inside?

I start with the inside, being in their body, in their physicality. The rest of it is really story anyway. The physical presence and the things that they won't say in the movie – and you'll maybe not even get a hint of – are the most important for me. In the same way that if I'm having coffee with a friend, all my reactions, the way I feel, are things that I'm not going to *say*. I often try and find a song that their mother or their father would have played when they were young. A memory of a song that wasn't their favourite, but they heard it a lot as a kid. Most of the time I don't talk to a director about all of this. I like to keep that part of it private. Then, when it comes to costume, I like to be in control quite a bit. I think that costume is so important, because this is how the characters present themselves. But I get to compromise there, because I can't help it – being really a kid still – I want to look attractive, you know? *[laughs]* So, sometimes I fight for particular ideas about costume. But I like to be aware and to notice that sometimes there are vanity issues.

How old are you at the time of this interview?

Eighteen.

How many features have you now done?

I've done four but two of them haven't come out yet.

Well, that's quite a lot to have done by eighteen. Let's go back to this thing about appearance and working from the outside in. When you said the physicality of the character, did you mean clothes, hair, make-up or other aspects of the physical body?

The physical body. The way they walk, the way they sit. How they are on public transport is really fun, I find. I'm thinking of how they behave in a public space. It's not about talking to people. More than anything it's how they watch people. It's so interesting how much somebody blinks, or where they avoid eye contact.

You were saying sometimes you're mindful about slipping into vanity. What do you think about the specific pressures on young, female actors about appearance?

It's such a huge subject. I've found it stressful. But I've had a sense of humour about it which has got me through. Also, I think that the pressure manifests in what you believe. Young girls believe that they're meant to appear a certain way, but I think that people respond ultimately to truth, to honesty. I think that's where beauty is. Not when we try to create fantasy man or fantasy woman. The nature of a fantasy is that it's not quite there. You close your eyes, you try and see it, it's grainy, it's not real. And then we search for the fantasy in a world that is real. We strive to be these things that aren't possible. We know it, when we close our eyes and really think about it. I feel I don't have time for that world. I don't have time for the stress and the pressure of, 'I am a young woman, I need to look attractive.' It doesn't need to be an issue. If you don't buy into it, if you allow yourself to be as you are, then you'll get at least an honest response.

That's a constructive attitude to have. What you're describing is how you deal with the pressures within. Nevertheless, there are very real, commercialised pressures from without.

Yeah, but I don't care for the people who care for it. I don't Google myself, EVER! I did, last year . . . I wanted to see my films come out, I wanted to see the posters come up, and then you read something that says, 'Her face is a bit funny' and KER-BAAAM!! You go down, down, down! So now I just don't look at it. They're having a good old time saying I look weird, or I look good, or I look flat-chested or whatever, and they can have a lot of fun doing that.

You've seen those kind of remarks?

No, I got off it way before I started hearing stuff like that. You know, they said so much shit about Lena Dunham! Which is just repulsive! And I love her!

Me too. One can stumble across such cruelty on the Internet.

Oh, yes! Who are these people? They don't take any responsibility for what they're saying, so you shouldn't have to take the shit they're saying personally. They can have fun saying their stuff, I can have fun not knowing about it. That actually suits me fine!

I wonder how much it has influenced your work growing up around film sets, as well as around a mother who's a director.

I wasn't allowed on a lot of them because there was too much sex. *[both laugh]* I was *never* allowed on the set of *In the Cut* (2003).

I had *no* idea what kind of films my mum really made *[chuckles]* for *so* long, because I was just too young to see them.

But nevertheless you've grown up in the force-field of movie-making.

Yeah, I saw a lot of pre-production and post-production. I love the whole process, because I was so exposed to that. I got really obsessed with the *weight* of a scene.

The weight of a scene? Can you say more about that?

I don't know quite how to explain it, but watching editing I became very attuned to subtle things. I would notice that they would use a different take, say, for just one word. There were often times where my mum would tell me to be quiet and I was never quiet . . . I'd be quiet in the car on the way and then I'd get there and I'd just be horrible and annoying . . .

You mean, in the editing room?

Yeah. And tell them what they should do.

How much time did you spend in editing rooms?

Oh God, I spent nearly the whole of my primary school in the editing room. I pretended I was sick, like, every day . . . My poor mum. I would just sit in the car and hold on to the seat and be like, 'I'm not getting out.'

To go to school?

Because I had such huge anxiety attacks. I found it *so* stressful to go to school.

And it wasn't just because you'd rather be in the cutting room?

I would *much* rather be in the cutting room, but it was because I had this *huge* anxiety. I couldn't handle school.

Well, I want to ask two questions arising from that. One is what was it that was anxiety-provoking about school? And then, second, what did being in the cutting room teach you?

I had a huge amount of sensitivity and I hadn't learnt how to be with other kids. Now I feel like the sensitivity is probably the best thing about myself. I could always speak publicly in front of many people, but I couldn't carry on a conversation with another eight-year-old. Actually, I think maybe I faked a lot of my anxiety attacks.

It was a good acting job?

In high school I faked all the time. I knew I was faking it . . . it helped if you *believed* it a little bit. *[laughs]*

And what did you learn in the cutting room? Because I refer to the edit as 'the great teacher'.

Yeah, I think so as well! One of the most exciting things for me was watching great actors and seeing how powerful it was being able to try different things in a performance. So if I have an idea, I don't like to cling to it because there are so many different ways that a truth can happen. That's what's most exciting for me, finding the truth in the scene and letting go of my plan, allowing it the space to breathe.

How about the necessary conditions that a director must provide in order to allow the actor to be that flexible and find that space?

Something that my mum always does which I think is very smart and clever, and that you do too, is to never give negative feedback. There's never huge, over-exaggerated praise either, and I *love* that. I think that's the smartest way to work because it means that as an actor you don't find yourself working for the praise. The scene's always treated as work that's to be done. We're not going to finish the scene until it's good, ever. And then it always ends with, 'That was good.' So it stops the judgement, because it can all be interesting. When you see a director look scared and go, 'Eurgh, that was a bit . . .', you get self-conscious and you clam up because you want to do it right. You start having this stupid idea that there's a right way to do this and there isn't.

So the director's facial expression is important?

Yeah, it's true. What I think is great is when the director takes the responsibility of being calm, being the centre of gravity, being able to have some empathy and generosity and patience and *strength*. I'll keep it simple: I think if the director looks scared, that freaks you out. *[SP laughs]*

Do you like to rehearse?

Yeah, I love it!

What do you love about it?

Well, it's acting, but you don't have to stick to it. I understand why some people don't like doing it because they say they'll have too many ideas about it, and then they won't be able to do it. I just enjoy it. The more that you can do it, the more you can feel the world, the better for me. What I love about rehearsal is you can leave the script and have time to be able to be sort of dumb about things.

And what about working on the text? Are the lines, or what's in between the lines, more important for you to explore?

When I'm preparing for a scene or an audition, I never study the page that much. Sometimes that means the script supervisor has to be like, 'You're not saying that line,' but I have a good memory and I don't like to analyse the text too much. As a person, I don't analyse what I'm saying that much either, even if I'm being manipulative or conceited. If there's something organic in it, that's why it works. I'm talking now, but I haven't really thought that much about what I'm saying. So I only get analytical about the dialogue if I don't understand what's being communicated.

And what about ways of finding what you've just described, that impulse to speak from within? How do you find that impulse in the script?

I think when you read it, you have an immediate impression. I like to notice what the impression was, what I reacted to, and then later go back to it. You can tell the story without the script, do the scene without getting the words right and ask yourself what do they want? Sometimes I need to understand what my agenda is. If I'm feeling lost or I'm flailing, it's really helpful to find some very basic need and then just listen to what the other character's saying as well.

Really listen?

Really listen.

In your experience so far, do you like to work with the director on that inner world – the space between the words – if you can?

Yeah, yeah, yeah. I think that spaces say as much as the words so, I really love working with people who have the time and respect for that.

Time. How much of an issue is time in the whole film-making process for you so far? In preparation, in rehearsal, but also of course in the shoot.

There's never enough, but I love that. It's the point! On a film, the light's wrong, there's no time, and we don't have any money. Even when you *have* money, you don't have any money. Incredibly enough, we all turn up and we do it! I can't believe anybody makes a film! Do you know what I mean?

I certainly do!

Like, it's absolutely unbelievable that we actually make the movies! *[laughs]* So much goes wrong! I love being exhausted and grumpy and happy and grumpy and furious and cold, I think that's just how it is and it's good.

How much do you draw on your own experience and memory and graft that onto the experience and imaginary memory of the character that you're playing?

I never consciously go, 'Oh, they're just like me because . . .' or, 'I could *use* that.' By the end of playing a character, they're so close to me that *everything* that they've felt is me, I don't know how to separate them any more. By that time, I've felt everything that they've felt. You can draw on sadness in your own life but I don't find it helpful. I find it's too much like copying and pasting for me. If there's something that is similar, normally it works its way in. But if I start trying to think about the time when my Grandma died, my body completely goes . . . It won't believe me and it says, 'I'm not doing that.' I can hear it, like, 'Don't do it, you know it doesn't work!' But if there's a scene where you need to cry, sometimes you've just got to use everything.

You talked about getting to a point where you can feel everything your character is feeling. The character is grafted onto you and you inhabit her in some way. Can you talk more about where you, Alice, are in that process and what that empathetic leap consists of?

I always think that I'm the white noise in the scene.

As in, something in the way? Static, or . . . ?

Not in the way, but it's like tuning out. You're in the scene and then, 'Cut,' and for me it's almost like, 'Oh, I'm Alice.' What's so cool about doing a film – and what's so relaxing – is that it's not your story. There must be a way to live your own life with that same relaxation. To be able to see that there's a narrative of your own life. It's the same as a problem, you can make choices. You can allow the problem to be there without *being* the problem. And I'm struggling with that, but I find that film and story and narrative teaches me more and more about how to be a human. That's why I don't think that acting is cheating, like, 'Oh, I'm escaping.' I find it's actually acknowledging that I can't lie. There's a truth in acting that you're representing something, you're allowing a feeling to be there. I love that clarity, but I'm still confused if it's my own being.

Whatever that 'own being' is. Maybe acting teaches one about the construction of the everyday self but perhaps with a better writer? [both chuckle] When you're on the shoot, how conscious are you of the camera itself? I don't just mean the lenses, I mean the presence of the camera.

I remember when we were doing *Ginger & Rosa*, I was looking at myself in the camera lens and you said that in the editing room it's hard when you find actors chuck a sneaky glance in the camera. I love that you said that. It's that vanity thing, wanting to appear attractive, which I guess I do. It leads me back to when you were talking about the pressure on young women as actors. What is that about? You do it because you think it will give you power, you think you'll have control, and ultimately make you happy, I guess. But I don't think that's true. If I take away the idea that being beautiful will make me strong, happy, empowered and loved, then

I must stop believing that this is the solution. So every time I notice I do stuff like that – look in a mirror and try to look like whoever it was – I try and remember, 'Why was I doing that? What do I think is gonna happen?'

So, the camera can represent a sort of mirror? A reminder about what you look like from the outside?

Yeah, totally.

What about the camera as the opposite of that? A sort of doorway through to the viewer?

It's so weird. I find I'm never *not* aware that there is a camera in the room. I will never go, 'Oh, I don't even notice there's a film crew here.' No, there's always an awareness of it. How much I touch my face in reality and how much I can touch my face in a shot is going to be different, because it's another language. I guess you have to be able to communicate with the camera as well. There is always an awareness and a respect for it. It's such an interesting question.

OK, you've got the camera there looking at you and you've got the danger that you've just described of it becoming a mirror, a kind of bounce-back at you. What about the eyes of the director during the process of shooting? Some directors look at the monitor, some try to look at the actors . . .

Yeah I've seen both . . . 'video village', and then the way *we* worked. You were there and you were close. On another movie we would be sent off in a scene with the camera strapped to the car and it wouldn't even be monitored. We wouldn't know if we got the shot till we came back. I like to know that the director's there. 'Video village' is a bit weird, but you get used to it. I can get used to most things.

Which do you prefer? What enables you to do your best work in your experience so far?

It doesn't matter, because I will always find a way. That's how I feel about it. In theory, I like having somebody there, to feel their presence . . . as long as they are communicating with you. That's really it . . . 'video village' is fine but you need to be able to communicate.

Between takes?

Yeah, yeah.

OK, so let's talk about feedback and communication. What kind of communication is useful to you, and what kind of communication is not useful to you?

When you get criticism like 'You looked like this,' it becomes 'I was judging you.' That can make me self-conscious. But I find that even when somebody has said that, you can use the provocation. Though I love the way you gave very simple directions, sometimes very exact, tiny things. I love it when a director has a very specific direction, because you can feel the intelligence. There was a time when you just told me to stay still . . . stop moving my hands or something, something *really* simple, and, it changed the whole physicality. I loved that. It excites me when I can see how much attention somebody is paying.

It was the second scene in the coffee shop, if I recall, and by not moving your hands, all the energy went into your interior life.

Exactly! That was exactly what it was. I get thrilled, I get turned on when there is something so specific to work from.

So, negative feedback: not very useful; general comments: not very useful; specific: good; detail: good . . .

It's all good. I completely understand though, when somebody is looking at you and they go, 'Something not's working, but I don't know what it is yet.' They may not have a specific comment, but it does help if they don't just say, 'Try something else.'

In that instance, when the director knows something's not working, but they don't yet know what it is, do you think it's most helpful – from the actor's point of view – for the director to be honest? And just say that?

I think so, generally, as long as there's movement. As long as you can then move then into, 'So let's change it all up,' or, 'Let's have coffee.' As long as there's a forward movement, as long as there's *hope*, you know! *[both laugh]*

We've talked about the pressures about female appearance, what about the pressures of youth? What misunderstandings have you encountered about what it's like to be a younger person on a film set?

When we were filming *Ginger & Rosa*, I had a chaperone, who was my godmother. It was wonderful, really nice, but of course, you know . . . you want to flirt with people and you can't. *[laughs]* When I turned eighteen I went off to New York and Los Angeles to promote things. I was away for about three months by myself and, *my God!* You realise *why* you have a chaperone when you're underage! *[both laugh]* It's like, just the amount of flings and things that I embarked on once I no longer had the chaperone. None of them bad experiences, but, my God, a set is like school camp when you were young. It's like everybody's on heat, you know. You form these strange attractions that you can't even understand later on. I find all that side of it interesting, because you have such a strange intimacy; you get pulled together and then sort of pulled apart. You share such intimate things and then you never see these people again. I'm used to that, I grew up with it. I like it, in a way. I'll be very intimate with someone and then like, 'Bye!' *[both laugh]* So I almost go, 'Intimate and bye!' instead of, 'Intimate and longevity,' or whatever.

So the end of a shoot for you is not a difficult experience.

It's sad, but it's how I know things to be. People who I love, I don't need to be around them. I understand that they're there somewhere. *[long pause]* It is interesting no longer having a chaperone, but I think I've probably been a bit audacious.

Totally understandable. Now that you're a little bit older and can look back on your younger self, what do you think directors need to understand about being a young actor? Things they might not be able to understand from the outside?

I've only ever been treated well, I think, on a film set. I've actually been impressed at the generosity. I've never been in a situation where I felt abused.

That's good!

I've seen a lot of gentleness and respect for young people.

Good. Glad to hear it!

But I don't think that is how it is . . . *[long pause]*

What, generally?

Yeah, because you can see the way that the TV industry and the film industry *can* treat kids. But I've worked with you, I've worked with my mum, and Richard LaGravenese was *so* generous and kind to us. Never patronising. He had such respect for all the young people. You showed amazing sensitivity and my mum works a lot with children and does it really, really well. So, yeah, I've seen good stuff.

What was that like for you as a child, growing up around your mother working with other children?

I don't think I was the age of any of the characters at the time, I was always a couple of years off. I was either too old or too young to feel any comparison, so there was never a rivalry, thank God.

What about your relationships with the other actors on set? How has that been for you?

Sometimes I have difficulty with male actors. I love and adore them, but with some young guys, it's lovely, but . . . the problem is, I have as big an ego as they do, and I don't like having to pet their ego, and they don't want to have to pet my ego, *they* want petting.

Is that what you've found?

Well, a lot of actors need a lot of attention. They're the most wonderful, beautiful, sensitive people: crazy, talented, I love them to death, but sometimes I just wanna slap them so hard. *[both laugh]* Sometimes they pull faces, they make jokes, they do dances, they pull pranks, for maybe like, forty minutes, and then they have to lie down. They exhaust themselves. *[laughs]* They're entertaining but you get exhausted being entertained as well. I find myself doing it too, sometimes. Presenting myself to people. You're entertaining, you're witty, and then, about three quarters of the way through filming, you just go like, 'I've used it all up! I've been as adorable and charming as this Alice character that I want to be. I'm done. I don't have anything else.'

Have you faced misogyny from other actors of any age, so far?

I've had difficulty, yeah. I *[sighs]* I don't really know what to say. *[long pause]* I've found that there is a liberty taken sometimes in filming. The way one actor talked about girls, constantly, in a way that felt like a reflection on me, and made it hard to feel safe. But I don't think that's an actor thing, I think that's just an arsehole thing. *[both laugh]*

Sure. What about when the film finally comes out and you all meet again and get to do press junkets, how is that whole side of the work for you?

I realised last year that the pay cheque you get for doing a bigger film, the fee for your acting services, is actually for doing the publicity. They pay you for how much you're going to sell it for them. Someone actually said it to me. I was like, 'I'm not going to do anything,' and they're like, 'No, you *have* to, this is your job too.' I didn't realise that publicising a film was my job but it is, apparently. *[laughs]*

When you're selling the film you're also being photographed and addressed as 'yourself'. Tell me about the experience that you've had of navigating that terrain.

I don't think publicity really does anything to help the film that much. And I find that if you try and be yourself, it's impossible! You *can't*, because it's not an environment where there's any room to be yourself. I found it was best not to even try. Emma Thompson said to me that when she was in a comedy group with Stephen Fry and Hugh Laurie, they would bang on a drum and say, 'Come see our show.' She said, 'You're still just banging on a drum, all you're saying is, 'Come see my show.' So, going into it with that in mind – 'Guys, I made a movie, we'd really like you to see it' – kept me sane. That's also why when I look at a script, I have to know that I can talk about it, and eventually talk to death about it.

So believing in it becomes one of the criteria for choosing it in the first place?

Yeah, I think so, but that's really just so that you don't do something for money. If you're going to do something, you want to make sure that you can do a good job and can do some work you want to share. And even if you fail, that you *tried* to achieve that. I don't think it's possible to know what a film is going to be. The blockbuster world is like meeting the parents. Film is the love of your life and you have to meet the parents. You don't have to like the parents, but you have to be polite to them. You just don't want to move in with them.

Do you think that there is a metaphysical or spiritual dimension to the work of acting? Do you have a sense of that?

Yeah, I do, more and more. Instead of feeling guilty about, 'Ooh, I'm escaping into acting,' I'm looking at the most basic sort of need. Why do we tell stories? Where does that come from? It comes from us. There's something about sitting in a dark cinema, as well. You can take the 'self' away in the darkness. It's been interesting for me recently to notice the purity in why I seek to do this.

ELLE FANNING

The search for the right teenage girl to play the lead role in *Ginger & Rosa* had been going on for a year (including over a thousand girls auditioning on Facebook), before I was introduced to Elle by Heidi Levitt. I had loved Elle in *Babel* (2006), a part she played when she was seven, and was startled by her vivid and touching presence in Sofia Coppola's *Somewhere* (2010). But as a blonde twelve-year-old living in Los Angeles I was concerned she might not be able to embody a sixteen-year-old redhead in a story set in London in 1962. Moments into our first meeting, as she launched into a difficult scene with confidence and courageous vulnerability, I needed no further convincing. My gut started to tremble and I knew I had found my Ginger.

The working process with her delivered even more than I had hoped for and we became very close. By the time we came to shoot she was all of thirteen – a year of her life had passed as the film went through the usual struggles of development – and the opportunity to work with a young woman at such a crucial moment in the evolution of her life's work was thrilling for me as a director.

Once the film was finished and we had navigated the sadness of separation from such an intense experience, and then, nearly half a year later, had stood up together in front of audiences at premieres, we met for this discussion in her home town of Los Angeles. At each of our meetings she had grown a little. She sat opposite me on the sofa – tall, blonde once again, following her transformation for our film into a redhead – confident and enthusiastic. The conversation repeatedly returned to our recent and still vivid experience of working together. I tried to keep the interview more 'objective' at first, but then surrendered to the impulse to talk in a more personal, direct way about what the experience had meant for her.

What do you love most about acting?

When I was really little, me and my sister used to play around the house and I loved imagining being something that I'm not. And when I was super-small I didn't know yet that there were actors and actresses. Then when I was older I realised, 'Oh that's a job, people really do that. I can grow up and I can do that.' *[SP laughs]* I've always loved acting because I feel comfortable imagining. It's just like dressing up and playing pretend. I like playing pretend.

So when you're playing pretend, how do you achieve something that feels real?

I try to get to know the person that I'm playing so well that it becomes like I can't react in any other way to a situation in the film, because that's just how my character would react. And I'm that girl, I'm that character.

Do you think that for children the pretend world, the play world, is in fact a serious and very real world?

I remember that it was sort of an escape, but then you get caught up in the different characters that you like to play. Or you have these imaginary friends and it's not like something separate, it's a part of your life. You could be talking to your mom in that character and she might not be able to tell the difference because it merges . . . all the different characters that you've been playing sort of merge into one to create you.

Pieces of a jigsaw. When you're thinking about doing a film, how important is the script to you?

It's important but I don't think it's everything. Reading the script is like a possibility. You read it and it's not how well it's written – maybe you like it because of that, but it's not just because of that. It's the story and to me it's always the strange, funny things in scripts that stick out. If a script makes me want to think about it – maybe if I don't understand it all the way, that makes me want to do it.

How much do you study a script before you think about doing it?

Normally I only read it once. That's in the beginning and it's sort of an instant thing. I feel like if you have to think about it then it's probably not something that you would want to do.

So it's an instinctive reaction.

Yeah it's instinctive, an immediate reaction that you get that intrigues you. It's not that it's good or bad, it's that it's interesting.

How about the first meeting with the director? How important is that?

I think that's *very* important.

Tell me about it.

I think that's more important than the script, because if you don't like the director, if your personalities don't click or you don't get a good vibe off someone, then you don't feel like all those possibilities that you liked when you read the script are possibilities any more. You feel it's not going to be creative in the way you thought it was going to be. You want it to be something that once you meet the director, is even better and then, after that, it's something that you just can't live without, because you love the person, more and more.

So when you have that first meeting with a director, what do you look for? What are you wanting to happen?

I want an openness, because I feel like I'm a pretty open person. I want to be open with the director because you're going to have to have such a strong relationship. And if you have a lot of hard scenes, with the harder emotions, you need someone that you feel comfortable with so you can open up and be yourself. A few times, I've met someone and I feel like I'm not myself around them and that's not good because I feel, 'How can I be another character when I can't even be myself around that person?' So you have to be able to be truly you and you have to see that the person is truly themselves as well. So you're being open and they're being open and from there it goes.

What's been your experience of auditions? Do you like doing them? Are they tough?

I've never really liked auditions, they've always scared me. I get so nervous, like being physically ill. I really get so scared even if someone's like, 'It's fine, don't worry . . .' Because even if someone says, 'It doesn't matter,' it matters to me. But if the audition goes well, it's one of the best feelings. You feel so accomplished. Like, 'I did the best that I could do.' But I do get so nervous beforehand and it's not a very enjoyable feeling.

What kind of things make you nervous?

Forgetting the lines, for example. And then I'm like, 'Why do I even worry about that?' Because when you eventually do the movie you often don't even end up saying the same things. So I do get nervous but the feeling afterwards is pretty great.

Did you feel that nervous when you met me?

Yes. *[laughs]* But you know what was different with you? I was so nervous beforehand, because we were going to do a lot of scenes, but then we did the scenes a couple of times and I felt a lot more comfortable. It was like we were on a set and you were giving me direction. Those are the best auditions when you get to do each scene about two or three times and you get to see how you guys work, how the director and the actor work together. Taking notes on things and getting feedback, that's when I feel more at ease.

Are there things you wished some directors knew about auditions that they don't seem to know?

I think that people are terrified – even if they don't seem like they are. I think everyone is. Maybe some directors do realise that.

What do you think can make it easier? Or do you think it even can be easier?

I don't think it can be easier. I don't think you can make it easier.
It's just that worry of, 'What are they going to think of me?' And
you're kind of thrown into a position of saying 'Hi', and then doing
the scene without even getting to know the person. So you're having to show all these emotions, which sometimes you haven't even
shown to your closest friend, and you're opening up to this person
who you've just said hi to in a room and they're all like staring at
you. *[SP laughs]* And you're showing all this stuff that you've never
shown anyone else before, just to try to be unique and memorable
and you're worrying, 'Am I being unique enough?'

What about learning lines?

I like the process of it. It's sort of like my textbooks. I have my
highlighters in different colours and I highlight all my lines. That
way you can kind of soak it in. And then I have to read it – and I
always have to do it in the bathtub – that's what I do, I learn my
lines in the bathtub.

That's lovely. So your body's relaxed.

Yes, my body's relaxed and I'm sitting there reading. If I'd look at
any of my pages now, they would all be soaked with water and all
the ink smeared. But once all the ink is smeared then I think, 'Oh
good, I've done my job.' And it's funny because the water makes
the lines go away, so it's hard for me to read them any more, but
then I know that I've absorbed it and can just say it. So that helps
me – and of course just going over it in my bed before I go to sleep
– because I think a lot in my bed, about everything. I remember
one time I had an audition the next day and it was really wordy, a
lot of paragraphs and stuff, and I didn't know it the night before.
I was thinking about it – and I feel like I was dreaming about it
– and the next day I knew the lines. It was just like I soaked it up
while I was sleeping. I woke up and knew them.

My experience of you was that you were always pretty much word-perfect anyway. So whatever it is you do to learn, it works.

With *Ginger & Rosa* I don't really remember ever having to learn the lines. I would look over the scene the night before . . . And I basically knew them. We did a lot of rehearsals, which helped.

You didn't have to consciously learn the lines because you knew the material so well?

It helps if you know why you're saying stuff and if you know the background of a scene. It's like, well, that's what you have to say because you're responding to something. You're talking about something you understand.

How important for you is the physical appearance of the character: the costume and so on?

It's very important to me. It doesn't matter that I feel comfortable. If your hair's a little odd or you are wearing something that you would never wear in your own life, then it's probably the right place to be, because you're someone else and that's how she would be. You have to capture that but it also has to feel natural, like you would wear it. But you have to feel sort of uncomfortable to feel comfortable.

So if it's right –

– it's right but wrong.

So working from the outside in is important for you, but is working from the inside out more important? The inner life of the character and so on?

I think it's more important to work from the inside out, because once you get to the outer part, which is what people see, you already know your inner part, so you can do the outer part very easily. If

you work from the outside in and you've already picked your costume, say, and then you get to know your character, you may find
the character would never wear that.

*So if you're working from the inside out, how important is rehearsal,
in your experience thus far?*

Before our movie, it wasn't that important to me, and now, after
filming with you, it seems extremely important – like the most
important. Because I don't think I would have been able to do anything that we did together if I hadn't done the rehearsals.

Why? Tell me about it. Let's figure out what was so valuable for you.

I think it was listening, because I didn't talk much during the
rehearsals. I remember people were arguing and not understanding
at first, and then they understood. It's about getting to know other
people's views, even of your own character. Looking way deeper at
all the layers and then building on that. And then also of course
getting to know the other actors before filming, because you have
to be so close with everyone. If you go in on the first day just having
met them one time before that, then you won't feel secure, maybe
even a little standoffish. You created an atmosphere where it's OK
to share your feelings, it's OK to share your opinions and I'm not
going to judge you. So the rehearsals were like a no-judgement
zone. And then also it's about reflecting back on memories too.
That day when you got me and Alice to talk about what our characters really thought of each other . . . that helped me a lot.

*When you went through the whole script – from memory – saying
aloud what you as the characters weren't saying in the text but wished
you could say to each other?*

Yes, that. Because I remember referencing back to that rehearsal
when we were filming. So even if I wasn't saying anything during

the scene, I could be thinking about that day, or about what Alice had said. It was like creating memories. Because my character has been on the earth for a lot of years and I'm just coming in there for about a month. So you have to create some memories, at least, and the rehearsals are the period where you can do that.

So you discover a condensed version of a whole life through the rehearsal period.

Yes, yes. After working like that with you, I'm sort of nervous to go onto something else where my character might be dealing with a lot of issues, if I won't have the time to do rehearsals. Obviously you could do it on your own but it's not the same.

What do you think you have internalised from the process, that you can take away with you, even if you don't get the structure of rehearsal that you would like? What do you think are the most valuable lessons?

For me it's questioning. Because we did a lot of questioning. And now I can take that away and feel more comfortable asking questions about things. Before in meetings with directors, they would ask, 'Do you have any questions about the script?' and I always said no . . . and then I'm like, actually I guess I do. But when I read the script I don't think of questions, I just think that's it and it can't be changed. But it can. So I can take away that I can question it and feel comfortable asking, because it can always be changed. It's just paper, you know.

How would you describe the particular challenges that you faced as a younger actor? You've been a working actor through so many different stages of childhood.

It's either not paying attention to me or paying attention to me way too much. Treating me so carefully, like, every step asking, 'How was that for you? Was that OK?' It's like, 'Yes.' *[SP laughs]* You don't need to do that. You can just treat me like everyone else. I'm here doing the same thing as the other actors.

You just happen to be younger.

Yes, I just happen to be younger. But they're obviously trying to be nice, which is fine and I am young, but still my mind-set is not really on that. I thought of myself as a part of everyone else so I didn't like to be singled out.

What do you long for in a director? What do you wish more directors understood about you as a younger performer?

I wish that sometimes they would care about my ideas a bit more. Because in a weird way, even though they're older than me, sometimes I have a different insight and maybe that insight could help and not just be like, 'Oh you're just a little kid, commenting on something.' Sometimes I have an idea and I want to try it, and they won't let me. I feel like, 'No, let me experiment, because I know I can do it, I can show you and I can make it work.' Then, if it doesn't work, it doesn't. But I wish they would be open to accepting ideas that could maybe enhance, or could also make it worse.

So to be more respectful. And to give you the space to offer up ideas.

Yes. And I think it's never good to get into a routine of a scene. If you start doing the same things too many times, then the words become not even words, just sounds that you're saying. And in a weird way if that happens and you don't spice it up, then you start saying it in the same rhythm every time. You need to be able to try different ways as well.

What do you think are the most important things the director needs to know to get the best out of you?

To sometimes just let me take it all in a little bit and step back and feel the moment, instead of asking me questions about the moment. Just have like a silence – I don't mean everyone on the set. I feel a little uncomfortable if it's big scene with a lot of emotion and everyone goes quiet. I like it when I really feel like I'm on a movie set with the camera and everyone is working. It helps me to know that people are doing things and not just waiting on me. Like I don't ever want them to say, 'Oh, let Elle have a moment.' That doesn't help because then you feel pressure like, 'Oh, they're all waiting on me to find an emotion.' I always say, 'Whenever you're ready, then I'll be ready too.' I don't need everyone to be silent and staring at me. *[laughs]* That doesn't help! *[both laugh]* It's nice if I can sit down in a corner and think, and whenever they say, 'Elle, we're ready to shoot,' then I'll just go and we'll start.

How much do you draw on your own direct memory when you have to work on a big emotional scene?

I find that thinking back on my experiences probably doesn't help me. It gets my brain too scattered with a lot of memories when I need to just focus on something. And it's never a memory I need to focus on. For me it's that moment, that time of standing or sitting and feeling the vibe around me, feeling with all the senses. I rely a lot on my senses. Just focusing in and blocking everything out, but also taking everything in at the same time.

That's really interesting. So for you the clue to getting into an emotional scene is actually being in the present moment.

Yes. Completely. It's a funny thing, sometimes I feel like I can't be too heavy or too sad about it because then it just won't happen. I need to feel a lot of different emotions. After the take you can't stay in the same mood, you have to let go and laugh and that will help you get back into it. If you're happy or you feel something different for a while it will help you.

Do you think that the working regulations for child actors have helped with that because you have to stop every hour or so to do lessons?

Yes. I honestly think it helps. When we were doing the huge scene in *Ginger & Rosa* and I went down and did math and then came back up and carried on filming, it made me think about something completely different for a while, and it helped. The fact that you have to be completely focused on something else as well is good too. You're so in there and then it's like restarting, like at the beginning of the day. Because the beginning of the day is often the best, it's the newest, it's the freshest. So being able to stop and do something else is like beginning the day again. You come back, but you've not been thinking about it too much for a while, which is good.

You were telling me the other day that some of the other actors were worried that the big emotional scene was too much for you. Tell me your thinking about that.

I guess I can see why they would think that, but for me it's so not. It's like a spiritual thing in a way. It's very cleansing to express the emotions at the highest point. It's honestly not traumatic at all. Like not even a little bit. *[SP laughs]* It doesn't affect me in that way at all. I knew when I read the script that there were a lot of scenes like that. So it's like – OK, we're going to do that one day. No, it didn't hurt me at all.

You said it's spiritual. Talk a little bit more about that – and what it means to you.

It's like an out-of-body experience, because you're not looking at yourself. You do later, when the movie comes out, but at the time you're not. You have to look inside yourself so much that it feels like you're looking down at yourself. And you discover things that you might not have otherwise discovered while you're in those moments. And it brings up a lot of questions. Having to do big scenes like that feels cleansing and then afterwards you get to know yourself even better than you did in the days before. I remember when I came back to do the ADR, I felt like I had grown up a little bit more because I had experienced those scenes.

You've grown up through the film?

Through the film and in myself because I had a lot of new experiences that I had never had before. It made feel older. I have never felt that before, never. You know people ask you on your birthday, 'Do you feel older?' but I felt older after filming. Because I don't think I have ever, on a movie set, expressed so much until our film. I'm pretty open, but I had never been that open before. And I was like, 'Wow, I shared a lot of things with so many different people.' I guess it just made me grow up. My ballet teacher actually said that, right when I walked in when I got back to Los Angeles. She said, 'You're way more mature than you were before.' Like, 'What did you do over there?' *[laughs]* It just sort of opened my eyes.

You said you look inside a lot when you're working. At the moment of shooting, does it feel as if a part of you is also thinking and observing what you're doing? Or are you just in that moment?

It's more beforehand that I'm looking inside. When I'm filming I honestly lose a concept of time. I don't even realise how long it's been. I'm just in it and then afterwards, after you've said 'Cut', that's when I can look back and see how I could improve. But once you're there, you're just there and there's no turning back from that point. You're just doing the scene.

What do you find are the most useful notes or directions in between takes, and also what are the really not useful things?

I think it's better not being too detailed. When you've gotten to know a director well, it's like they can just do a little hand signal and you know exactly what they're talking about. It could be as simple as that. But if they say, 'Place your hand just like that,' then you feel you've sort of lost your freedom. But if you bring in another layer, one more thing to think about, like, 'Remember what was happening in the scene before this' – that's helpful. Just thinking about the previous scene would make your hand go somewhere it wanted to.

So, in other words, notes about the inner life are more helpful to you.

Yes.

And what about useless directions. What is your worst dread?

Wow!

It's helpful for directors to know about. It really is.

I think that it's maybe being too particular about which emotions to feel at any one time. Like, 'Oh and then you get happy, so you smile there.' Or, 'That makes you mad.' Why does it make me mad or why am I smiling? Maybe I don't feel like smiling. Just let it happen the way it's going to happen. You don't want it to seem like a fake thing, or that you're just doing it because someone told you to.

What do you think are the key ingredients to developing an atmosphere of real trust with the director so that a hand signal or nod becomes possible, that kind of shorthand?

It probably takes more than two or three meetings to really get there. Because in the first one there is something about them that you like and then in the second one you realise why you like them and then in the third one you're like, 'Now I can begin to be close.' And it's not always that you're so much like the person. It doesn't even have to do with movies. It's just like how you would choose friends. It's the details of how they are which makes you want to be with them. And if you want to be with a person all the time, of course something is going to develop and you're going to feel comfortable.

When you're approaching events and situations that you have not directly experienced in your life, what do you do?

I try to put myself in the person's shoes and I try to understand the concept as much as possible. Like with ours: how it felt living back in that time, and fearing that the world was ending. So I first try to put myself in that position and think how I would feel . . . though it's not so much what you would feel, it's what they're feeling. But you have to get in touch with yourself first before you can get in touch with the person that you're playing.

And you make a distinction between the two?

I make a definite distinction between the two. Then there's always something that you have in common to add in and that helps you, something you both relate to, so it becomes more personal, and that's what makes it real, I guess.

How do you feel when you watch yourself on screen?

I'm sort of OK with it. I feel like I'm someone else but when I start to pick up on things that I do in my real life, like hand gestures – then that makes me a little uncomfortable. And it's funny watching the movie and seeing how subtle things look, when inside my body it felt *huge*. And it's like, 'That's what I looked like when I was doing that?' Like it wasn't a bad thing but it just looked a lot smaller than it felt while filming.

That's a very important point about how subjectively something feels and then objectively how it looks. That's when the director comes in, right?

Right.

Sometimes we can feel the intensity of interior life through the actor's restraint. It's a direction I often give – 'Don't try and show it – just feel it and think about it and we will feel it too.'

I felt like I was feeling it so much that there was no way that it wasn't going to show like crazy in my face. I remember there was a particular scene – on the boat when they were talking and I was watching and Roland said, 'Isn't this boat marvellous?' I felt like I was feeling so much, like, 'What's going on? What's this? What's that?' but it came off a lot more subtle.

Yes, but it's very tense.

Oh yes it's super-tense.

And in your face – we feel it.

It just felt so much larger. Maybe that's just me because I'm watching myself.

No, we as an audience do feel that largeness. It feels incredibly real and we get drawn into what Ginger's feeling by the power of how strongly you were feeling it. You've worked with a lot of directors already. What advice would you give to young actors about how to get the best out of that relationship?

Don't be afraid of them. I think that there's a stereotype of directors. That they're just like screaming all the time and have the hat and the chair, with the megaphone. *[SP laughs]* And I think that's because you see pictures – and they did look like that back then. I've never had anyone be mean to me but you do feel a little scared and feel like they have all the power over you and you have to do whatever they say. And I'm just starting to learn that instead of it being like a king, controlling you and ruling you, it's more like a partnership. It has to be a strong partnership for it to work. It will show if you're just performing because someone is telling you to. You have to be able to feel comfortable to be the other half of someone else. So you have to come into it with 'it's OK, you're your own person'. The director of course knows more about the story than you do, especially if they've written it. And they've lived with it longer than you have, so definitely listen and respect all of that, but you can also put your insight in. It doesn't have to be about some strong person yelling at you all the time. And also it's not really like that anyway, so don't prepare yourself for that. It won't be like that.

What does truth mean to you in acting?

I think the truth is basically everything. It's like confidence, being comfortable with being yourself and being able to be free and real. If something comes at you in a scene, that you're not expecting, you're able to come back with something that's natural and real and not have a guard up, or a barrier. It's just letting it all down and being naked and letting it hit you. It's not about performing all the time. You just take it in and react the way you would react. It doesn't have to be a huge deal – not everything is a huge deal in different scenes – some things can just be there and true in that way. Yeah, just don't have a barrier.

Let's say the film is finished – what about the attention coming your way as a consequence of the work? What effect does that have on you? Does it feel connected with the work or does it feel like a completely separate entity from the work?

I think that after filming, from right when you wrap, it's that feeling of, 'I want to see the movie, I want to see the movie. What's it going to be like?' And then you see the movie for the first time and it's really sad to me, because I feel like I'm never going to get back that feeling of before I saw the movie, when it was just something that was out there. I knew I had filmed it but I didn't know what it would look like. So when you see it for the first time, you're so happy, it's like a wish came true, but it's also . . . *[pauses]*

. . . a feeling of loss?

A little bit a feeling of loss, because you miss what you felt like before. And then when you do all the promotional bits, it's exciting to see what other people think and also reunite with the cast again – it's more of a fun experience. I don't know if it relates so much to the film. It's a separate part, it feels different. And as much as you try to explain in interviews what it was like shooting the film, they're never going to understand because they weren't there. They'll never get it.

If they could get it, what is it that you wish they could understand?

I wish that they would understand that for me it really is not like 'the glamorous movie'. For me it's something that's so different. You're thrown together with these people and you always come out of it feeling like you just created a huge family together and you've created a baby and everyone's put their heart and soul into it. They're only there because they want to be there. Especially with our film. I felt like they were there because it was a special story that they wanted to tell. I guess you can tell what makes a film good, because everyone works so hard. I wish people could understand just how strong the relationships are, and that it's definitely work. That's what you want people to know: the work that went into it, because people don't normally understand that.

People just think it's learning lines, then turning up and standing on a mark saying your lines, but it's not that at all. To me it's the behind-the-scenes stuff that they will probably never get. I think that with our film a lot of people thought we just sat around and were sad all the time. We had those moods but then we snapped right back out of the mood within a second and everyone was laughing.

Do you think that's a general misunderstanding as well, not just about the sheer volume of work, and the pressure of it, but also what work really means? What does work mean to you?

I definitely think I worked most on this film, meaning that I got to know the person I was playing, plus the other actors in the film and the characters that they were playing, more than I ever have before. I got to know all the other people's personalities. That was due to the rehearsals: them talking about their characters and being there to hear it. And I got to absorb and think about things. It would come in bursts of, 'Oh yeah, Ginger could do that and I could draw on my experience . . .' Because you had me thinking – I remember in the second meeting you gave me a homework assignment, because I said I was going to have a sleepover with my best friend the next night. And you said, 'Oh maybe you could pick up on things that you guys do together.' And I was like *[gasps]* 'I'm going to do this,' because it was like an assignment that you had given me. I remember at her house I was thinking about what we do, because I really wanted to contribute something in that way. So it was work because I was thinking about it as much as I could.

What's the most joyful part of the whole process and what's the most painful part of the whole process?

I love all of it, I just love it. The most joyful part is to try and make people understand a story that they've never heard before.

Because people go to the theatres – sometimes they've seen a trailer, sometimes not – and you're telling them a story from beginning to end and you're getting to act it out and also have people enjoy what you've been doing. And when you're shooting you get to meet everyone and travel to really cool places. And be able to get so close to someone. Because there's always someone on the set who you get extremely close to, that you know that you'll see later. Even if you don't stay in contact with them, you know if you see them on the street, it will all come rushing back. It's like making little micro-memories that you can relate back to. Sometimes I see a colour, a random object and it brings me back to a film, to that fun time or that difficult time and that's what I like.

And the most painful aspect?

I think the most painful aspect is being torn apart at the end. That's hard. It's always hard for me. That's definitely the most painful. Because you've seen each other every day, like every single day for months, and when someone says it's over, it's over, that's it. And you don't really ease away either. 'It's wrapped' – and then the next day you're flying home and it's like, 'Whoah! I'm back home now and I'm not going to wake up and go to the set tomorrow.' It takes a while to get over that, a couple of grieving days, I think.

Only a couple? [laughs]

No, a lot!

Do you think your dance training has affected your approach to work?

I think it has – I started when I just turned nine. It's the discipline of dance training that I think makes me discipline myself when I work, so I can be tuned in all the time. And also being in touch with your body – to be able to show different emotions with your body – because it's so expressive. Even if you slouch. It's not to do with good posture, it's to be able to show you're nervous or worried. Dancing makes you in touch with that.

And what about the sports background in your family, do you think that has also helped?

I think it has. Because my parents have that sports background, they've influenced me and my sister to know that hard work equals results. Even if it might feel really difficult at the time, you're going to be so happy with the end result and proud of all that hard work. It's a lot worse not to do anything, then have a bad product and feel bad about it afterwards. The sports background helps in that way. Sports people have a real practice schedule and a film set is like that. Filming is like a practice, it's not like a play. You get to do multiple takes, so it's like you're practising each time. Each take is a practice. And then you get it. Out of all of those takes, maybe the seventh take, 'Oh yeah that was the good one, we got it.'

The relationship between actor and director – this is difficult to talk about because we've just been working together. But maybe that's OK. [EF laughs] What was it like? [both laugh]

[Elle laughs – they hug] I think with you it was . . . *[sighs]* we're both girls so we could relate in that way. And I felt like I could talk to you about anything, even not to do with the film. I felt like I could really trust you. I could talk about anything that was going on in my life. And that helped me to feel so open towards you that I could express anything. And also we got so close and it was because we really bonded together from our first hug. It was just there. And being in East London you were in your element, but I wasn't in mine, so you were showing me around your place. And me being away from home, you were like my home, my centre at that time, and that made me feel comfortable.

Do you think that ideally that should be the core of an actor/director working relationship? Do you believe that trust and openness are the essential conditions for doing good work?

I think that a hundred per cent. Definitely. You have to be able to relate on a human level so that you can just be yourself, plus more, plus your character.

Did you also experience cutting through to what lies beneath the surface, going beyond what is normal in an everyday relationship? And cutting through it really fast?

Yes, you have to speed up the 'hello, how are you?' process. You have a connection because you both love film. You have to learn to look through someone and get to know them very fast, to be able to jump into it. It all speeds up . . . and then it goes so slow. Once you're filming you get to really experience people. With you I felt like we got to know each other really fast and then, while we were filming, we took it step by step, one point at a time.

So time slowed down . . .

. . . and we got to know each other better and better even though we sort of rushed it in the shoot. But you have to dive right into it together.

CHRISTINA HENDRICKS

Long before I met her, Christina's portrayal of Joan in *Mad Men* had me gripped and entranced. I looked forward to seeing her poise, strength and apparently confident physicality in every episode. I also found, paradoxically, that her qualities provoked a protective feeling in me. It was partly this response that led me to feel she might be right for the role of Natalie in *Ginger & Rosa*, a role that was so utterly different from the one she had become associated with. Christina sent me a stunning rendition of a scene, which managed to communicate Natalie's suffering without at all playing a victim. When we spoke on the phone later, her approach to Natalie was original and refreshing. She said she saw Natalie as a woman of great spirit who had simply been 'dampened' by the time and circumstances she lived in.

Christina turned out to be an extremely hard worker, schooled in the relentless precision of television production schedules. She was also great fun. Dancing with her at our wrap party in a pub in East London was joyous. But I also witnessed the invasive quality of people's interactions with her and the effects on her of her pursuit by paparazzi.

We managed to find a time in her packed shooting schedule to speak on Skype. She was reclining on a bed, leaning against a white wall, somewhere in Vermont – unmade-up, unadorned, and radiant. I was in my studio in East London. Even on my small computer screen the quality of light reflected on her skin was dazzling.

What do you hope to find when you get sent a script?

I hope to find a character that is fully established and with language that I feel people truly speak in, so that as I'm reading it doesn't become a struggle of how to interpret it, or change it. A script that is fully realised.

Which is more important to you, the script or the director, when you're choosing to do a film?

That's difficult, because if you find a script that you really love and you don't know who the director is, you'll find a million reasons to convince yourself why that's OK. And if you're not that sure about the script, but you love the director, then you feel like that director's going to take care of the parts of the script that you're not sure about. So you can justify both, I think.

What about the first meeting with the director if you haven't met them before? What clues are you looking for to feel this might work?

If it's a director that I know and respect, I'm just trying not to say something stupid. *[laughs]* If it's a director that I've never met before, I'm looking for clues of how prepared they are and how well they seem to know the characters rather than just the technicalities. I really enjoy it when they start to talk about the relationships between the characters, because then I trust that when I'm going to have those questions, they'll have the answers. It's a strength of competence on their part.

How is the process of being up for a role before it's definite? You're in this kind of 'limbo land' before it all goes ahead. How do you deal with that?

Well, sadly, I feel that I have very little power in that regard. Luckily I have a manager that I trust very much and who is good at following up with people. I'll call him, especially with something that I'm passionate about, probably a couple of times a week, and I'll say, 'Have you heard? Did they call you?' If we feel we need to send over a project that I've done as a back-up, like, 'Look, she did this too,' we'll do that. When you're in that limbo period, I think the offer's probably out to someone else and you're waiting because you're on standby. Or maybe there's a struggle between the producer, the studio and the director. I think people generally have a very strong feeling about who they want. I could be wrong – that's a question to you.

Often, but not always. Sometimes it's about working out an ensemble. What about auditioning in its various forms and guises?

I absolutely despise auditioning. I think I'm not very good at it. Everything weighs on that one moment. I often start and then stop after a few moments because I feel I started out in the wrong way.

I'd rather just reboot, and then give the performance that I was hoping for. I sometimes wonder if that's been detrimental to me, but I'd rather they didn't see that horrible first performance that I was about to deliver, which felt false and anxious and strange. Often you've been waiting in a room next to other people who are up for the same part, so you start to compare yourself to them, especially if they're better known than you. And of course you feel they're going to choose that person. You can get yourself worked up and then that can work against you.

How do you think directors and casting directors could make the auditioning process more humane?

I love when a casting director has a reader in there who's an actor. Then I feel like the casting director can actually watch you. Often they're reading with you and they're looking at the page half the time. They put you on camera, but sometimes they're trying to watch you and read as well and you go, 'Sorry, that's my line.' To act to a flat performance of someone staring at a piece of paper makes no sense to me. Acting is about listening and hearing and having a conversation with someone. So to me, having an actor to read with is incredibly important, but it's rare. You can't ever expect it. So when you prepare for an audition you have to anticipate not only working on your own material, but also working on the pretend reaction of the other person.

What do you wish that directors understood about the auditioning process from the actors' point of view?

Most actors have a similar complaint after we leave an audition. We go in, we do it once and they go, 'Thank you very much, that was great.' Then you get a message from your manager saying, 'They really wish you'd done it a little bit more like this,' and you think, 'Well I'm a goddamn actor, give me a note while I'm in the room!'

When I'm given the material I have a hundred options, a thousand options, a million options, and I've chosen this one. I've never met you, I don't know the tone, I'm making all these guesses. So often they just want the answer to walk in the room and I don't think that's fair. So I wish directors would spend a little time. It doesn't have to be a work session, but give some notes, and let me try it again. Actors want to work, we want the opportunity, it's fun for us. Maybe some people would take notes as criticism, but I think most of us take it as an opportunity.

Let's assume you've got the role. How can the director best help you prepare?

Depending on the project, you don't always get a rehearsal period. When you do it makes all the difference in the world.

Why and how?

As with auditioning, there are a million choices. When you're all on the same page, talking the same language, there is a shorthand when you get to the set. The time that we had in London, and the time that I had just now in Detroit were extraordinary. We all knew what our relationships were when we walked on set. The film I'm doing in New York right now, we're still asking those questions just before we do a scene and the director is surprised that we're asking. Therefore you're working it out in takes, which I think is a waste of film, a waste of everybody's time. And the anxiety that it brings to the room is not appropriate. Being able to sit in rehearsal and talk about history and back-story and *why*, when you're playing make-believe, I think *has* to happen. If you've had a moment, and shared something that was real, it will translate. I believe that.

How important is working from the outside in for you? Appearance, clothes, hair and make-up and so on?

I think the way we present ourselves in our lives says very much about who we are and so it certainly also says very much about who our characters are. Hair and make-up is a little less influential to me, but dress I think is important. It tells us how that character wants the world to see them, or how they feel about themselves, so it's a huge tool. It's the first thing an audience sees and they have an immediate reaction to your appearance and your demeanour. Most actors would say that they get very hands-on and personal with it and that's why the costume designer and the actor have a very intimate relationship. Sometimes it can be rocky because the costume designer can have a strong feeling of something and if the actor has a very strong but different feeling, you will butt heads. It should really be a collaboration.

Do you like it when a director is engaged in that step-by-step, careful preparatory work?

The director's had the material in their mind for far longer than you, so when they are involved in the process, you learn what they feel about the character. For me, it's about getting constant clues that I can string together to develop this person. As many clues as I possibly can. And so, if the director is like, 'I think that she would wear this . . . and she would always wear a belt,' you think, 'Well, why does she always wear a belt? That's interesting.' And then, if the director, once they've cast you, adjusts what's in their mind to what suits you, it's wonderful.

And the work from the inside out? You talked about asking questions and thinking about back-story in the rehearsal process. What about other aspects of working from the inside?

I've started working with an acting coach, something I've never done before. Her process is working with dreams. And it's not dream analysis *per se*, but giving yourself a dream assignment about the project you're working on and the clues that your mind gives you, when you wake up, about how you are emotionally responding to the material. It gives you a place to start. Sometimes you open a script and you think, 'Where do I begin?' It can be so daunting, especially if you don't have a rehearsal period and you don't get to sit and talk with the director.

What pushed you into deciding to work with a coach?

The director on the project in Detroit (Ryan Gosling) hired her to work with all of us. He works with her all the time and he had used her in the process of writing the script. We all sat in a room together and then we acted things out with one another and went through the emotions we were feeling during that time. Some people would say it was like acting school, but I never did that, so it was new to me and incredibly helpful. I realised how important it was to be vocal, because you ask yourself a million questions but if you do them out loud, somehow it's more helpful than sitting there thinking about it alone.

Do you think in an ideal world you'd do that intimate work with the director?

Oh yeah. It would be phenomenal! Ryan was there with us for the entire process as well, so it was all integrated. And with *Ginger & Rosa*, sitting at your table the day that you said, 'Ask someone else the questions that aren't in the script that you would like to ask them.' That's a similar kind of work: getting intimate and not being so literal, being vulnerable enough and feeling silly enough to ask the questions. If you're an adult and you're working with Annette Bening sitting there, for God's sake, and Sally Potter sitting there, you don't want to look like an arsehole. And yet you allow yourself to do it, you become vulnerable immediately and you get the answers that you need. I found it enriching and incredibly useful. Even more useful than just going through the lines, which is also important.

So in a way it's the spaces between the lines and the context around the lines that gives you the ground from which to work?

Yeah, and I found that knowing what it feels like to have a question asked, or to be looked at like that by another actor, as we did that day, was very useful later, doing the actual scene. Someone asks you a question and you think, 'Oh, that's how that character feels – or that's how that actor playing that character feels – and I'm going to remember that when they look at me in the shoot.' Because you can be intellectual about the lines, but if you feel the underlying hurt or the yearning that the actor or character is feeling, it's more emotional.

In contacting the emotional layers of a character, how much do you find that you draw on your own personal memories and experiences?

I would say, almost always. There are some things that are written that are very easy to relate to and feel and you just do, but most of the time these characters are going through things that I have not experienced. Rather than conjuring up a memory of my own I try to conjure up the feeling attached to that memory and then apply it to what the character's feeling.

When you talk about your character, what do you think a character really is? Is it also you? Is it you grafted onto this fictional other? How do you relate to this other 'self'?

It's a very confusing thing. A character can only be an interpretation of what I've learned and known in the world, so the character is limited by my experience. Some people will say, 'Oh, that actor always plays the same character,' and sometimes I say, 'But are they? Or are they just being very natural with their interpretation of what that person is going through?' It's tricky. It's very, very tricky. You have to bring what you know, with everything that you're feeling, into new circumstances. If you were this person, you had a different accent and you lived in a different city and you were brought up in a different way, it's still essentially how you would be in those circumstances. That's all we have.

What do you need from the director during the shoot?

I respond much better to a director that's really listening to the performance. Some directors are quite technical. They are concerned with many other things at that point and leave you to do your thing. I need someone who's really listening *emotionally* to the performance. To say, 'And knows how to speak to an actor' is such a broad term, but there is a way to ask an actor to do something.

What is that way?

If the director is truly in tune with the story and truly knows the character, then it's quite easy for them to say, 'Let's think about this, what about . . . ?' An actor responds to that. There's nothing worse than someone just going, 'That's so great, but faster.' That is the weirdest note! That is not a human note. That kind of thing makes you crazy, but when it really is about story and emotion then the actor responds. I *like* notes. And I don't know an actor alive that doesn't love a little bit of encouragement at the end of a scene like, 'That went well.' You want a little feedback and a lot of directors don't give it. They're just like, 'Great, we got it, let's move on,' and we're all like, 'But did it go well? Are you happy? Did it happen?' You know, we want a little . . .

A little pat on the back?

Yeah! We're a very, very needy group. *[laughs]*

I think it's very reasonable to want feedback when you've just given so much.

It's extraordinarily emotional and you're doing it in front of a room full of people who are worrying about what they're doing, making sure that the focus is right and the lighting is right and so on. Everyone's doing their job, and you're pouring your heart out and no one's saying anything and then you move on. It's strange. It is nice for someone to come up and go, 'Great, we've got it, this really worked.' Then you think, 'OK, I did my job right.'

What about the director looking at you during a take, as opposed to looking at the monitor? Does that make a difference to you?

I can sometimes be distracted by a director if I can see them in front of me. I am aware that there are going to be people in your eye-line, doing their business all around you, but when it's the director right in front of you, I feel the need to perform for them, rather than for the character or the story. I feel like I'm looking for approval, which is distracting. Yeah, I get distracted by wanting to make them happy.

Is that because of what you're seeing on their face, or it's just inherent in the relationship?

I think it's both. As an actor, you're an observer. You're constantly watching people's behaviour, and even if their face isn't changing, there's body language and you know when someone's happy and when they're not.

So directors should be more aware of what they're communicating?

Yeah, or not. Maybe they want you to know if they're happy, or not.

What else is important for directors to understand?

I need to feel like I can say anything. I need to feel comfortable enough to come and hug you in the morning without feeling self-conscious about it. I need to be able to say, 'You know what? I was thinking about this all last night and I need to talk to you about it.' With some directors you feel like you don't know what your relationship is yet and that you have to tiptoe around. That doesn't work for me, because I feel like then I'm constantly trying to get approval in order to get into that comfortable space. You can't be scared of a director. It's a very powerful role and the director needs to make everyone comfortable. *[pauses]* And whatever you say, we will remember for ever, because we're incredibly sensitive beings. When you say something it will affect us greatly.

What about awareness of the camera itself? How aware are you of the lens?

I've actually been able to block it out quite a bit. It is a very large and obtrusive object but you have to pretend it isn't there. Obviously if it's a close-up and the camera's right there, there's nothing you can do, but sometimes there will be several cameras going and I intentionally don't look to see where they are. I try to just do the performance each time, even if I'm off-camera. I try to do the scene as if I'm in a play. If the camera's there to catch it then it will be there, and if not, then I will have had a rehearsal.

Is it helpful to know what lens it is?

I don't know jack about that. Every once in a while, if I'm in an interview or a commercial, I'll ask, 'How tight is it?' just so that I don't worry about the physicality of my body or to make sure my hands are placed in a certain kind of way. If there's a scene that's intimate, maybe a love scene, I'll ask the make-up artist to keep an eye on me. I'll say, 'Let me know if I'm doing something weird with my leg. I don't want to think about it, so could you think about it for me and come and tell me to adjust something that's awkward?' Then the audience isn't distracted by awkwardness. It becomes a nicer image, a nicer painting.

What about the question of appearance, given the amount of pressure there is about this, particularly on women. What specific challenges do you think you face as a female actor or actress? You use the word actress don't you?

I do, yeah. I know some people are against that but I am the female version, so I use actress.

Fine by me!

[laughs] Listen, you try to make sure the clothes are as flattering as they can be. You try to make sure that your good bits are complemented and your bad bits are hidden. Once you're on camera it's going to catch everything. You're in 360° all the time, so there's nothing you can do. You just have to say, 'This is who I am. I'm gonna act the shit out of this and if you're sitting there worrying about my body or my face or my hair then either I'm not doing my job or your priorities are off.' But we all do it. We are all influenced by image.

And the actor's body is their medium, right?

It is and you have to be aware of how it affects people. Therefore, when you choose your costume, or you choose how you walk, or how you lean towards someone, you have to be aware that your physicality is part of that and will always be and that's one of your great tools.

Do you think that a happy shoot is necessary or a bonus? Do you think it bears any relationship to the final result?

I don't know that the audience can see it in the end result either way. I think when you go back and watch it yourself, all you can do – if it was a bad experience – is conjure up what that process was. So it's hard for you as an actor to watch it and think, 'Oh that scene went well,' because all you're thinking is 'That was the worst day!' You can't watch it honestly. But I don't know if the audience knows, because I've had those experiences where I'm like, 'Oh no! That scene!' and then people go, 'But that scene was so great!' So I don't know if it translates.

How do you navigate the fact that the shoot is such an intense process, the relationships are so intense and then, suddenly, it's over? What does that mean to you and how do you deal with it?

I often maintain a lot of those relationships. Sometimes I can't just say goodbye. It's important for me to have those people and those memories in my life. But I understand that not everyone can do that. A lot of people need to move on. There's also a certain *relief* to the end of some of it because it *is* so intense that you think, 'Ah, OK. We did it. We can wrap it up. Let's all give each other a big hug. We really did the shit out of this.' *[both laugh]* And then you can move on emotionally too. *Ginger & Rosa* was really just, every day, tugging on your heart-strings. Putting yourself in that place every day is a *lot*. I got a phone call from my mum the other day. I was on set in the film that I'm working in now. After the third scene, my son dies, and the entire film is me grieving, suspecting foul play and trying to get answers – it's *so* intense. I checked my voice messages. My mum said, 'You haven't called your grandmother yet to thank her for the birthday gift she gave you,' and I thought, 'Are you fucking kidding me? Do you understand what I'm doing every day? I'm in every scene and I'm like *this*!' I don't think people understand, even if they love you. Thank God my husband's an actor so he does understand. It is *so, so*, intense! We're *living* that! Every second. So sometimes, when it's done . . . thank God!! Thank God it's over!

*And what about when you all meet again when the film is done.
How do you feel about watching yourself on the screen?*

I am, of course, immediately critical. But I learn a lot from watching my own performance. Often I'll think, 'Oh God, that's really weird. I thought I was projecting this and it came across like that,' and that's interesting to know. I also find the edit very interesting. You think that you've done a certain performance and you feel, 'I would never have chosen that take.' But they've been in that room for a million hours and they've chosen it for a specific reason. You have to acknowledge that and see how it applies to the storytelling, so I find it very educating.

*What about the interface with the press, the publicity and the
junkets, which is a huge part of the work these days. How do you feel
about all that?*

I feel like you bounce into a different person. There is you as a performer, an artist and an emotional being, and then you have to pop into 'politician mode'. People are going to say the most bizarre things to you about the performance and about the movie when you're still raw from it. It's so important to you, and they say shit that will hurt your feelings, left, right and centre, even if they think it's a compliment. It is so strange. What dress you're wearing to the party becomes more important than your performance, sometimes. I'm not particularly fond of it all, to be quite honest, but I'd be naive not to realise it's the business side, and this is the full career. You don't just go and do the art bit, you have to do the whole thing. And if you're going to do it, you might as well do it well.

*What about fame and celebrity? How has that affected you? How has
it affected your work? What's it done to your real feeling of purpose?*

Well fame has gotten me work, so, I thank it for that.

That's a good attitude!

I walked into a million rooms where they were sifting through headshots, looking for my résumé and eating a sandwich during my audition. Now they listen when I audition and when I walk in they go, 'We love your show!' So they already have a positive feeling, which is amazing. So I have to thank it for that. I don't think it affects my performance. I don't think about it while I'm working. But it does make me unhappy, I have to say. It's such a double-edged sword. It gives you so many opportunities and it makes life so easy in so many ways. It makes the airport *really* great. *[SP laughs]* It makes travelling so much better!

Why, what happens?

People take your luggage and walk you places and you don't stand in long lines . . . it's ridiculous how much better it is. And yet you always feel a little bit like you're being hunted. You always feel like someone wants you to fuck up and they're going to be there to capture it on film. I got out of a cab the other day and I hadn't even looked up yet and someone was in front of my face with a cellphone, so close that I thought something was being thrown at me. I was startled and my immediate reaction was, 'What the fuck are you doing?' and he goes, 'Oh, I love you, I wanna take your picture,' and I said, 'How rude to push your phone in my face like that!' – and then my reaction afterwards was that I shouldn't have spoken to him like that because he's going to tell everyone I'm a bitch. I felt attacked and scared but I was worried that I didn't come across professionally.

Is there an aspect of your work that you think is invisible to most people?

That we just turn around and act mad is astounding to me. It's horrible what we do to ourselves! *[laughs]* We are exploring our emotions every single day in a way that a lot of people don't. It can be a rollercoaster, more exhausting than running a race. It is taxing, upsetting, interesting, enlightening and filled with love every single day. It could drive someone crazy.

I've been sitting here looking at you on this computer screen and even on Skype you look so beautiful, Christina. How do you relate to your own beauty? Are you aware of it? What do you see?

I am very self-conscious about myself physically. A lot of attention has been brought to my physicality so it makes me think about it more than I'd want to. I don't enjoy thinking about it, but I like my face. I feel like it's expressive and still looks like my kid face. That's something that I know and am comfortable with. Everything else changed, but my face stayed the same.

Did it feel strange for me to make a remark to you about your beauty? How did it feel to receive that?

I got self-conscious, because as I was getting ready to call you, my husband said, 'Don't you wanna do yourself up more?' and I said, 'Sally knows me so I'm going to be, you know, fresh out of bed.' But when you commented on it, I started thinking of things that I should have done, like put on some make-up.

Oh no! What I'm talking about is the raw you. I don't care about make-up. But looking at you is pleasurable. The fact is that film is a visual medium, people are staring at the actor, they're trying to stare into them. I find the relationship of looking and being looked at is very little understood.

Yeah, and we all do it. I do it. I watch films and I stare, and I judge, especially about whether I'm getting a real thing given to me, or not. What am I feeling? What am I watching? What am I receiv-ing? We are storytellers. We are players projecting and hopefully telling the story in the best way possible. And the best way possible is that you're feeling the things that the writer originally wanted to tell. You really just need to tell the story right.

Then, in a strange way, appearance is more like being transparent, if what matters is whether it feels real or not.

I know it only works for me when it's real.

You can tell immediately?

I can watch myself and say, 'I never fully got there in that,' and I *hate* it.

And when you did get there?

Then I think, 'Yes. That's what I was trying to say.'

JUDE LAW

I met Jude to talk in his house, on a rainy day in May. We sat
in a room with dark-red walls looking out towards a green, wet
garden. The last time I had been in his house, several years previously, was to talk about *Rage* and his role in it, that of an American man occupying the female persona of Minx, a model working
in the fashion industry. We had talked about the part, and about
the nature of beauty, including his own physical appearance. Then
Jude picked up the script and started to read one of his monologues
(all the characters in *Rage* talk in soliloquies, addressing an invisible

child behind the camera who is conducting interviews backstage at a fashion show). A voice began to emerge that made my hair stand on end: low, seductive, and utterly different in intonation and accent from Jude's own speaking voice. We both realised that Minx had arrived.

Jude occupies a terrain in movie-making which many actors might envy but which places certain narrow expectations on him. His matinée-idol looks have tended to stereotype him as a romantic lead and have led to intense press scrutiny and outbreaks of paparazzi-stalking of his personal life. Despite his strivings to free himself from this straitjacket, often through 'character' roles that are far from his everyday identity, or by working in the freer and in some ways more demanding world of the theatre – playing the hugely complex role of Hamlet, for example – his image as a romantic film-star persists. In private he is articulate, serious, charming. Professionally, I have rarely worked with anyone who was more courteous, enthusiastic, or more dedicated to getting it right.

Before I started recording, we were talking –

– about confidentiality.

Yes. Because I didn't want to break my confidentiality with actors by talking about them, which is why we are talking today.

One of the stages of our work is to go out and explain what we've done or defend what we've done . . .

– more often [laughs] –

Yeah. And it's become a rather handy in-road for journalists to say, 'Oh talk about the process. What did you do to create this character?' It used to be a useful thing for me to hide behind and say, 'Oh, I read this and this . . .' but now I'm starting to feel, 'It's none of your business.' Because what you get from the experience of sitting in a theatre watching a play, or a film, is what we want you to see. If you take a journalist backstage and say I did this, and the director asked me to do that, it's like showing all your tricks. So I started trying not to talk about it. It also started to sound terribly predictable. I like not knowing. Just to see the work and to say, 'How did you get there? Goodness me. Wasn't that extraordinary.'

Sometimes the language one resorts to is a kind of untruth and that's what feels really tricky. We're not talking about –

– what actually happened.

– because the real process of course is much more mysterious.

Yes. Everything you feel that you can mention – that sounds meaty enough to make sense, or to anchor this bizarre process in – is only ever the platform from which you leap off. And it's the leap and where you fall and how you feel while you're falling and who manages to push you in a direction whilst you fall – that's the process.

It's precipitous.

And yet they're the things that you really hold on to. It may be a cliché but you prepare and prepare and then you have to forget everything.

It's not a cliché. When you get sent a script what do you look for? Or hope for?

The things that I used to look for have changed. What I've learnt from past experiences has now informed the decisions I make. More often than not, if the director is someone I really admire and who excites me and who, in my opinion, has always done something interesting, then the script doesn't necessarily bother me. If I read it and don't get it, but they did, then surely there is something there that I haven't seen. I don't trust myself enough to think – 'No, I'm not going to do this because I don't see it.' I'll go and say, 'I don't see it *yet*.' And that's the beginning of the relationship and the process. So I'm probably more led by the person that I'm about to work with. Which is odd, because I'm also someone who used to say, 'Oh, the script is everything. The script is the map. If it's not in the script then . . . No great film was made from a bad script,' and blah blah blah.

But actually . . . ?

But actually I think I'm willing to ignore the script and go with someone who I think is going to take me somewhere interesting. But what do I look for in a script? I like to be moved. I like the opportunity to fill in gaps. It's an experience that you also get with good literature. I like reading things that somehow conjure up something between the page and your head, in the empty space. It's more like a suggestion that creates a wonderful spell. That kind of writing is rare and magical. The obvious answer to your question is also when it's a character that I've never played before. One that perhaps frightens me. I think the best parts, the best experiences I've had are the ones that I've shied away from for quite a long time, or not really wanted to do. Because what I realise is that I get a sort of sick excitement. 'God, this could be extraordinary but how terrifying to go there.'

So excitement and fear are adjacent to each other, in a strange way.

Yes. As they are when adrenalin kicks in. You get that slight nauseous feeling *[inhales]* – you know, but also a thrill.

You talked just now about the primacy of the director for you. What qualities do you look for in a director – especially if you haven't met them before – in that first meeting? What clues are you looking for to help you to know this is a road worth travelling?

The first thing that comes to mind is I want them to be kind of nice. If they strike me as someone who is either bullish, a bully or impenetrable – an awful lot is about how they treat the people around them – then I know I will find that relationship very hard to survive. I don't think I could feel open, if I walked on a set and people were being shouted at and there was an unhappy atmosphere, even if they were delightful to me. I think I would seize up. I've been incredibly lucky that so far almost every instance of how I've read the person has been accurate. I've never been on the set of a bully, someone who is aggressive and abusing their role. What else am I looking for? Clarity. I love the idea of stepping into someone's vision. Of course I love being seduced too. I love someone saying, 'You're going to do this and it's going to be wonderful.' I like to feel the spell, the conjuring of where they can take you and what they think you can do. It's inspiring, it's like being taken out of yourself. Sometimes I feel incredibly clear about my capabilities but not clear on how to get there. That's the job the director does. I can know how large the circumference of what I'm willing to do is. I can feel it but I don't always know how to access it. And so if you feel a little bit of that in a conversation with a director, it's enlightening and inspiring. Having said that, I also think back to directors who have had incredible careers and I've had the good fortune to step in and work with them, ten, fifteen years down the line. There is something wonderful about just sitting back and listening and watching when you know someone has done something pretty brilliant in the past. Just being a pupil is, I think, very rewarding.

A state of trust.

Very much so.

What's important to you in the first private read-through of the script with the director?

The leap of faith that you can make mistakes and be awful, because normally that's how you feel. Awful. *[laughs]* I always step into those environments thinking, 'They're going to change their minds as soon as I open my mouth.' All you can hear are the mistakes and how clunky it is. Maybe we've not yet chosen the accent or whatever it may be. And of course those mistakes would often override anything positive, whereas what I've realised is that mistakes are actually a blessing. It's like, 'Let's get it out there. Let's make an absolute mess of it right now. And I'll show you how brave I can be.' I'll do it and then turn around to the director and go 'OK. Now fire me or tell me what the hell to do.' *[laughs]*

So in a way that's all it is. I don't think I've ever been in a read-through and felt, 'Gosh, yeah that's how we're going to do it.' That would be fake.

What do you need from the director at that moment of taking the plunge?

I suppose you need them to acknowledge the discomfort and the . . . well, I was going to say falsity, but of course in a way everything we do is false. It's no less real doing it around a table than it is pretending, 'This is my house and I live here.' But you want the director to make you feel safe. What they're doing at a group read-through is weaving a family together, introducing everybody, bonding everybody, gathering the team for the first time. You're all there looking at each other and that ritual – now that I think about it – is very important. There you all are in the same room – not off in your different departments – looking each other in the eyes, maybe sharing a laugh or a tear because you're all suddenly thinking, 'OK. Here we go. This is the adventure.'

Do you prefer to have first done a read-through in private with the director?

Yes. But that's something I've only really put my finger on recently. With you and me it was very specific because it was an isolated and individual experience. How you conceived the piece – and why I was intrigued by it and by the process – was because it always felt fragmented. It felt like, 'This is the world of my character, alone. Only.' And so all the work we did was always going to be personal and one-on-one. Since then, funnily enough, what's happened more and more in my process is that I've sought that experience of working with the director one-on-one before we've been in a more communal environment. In fact my whole process has changed quite considerably since we worked together, because of the way we worked on *Rage*.

How?

Just the amount of work I like to do now before I feel ready. And I'm astonished, looking back at the work I did before we worked together and what I thought was enough, which I now realise wasn't enough. I can feel solid in a role, when I've had that one-on-one experience and asked all those questions and looked at everything. I demand it now. Not by 'being demanding' but just to say, 'I really need this time with you to ask you this, this and this.'

I'll never forget one of the one-on-one moments we had in this house in the first read-through. You found the voice. And it was like – like watching something emerge.

[JL laughs]

What do you wish more directors understood about actors?

It's a terribly hard question to answer because the individuality of a director is what makes my job all the more rewarding. It's the same medium being translated, perceived and manipulated by completely different processes and styles. Each director recognises different things in actors. And if I'm honest, I rather like the opportunity to be as malleable as possible. For example I can think of a director who chooses to do just two takes. They make that decision, that's their process, just capturing something and moving on. Sometimes after a day or two with a director like that I could say, 'God, I've got so much else I could discover here, why are you ignoring that?' But they've made a conscious decision to grab something that they saw in you that was raw and ready to go and they don't want to sit around questioning it. And the longer they do, the further away from the line they wanted to follow they will get. And they're not being rude, they're just saying this is what they want. So with that person why fight your corner, saying 'let me experiment, let me explore'? Then at the opposite extreme you could work with someone who lets you do twenty, thirty takes and you say, 'What do you want from me? I've tried everything and I'm exhausted. Don't you realise we're going round in circles here?' In that situation it's better to think, 'OK there's something they haven't got yet, let's keep looking.' But your question was very specific. What do I wish more directors recognised?

Understood.

Understood. Understood about us. Hmm. I think they don't always know just how hard it is. And that the re-setting process, unlike putting all the props back to the same place, you know, closing all the doors or whatever it may be – it's not quite as easy for us. But of course we're going to go and do it again. If I have experienced a lack of understanding it's usually because the director's mind is on something else. Sometimes they have a million things to think about so I don't always walk away blaming them or feeling taken for granted. I've worked with people who don't necessarily want to follow a process as much as I do but they've never said, 'Look, I'm not bothered about this, leave me alone, I've got better things to do.' If I've asked for more input, or I've explained what I'm going through, they tend to be communicative and helpful. I think I have been very fortunate. Actually it's about us understanding them as much as it is about them understanding us.

Lovely answer for a director to hear. [laughs] Let's talk about preparation. What's the difference between preparation and rehearsal for you? Is there one?

Yes, there's a huge difference. And that's something I've really discovered in the last five years. I've learnt that there's a hugely rich bedrock, a root system, where you can go, and only you can go, where you create the back-story, the intimate details, the intricate nuances of what made your character who and what they are. It feels like the most solid and wonderful foundation that gives you great confidence to proceed with anything you then choose to do. And the rehearsal room then is to me about playing with the given text. But you can bring everything to it that you have prepared from the day of the character's birth. Without that I now feel unprepared. I do think there are a lot of questions that can be answered in the rehearsal room, but there are an awful lot of personal questions to do with the character that I think you need to resolve before you get in there.

Do you prefer to do that kind of exploration alone or with the director?

I like to do a little bit of both. I think it's great to allow your imagination to inform it and it's obviously helpful to get a director's input, because you want to be on the same page. Creating that back-story is going to affect what you then bring to the script and the rehearsal – and ultimately to the piece – so you have to be in tandem. But it's a wonderful bonding process you go through with your character: a state of possession. The rehearsal to me is then all the richer for it because you're not having to go off the text and then recount all this stuff, you're able to work with what's in front of you and apply all of your preparation to it.

Secretly, so to speak.

Yes.

Do you always like to rehearse for a film?

I think it's helpful to get things out there. I personally feel better saying lines over and over and gradually owning them and understanding them. I feel that if it's about capturing the truth of a moment, it becomes more truthful, more honest, if it's already embedded in you. It's not about trying to capture a truth as if you're just saying it for the first time. I also like the opportunity to make mistakes and ask why they were mistakes. Find out what can be improved. I think there's also something about parameters. You can push something too far in a rehearsal – and feel safe that it's too far – and know what that parameter is before you say, 'OK, that's too far, so how do we come back from that?' It can go in every direction. You can be bigger, louder, quieter, softer. And it's very important to see how other people are going to work. Although surprises are wonderful too, when you're confident and free enough to allow them to do whatever they want and not be thrown by it. There's a little bit of trust that has to be built, but . . . I'm not someone who is easily scared by someone who changes things. 'Oh, you didn't do that in rehearsal.' You're testing boundaries aren't you?

How important is the look? Working from the outside in?

I tend to do them simultaneously. I love working on the look. Both affect each other. I don't necessarily have an order where one leads the other. But I do tend to have a very immediate image of someone in my head that I tend to sketch and it's interesting how often I go back –

– physically sketch?

Yes, I sketch on paper. And it's interesting how often I go back later and the character looks exactly the same. It's also about the great work of people around me, where ideas and suggestions spun off my initial instinct are improved by people's understanding of what they can do with a hairpiece, or whatever it may be. It sometimes seems terribly theatrical to talk about the 'disguise' but I feel very free when I'm as far away from me as possible. I'm not talking about prosthetics. It's amazing how tiny things can change you and how by changing you, you suddenly feel free of yourself. Little tiny details can slot you into the physicality of a world, the embodiment of the person you hope to play. And that journey, that marriage, I find absolutely glorious. It's only when they become a physical entity that I feel that my relationship with them truly starts. I kind of fall for them when I embody them physically, because suddenly it feels that they're not me. It's the separation process as much as anything. I can sit back and look at them. That's also when that inner journey that you mentioned, and the outer journey, meet. There's a wonderful moment when the two marry and you find out why they walk or behave in a certain way.

How much do you consciously draw from personal experience when you're working on a character?

I don't tend to mark through a script and note, 'Oh this is similar to this, this is similar to that.' You tend to discuss it a lot more with a director. But I don't write lists of things that refer to me. I will talk and write about key moments in the character's past or even make diagrams of who may affect them, but then, on the day, I use my life almost as an immediate – there is a technical term for it isn't there? Visualisation? – I use my relationships and I use imagined dynamics to create emotions in myself.

Do you ever share what those are or do you keep that as your secret armoury?

I've never shared them.

Would you ever want to or is it important to you that they remain private?

Not necessarily. It wouldn't weaken them, I don't think. And they're not terribly surprising. They're about imagining the pain of loss, or the pain of unhappy circumstances, with the people I love the most. Usually they're the immediate things one can tap into and it's amazing how effective they can be.

But you save that process until the moment of shooting? It's not something you tap into in preparation?

No.

Subtext or text?

Which do I prefer?

Is there a hierarchy of importance for you? What your character is saying or not saying, or not able to say? The spaces between the lines.

If I look back I was someone who learnt on the hoof. I've gone from being someone who used to concentrate more on text to someone who tries to pay more attention to the subtext. I'm more intrigued by it now. I love the written word and I love playing with the beauty of language and sounds, but that's not always required. On stage we have the opportunity to work with the great writers, Eugene O'Neill for example, poets and masters of the English language. It doesn't mean that you can't then play with subtext, but to not enjoy and relish the written text would be dropping one of your main assets. But on film, or in a more contemporary setting with a part that maybe doesn't say very much, I think it's all about the subtext. I've learnt to embrace that more and more and enjoy it. You've connected me with something that I've not necessarily seen. What's happened in the past is I've been playing contemporary roles, people who don't have a lot to say, and by not enjoying the subtext, I've not given myself very much to play with. But I'm about to do a film and I keep telling the director, 'Stop giving me lines!' because I don't want him to speak much. The director keeps saying, 'But you could say this,' and I say 'I don't want to say anything.' I now realise this is because I know I can create a character who will say all through his silence.

I can see it as you're talking about it. I can see it in your face. [laughs]

The more he says, the weaker he'll be.

So let's assume you've gone through preparation in the way you want to, you've had rehearsals the way you wish to – the shoot begins. What do you really want from the director at that point?

Initially, on day one or two, until you're warmed up, you just want to be led by the director. You hope that all the promise of the type of person they were, the type of set they'd run and the way they were going to behave with you – all the things that were discussed around coffee and in the rehearsal room – are true. And that you don't suddenly feel 'who's this?' *[both laugh]*

'And why are they behaving like that?' No, you want them to lead. And you want to know that everything matters. I don't like turning up and people saying – even if it's not a big scene, and of course you hope it's not a massive scene to start with – 'Don't worry, we're just doing this little thing.' You feel, 'No, no, I really want to know that everything we do counts.' And whilst I'm ready to keep going and keep exploring, with a director, it's nice to feel a sense of clarity early on, where they know how to recognise when they've got what they wanted. Sitting on set for the first few days and feeling that someone is just sort of drifting and not sure is terribly worrying.

So it's important that the director knows when to stop.

Yes. Feeling that clarity is wonderful. And feedback is very, very important.

What works and what doesn't work with feedback?

Being told that what you just did was what we wanted and we got it. Hearing that and not too much, not too little – and hearing it with eyes locked.

Speaking of eyes being locked, how important is the director's gaze on you at the moment of shooting, as opposed to the monitor?

That's a really interesting question, isn't it, because it has transformed in the last ten, fifteen years. I land somewhere between the two because, again, I've been really lucky to work with both types.

By both types you mean those that stand by the camera –

– and those who operate the camera, like yourself, or Steven Soderbergh, who literally pop their head up to look at you between takes or are otherwise looking through the lens and it's glorious. I've had directors who don't operate, of course, because that's very rare, but they sit next to the camera. And I've had those who are off in a blackened tent and then pop out or you get beckoned over. *[laughs]*

And there's somewhere between the two. I love an immediate response from a director. I love the feeling of someone's eyes being on me and that being enough. I'm also terribly old-fashioned in that I feel that if you look back at the history of film – not that I'm against its evolution, moving this art-form forward technically

– but if you look back at the great, great films, many were made where a director would sit and have to trust their cinematographer so much that they would ask, 'Did we get it?' after a take. What they were asking was about the frame and the shot that they had planned. And based on that trust they would move on. I love that sort of intimacy. At the same time I'm sometimes intrigued to go and take a look at the monitor. If you're battling to do something very physical and it's not quite working, I can watch a playback and remedy it immediately, giving the director what they want. I'm often very confident about that. 'Stop describing it, show me, where do you need . . . Oh you need me closer to that wall and then to come further out there . . . Oh I see. OK.' And that's wonderful. That can make you feel technically included, as an actor, rather than, 'Oh, we have to just draw it out of them.' Just show me. I'm in control of this just as much as you are or the cameraman is.

So you want respect for your sense of responsibility and your awareness –

– and my involvement. Yes, my involvement in the process. And it is terribly rewarding when you know the director's right there. Also it sometimes prevents the tricky and unavoidable thought which can pop into your head – when you are in the middle of something incredibly intense – when you become aware that you're performing it for this object, this camera. If the person that you're performing it for isn't there then you can't help but feel, 'Gosh, this is so alien. What are we doing?' Having a real pair of eyes there with you on the journey lessens that happening.

And lessens the solitude.

It's a sort of emotional camaraderie. The journey that started in a discussion about an idea when, hopefully, truths were shared, then becomes a sort of bond. 'Wouldn't it be wonderful if we . . .' or, 'What I would love you to do is bring this out of that moment.'

When that moment finally arrives you want them to be there to share it with you. If they're away looking at you through a monitor you can feel quite isolated.

Do you experience the gaze of the director as a palpable doppelganger for the eventual cinematic frame?

Their eyes?

Am I being clear?

You are. And yes, I do. I mean . . . the director is the audience, is who you are trying to . . . *[pauses]*

– say it –

– I was going to say 'please' but that's not the right word, because I'm not always trying to please them – I want to get it right for them and for me – but you hope that by then it is one and the same thing. Sometimes in your imagination there is something else you're trying to achieve. It might be for someone who you hope will see this story and it will make sense to. Or it might be for a child. Do you see what I mean?

I do.

But the vast majority of the time the director is that external view, or doppelganger as you said, of what the final film will be. So you go to them and ask, 'Was that right?' because they're your eyes too.

And your mirror also?

Yes. Your mirror, your audience and ultimately – you can't escape from this – they are the creator, in a literal sense, of the universe of the film. And so they are the ones you go to to say, 'Did we get it?' or 'Are we there yet?'

You've referred to the notion of character several times. How does character relate to being, or presence, for you?

Being in the moment?

Beingness. Presence on film. What does that concept mean to you and how do you find your way into it?

Two things come to mind. Looking back I realise that maybe one of the reasons I was able to be an actor, is that somewhere inside me, I had antennae of when something was realistic or not. I could feel how to play it and knew how to lose myself, whilst also being technically aware enough of manipulating a circumstance, so that people believed in it. That wasn't necessarily character-based – it was more like a natural instinct of how to play a scene. The characters that I'm now creating are being layered on top of that instinct, because they aren't me. You know we all perform, in a way, to survive. Playing someone who really isn't you – no matter how intimately you feel you understand them – the antennae still have to poke through the layer of the character. So I'm hesitant to say, 'Oh I just lose myself.' Because I don't think I do. I may understand the character and feel confident that I can allow them just to free-fall, as it were, but I'm yet to say, 'Oh, I'm lost in these characters.' My antennae are as fresh as they were when I was just playing myself. Does that make sense?

Absolutely. You're consciously crafting. Part of you is detached at the same time as you're inside it. I remember a discussion we had about your relationship with your appearance and how that was going to resonate with Minx's relationship with her appearance. I think we used the phrase 'the curse of beauty'. Appearance can be a kind of veil of the self, can't it?

As with anything you live with, it becomes a part of you. It's what you're dealing with as a performer but also the thing you're dealing with in your life. My relationship with my face is changing. I've aged quite a lot in the last few years. People have been used to me looking a certain way for many years. I always saw the signs of age-ing – and in fact looked forward to them coming because I always saw them as signs of character, signs of life. Signs also of potentially not being over-looked as just being a beauty, but being understood as someone who was able to perform. And so you're right that it is something I've often thought about. Some of the parts I've enjoyed the most have been the parts where I've been allowed to mess myself up or hide behind little things. What's happening now – which is also interesting – is getting used to something I had wished for. Be careful what you wish for! *[laughs]*

Because of course now it's a double-edged sword. I'm getting used to being told, 'Oh no, you can't go up for that part, you're too old.' *[laughs]* 'We want someone young and beautiful.' No matter how much you thought you'd been wishing it, when they say it, it's cruel. And then you are immediately defensive . 'I don't look that old, you know.' But it's certainly not something that's hanging over me. I'm enjoying too much the opportunities that have become available.

But maybe this experience throughout your life has given you specific insights into the mysteries of appearance. The true correlation between appearance and self.

Very possibly so. I've certainly been aware of the effects of my appearance on people since I was a young boy.

Such as?

The way people respond to the way you look when you walk into a room. People's reactions, their immediate perception of who they think you may be.

Do they go weird around you?

I've had a whole mixture. It still happens. An obvious one if you're a young good-looking guy, and you're known, is you get a lot of advances. Flirtation and sexual advances. More interesting to me is people assuming that because of the way you look, you are arrogant or full of yourself and therefore they're immediately cold with you. I've so often had people saying, 'You know I always thought you were like this and I'm amazed that you're not at all.' Because they've built this perception of you based on the way you look and what that says to them. Men and women. I do the same. What's awful is that I'm someone who, because of my job and my physicality, has been aware of this first-hand but I still do it myself. I am aware of someone's work, or whose image I know, who I've then met and realised, 'Gosh, I've had this perception of this person I don't know and they are completely different.'

All the things that have been projected onto their appearance which you then have to navigate.

They live in me as if they are the persona and of course they're not at all.

Do you think there's any way in which this has confused you about who you are?

I think – gosh, this is me being really honest – I think they've at times brought out the worst in me.

Really? How?

Well, being reliant on them in social situations out of sheer laziness. *[laughs]*

And then at other times feeling a constant battle. I heard myself banging the same old drum all the time, about not being taken seriously in this business. Rather than being seen as someone who is a pretty boy – or a beauty – I wanted the challenge of being able to play other parts. I was always interested in having a go at a lot of different types of roles, not just one type. What scared me was simply about being seen only on one level.

Much more similar to the experience of a lot of female actors.

Yes. That's possible.

What's the key difference for you in performing for the stage and performing on camera?

I find it much easier to lose myself on stage, if only because of the duration of the performance and the duration of the physicality. Once the curtain is rising you know that for two hours or so you're on a physical roll, whereas on film, with the fragmented structure of the day, you still have to stay on that level even when you're not on camera. It's a sort of meditative state of mind and you have to summon up energy like a sprinter, whereas on stage it's like a long-distance run, so you're absorbed in that breathing. We talked a little bit before about the journey that starts with a discussion, through a script, through a rehearsal that you hope a director will then share with you on set. With theatre it's then handed to an audience. That emotional sharing of imagination, right then and there in the room, is so intoxicating that for me, it helps me lose myself. Having said that, I also adore the technical trickery, the magic of film-making, that you can splice and cut and stop and start and redo and capture a little moment. And then just when you think you've got the greatest scene the director says, 'Ah but now we're going to come right in and hit –' and you go, 'Oh fantastic. A close-up for that line? Go on, give it to me.' Or hitting the light and not having to say a word. It's magical. It's that wonderful alignment of a group of people coming together technically, to capture something. And the process that is intriguing me more and more is post-production. But fundamentally, I think the intoxication of live theatre is where I feel I can lose myself and feel indulged as an actor.

From the way you talk about it, it seems part of you can see from the outside how something is going to look when you're shooting. You've got a strong visualising capacity. When you come to see the finished film, when the post-production period is over . . . have you found that you are surprised by what you see? By what's been done to your work in the edit?

Yes. I think I've been surprised sometimes at how it's been manipulated and improved. I've been surprised in other ways too. *[laughs]* How bad it is and how lacking or . . . vacant. 'Is that it? Is that all we got?' – not just in quantity but also in feeling or in impact. It's been really rare that I've sat down and been completely washed away by a film I've been involved in, as I can be by other great films. And that's something that's taken me a while to come to terms with. It's something I say to younger actors when I talk about making films: 'Don't be disheartened when you watch your own films.' You can't help but remember where you were when you did that incredible scene – and it isn't in there any more. And that's alright. It can be interesting to look at films that you made some time ago. I don't tend to go back, but the older I get and the more films I make, it is odd how something will pop up on television and I'll just flick to watch a bit and think, 'Oh, actually, it wasn't as bad as I remembered.'

Because you're no longer flooded by all those memories –

– the experience is not as immediate.

Have you ever sat in the edit in post-production and watched every take?

Not for long enough, no. But I really want to.

Massive teacher. I watch every single take of each actor multiple times over and learn about all my directorial mistakes. 'Why the fuck did I do that?' and so on. Agony but fascinating. Difficult.

Do you ever get to that point and think, 'I missed it, I lost something,' or 'Why didn't I do this?' Or is it more, 'Why didn't I stop them doing this?'

Quite often it's, 'Why didn't I stop there? We had it.' But not always, because sometimes at take fourteen – 'Yes! It was worth doing.'

You got there.

'There it is.' And that's wonderful. And then sometimes I look at the difference between one take and another and I wonder what I did right? Or between one take and another and I think, 'What the fuck was I doing in between? Why couldn't I give that bit of feedback that would have . . .' and so on.

Fascinating.

Amazing lessons. Not a lot of actors I talk to are very interested in it.

I'm really interested in it, but I don't know whether I'm interested to watch myself. I think I would find that very hard. Maybe one day. But what I would like to do is watch a film being put together, certainly before I would attempt to direct. I want to see the extent of that process.

You learn everything you need to know in the cutting room. It's a marathon, talking about sprints and marathons. And you can make or break a performance. This is the secret that directors and editors share in the cutting room.

What I've learnt is that sometimes it does go back to a little fear you had really early on. 'Do they really know what they want? Why are they making this film? Do they really know what they wanted to get out of it?' And then you see the end product and you still don't know.

That's the vital thing about that preparation period. You've got to be able to ask those terrible questions before it's too late.

Yes. Which can be as basic as, 'Why are we bothering to do this?'

– at all.

If someone says, 'Well we want to make loads of money,' then at least we know they're being honest. But you can go, 'Fuck off I'm not interested,' or, 'Alright, great. At least we know why we're all here.' Because it's a lot of people, a lot of time, a lot of effort and a lot of emotional commitment. So let's ask that question – 'Why are we doing this?'

The more uncomfortable the question, the better, in a way.

Often so.

Fame and celebrity: the impact on your work – negative? positive?

It's had a huge impact on my work. As my children get older and therefore more independent and individual and communicative, it's intriguing for me to realise how long I have been in the public eye. In a weird way, in my heart of hearts, in a secret epicentre of my head, I'm still Jude who grew up in Lewisham. I live there still, as a little boy, as I think we all do. We all go back to the family home where we were young. Well, I certainly do. And I still know him and communicate with him. But even my children – who I spend ninety per cent of my time with – don't know who he was. And I am further away from him than I've ever been because it's been years and years – like second nature – that we've been going out and had private moments suddenly interrupted. Not rudely, not badly, we'll get onto that later – but just being interrupted as a matter of course. My kids are used to it. They don't find it offensive.

Strangers coming up to you?

Yeah, people asking for photos. People saying, 'Oh my goodness, is it you?' It's just . . . it's what my life is. And it's who I am as a dad. They laugh at my reaction, or they laugh at them rather meanly, or we all laugh at them when they're unusual. And it makes me look at my kids with respect and astonishment, that they're as relaxed and cool about it as they are. But then again it's all they've ever known. Their dad gets this sort of attention and it doesn't make them any less – or more – proud. So what I'm trying to say is: yes, it is my life, on the one hand and yes, it has had an effect, but on the other hand it's just become who I am. And who I am then informs what work I choose to do.

There is a battle in me though. Somewhere along the line I was just excited about being an actor. I was just excited to work. And then I became aware – going back a little to what we discussed already – that I wanted to get away from being perceived as playing 'dashing young leads'. If you look at some of my early work I almost fought too hard sometimes. And then I realised five or six years later, after having children, 'God, this is my business too. I've got to try and make some money.' And I started to play the game, as it were, to nurture a career. It was informed by being a father. Then I became aware that I had a responsibility to myself if this was a career that I wanted to continue. I wanted to define myself as an artist. I started to think who I wanted to be associated with, what kind of work I wanted to do. Being successful or 'famous' – to use a word that I don't necessarily like – is a strange responsibility. At the moment the business is very hard, as you know. The only way of making good money is to do stuff that you don't necessarily want to do. I've got kids and that responsibility looms over me. But I find it hard to say, 'Oh sod it. I'll go and do that and get paid a lot of money.' That must be my artistic conscience and how I hope to be perceived in the public eye. What's terribly disheartening is when people still think of you in a certain way and don't seem to be looking at the work you're actually doing. And that's a lot to do with the magazines, which you've no say about whatsoever. I only ever talked about work in interviews and then was dragged into a much more seedy side of it, simply because of the boom of celebrity magazines. That's had an effect on my private life and also on how people perceive me. They write up lies or they hassle you until private stories pop out. And that affects a general perception of who I am, which in turn has an effect on how people cast me. That has nothing to do with the work I've chosen and everything to do with a world I have been dragged into because my face sells magazines.

So the celebrity-hungry culture has had a huge impact on you.

Huge impact. Yeah.

What about when a film comes out and there's all this fronting-up process – press junkets and all that. How do you relate to that stage of the work?

I was led to believe for at least ten years or so that it was something you just had to do, and yet at the end you felt really depleted and exhausted. Occasionally you would have a really good discussion. But on the whole you just felt that you were putting on this front and you were selling and selling. And then as the business changed – and as my role changed – I started to realise that there was no direct relationship between selling the film and how I felt about the film itself. Sometimes I would enjoy going out and talking about a film, because I was proud to be a part of it. It can be interesting to say, 'This is what we were trying to do.' It's something altogether different when you're just out there flogging something. What I've also realised now is the fall-out. If you're out there once a year doing that, suddenly vermin scuttle around and pick up all the crumbs. So you're not just talking to the press in organised and constructed articles. There's always knock-on effects, articles that say, 'Oh, he said this and he said that.' And you feel that you've been dragged across the coals or that you've been nibbled at. And that's really hard work. So unless I can genuinely talk about the work, I'm not going to do it. Because I'm bored of me in that environment.

[laughs] When we make a film so much time seems to be spent dealing with the appearance of it, the mechanics. But experientially there is something at the core that's so other. Do you feel there is a metaphysical dimension to your work?

Well I have a belief, when I try and rationalise what I do, that I am part of the ancient and noble art of storytelling, looking to make sense of the future, looking to make sense of the past, looking to create feeling and thought and to conjure imagination. And that is as much a part of who and what we are as procreation. There is an Ice Age exhibition at the British Museum where it proves that man and woman, for thousands and thousands of years, when we thought they were just surviving, were whittling out creative and imaginative totems that explain their dreams, their lusts and their fears, and that in a way are no different to when we create a film or put on a play or dance or make music. It's all the same. I can still go and watch a film or a play and be moved deeply on a spiritual level. It can have a huge influence on my life. Without trying to lend myself any grandeur, I love being a part of that. And I believe in it deeply. I think at its essence that's what I do it for.

An hour and three quarters. I can't believe it.

No way. It felt like twenty minutes.

ALESSANDRO NIVOLA

Alessandro took on the challenging role of Roland in *Ginger & Rosa* with enthusiasm. He sent a self-taped rendition of some scenes (the first time I had encountered this particular method), which had authority and exuded a keen intelligence. When we met in London for the first time I was fascinated to learn more about his background (his father was a political scientist and Alessandro had studied literature at Yale). Alessandro is known for his willingness to approach characters that some actors would shy away from. In his own life, he is an affectionate friend and a loyal, loving husband

and father, but he is able to project himself compassionately into the minds, bodies and needs of men whose wounds manifest as shadowy, difficult or destructive behaviour.

During preparation he showed me a book of photographs of his Italian sculptor grandfather, who lived and worked in a milieu that resonated with the world of our story. He also devoured books from my library on anarchism and pacifism. He wanted to know what Roland would read, how his mind worked. He wanted to love him and he wanted the audience to understand him, as did I. When the film was finished and we stood together on stage to answer questions he said that one of the things that attracted him to the role was that I had put words of truth into the mouth of an untrustworthy character.

We spoke on Skype for this interview. I was in France and he was sitting in a chair next to a window in a house on Long Island, his laptop balanced precariously on his knees. Occasionally his young daughter wandered in to the room and he tenderly carried her out again. At one point he showed me images on his mobile phone of his transformation into another character for a recent film, again a man with a dark side. The interview was punctured with laughter and infused with light and birdsong from the open window.

What do you look for, or hope for, in a script?

Some kind of originality in the voice. Not just of *my* character, but of the script as a whole . . . and I can usually tell that in the first ten pages.

How?

Just something about the way that the dialogue is written, or the way that the scenes are framed. It's an intangible thing, but I can quickly tell if it feels original or if it feels cynical, pretentious or rehashed. Ninety-nine per cent of scripts – even the ones that are somewhat worth doing – don't really have that original quality.

Why is originality important to you?

I don't necessarily mean originality in terms of subject-matter – it's more to do with the way that the story is told. The reason it's important is because, if you want a movie to have any chance – just from a practical standpoint, and we're talking about independent cinema, which is really the only cinema that has any ambition – it's very hard to sell a film if there isn't something about it that is different from all the rest. But from an artistic standpoint, I guess what I mean by original is not necessarily that it has to be different in a shocking way, but that it has to smack of truth.

Hey! The connection's failed! I don't believe this!

Hello . . . ?

Sandro, I lost you when you said the word, 'truth'!

I'll make sure not to say it again!

[Laughs] What did you go on to say?

That you open a script, you start reading, and immediately, in the dialogue, you can hear if the way that the characters are talking sounds real. I don't mean that every movie has to be realistic, but there has to be something about the way that it's written that feels like it's getting at something in a character, or a situation that is true to life.

What about your hopes for the role, specifically?

I used to choose what jobs I was going to do just based on the role. If it was a good part, I would take it, no matter what. It didn't matter who had written it, what the rest of the script was like, who the other actors were, or who was directing it. All I cared about was: could I say the lines in a way that was going to be exciting to me and might give me an opportunity to play something different to what I've played before. But in more recent years, I've changed my attitude. I don't take jobs based on the role so much as I do based on the director. Because I realise that films *completely* belong to directors. So I started taking the attitude of, 'I can play anything, if it's with a good director.'

What's your definition of a good director?

Somebody who is highly intelligent, has a strong vision for the story that they want to tell and who has something about their personality that sets them apart from average people.

When you first meet a director, what qualities or clues as to the future working process are you looking for?

It's usually not so much what they say as how they say it. This gives me an impression of their personality. Obviously, if you have the opportunity to work with people who have made great films in the past then you don't really need to know.

Because the evidence is there?

Yeah. But if you're working with somebody who, you know, is younger . . . I don't want to rule those people out because they don't have a lot of experience, but it's less likely that somebody who's making their first film will make a good one. So with a first-time director I feel like a lot more is riding on meeting them, and getting an impression of what they're like as a person. What you really want to *feel* is that they have power. I don't mean in a fascistic way, I just mean that they have the power to drive their vision home. There are so many factors that can get in the way when making a movie, if somebody doesn't have the conviction – and maybe the slight eccentricity – to be able to stick to it in the face of a lot of nay-sayers, then I get worried.

What do you wish all directors understood about actors?

That's a good question. I used to feel like directors generally weren't sensitive enough about what actors have to go through to put themselves in the world of the film. But I've since changed my mind about that too. I have more sympathy for directors now, maybe because I've produced some things. And in recent years, I've had starring roles where I was more part of the process from its inception than I had been earlier on. I started feeling that actors really just need to get on with it. *[both laugh]* And that if the director has created the world of the film adequately, in terms of the look and background and has given you the opportunities to do the research that you want to do, then psychologically preparing yourself for the pressure is really not the director's job. That's your job as an actor, isn't it? Most importantly, what I want from a director is trust. The feeling that they believe in you, especially in the early stages when you're trying to find your way into a role and might not be that sure-footed. There's all this uncertainty and vulnerability around your process and you feel like you're on shaky ground. You want to feel like the director has no doubt that you're going to find your way. If you sense that in a director, it gives you a huge amount of confidence. But I can imagine that there are times when that would be difficult for a director, with panic setting in if an actor is showing signs of not yet having locked into something that they feel confident with, because there's so little time. Once you get into actual filming it just goes by in the blink of an eye. Suddenly it's over and whatever you've got is what you've got. I think that one of the director's challenges is to find an attitude of relentless positive reinforcement. And that doesn't mean neglecting to guide or push an actor in one way or another, but it just means like, endless hope!

*That's a lovely way of expressing it! For both sides I have to say.
[laughs] What are your thoughts and feelings about the audition
process, whatever form that may take?*

That's been a very tricky one for me. I stopped auditioning for five
years at a certain point in my career because I despised the process
so much and I was bad at it. I think that there was some part of me,
once I'd amassed a certain amount of work, that felt resentful about
it. I just felt like, here's a first-time director . . . what the fuck have
they done? I have ten starring roles in movies that they can look at
and know what I'm capable of. So just watch the damn things and
get back to me.

What changed your view?

Some of my best performances came in those five years from roles
that I didn't have to audition for, but on the other hand, I was
ruling myself out of some great roles, and I was ruling myself out
of working with the best directors. Because the best directors have
a high status in the industry and can make anybody audition. I
didn't realise it at the time, but the biggest movie stars were auditioning. So I decided that I had to reassess my position. *[both
laugh]* And eat a little bit of humble pie, and figure out a way to
do it. I was aided by the onset of technology that allowed me to
tape myself, so from about three years ago I started doing these
self-taped auditions and I treated them like I was filming a role.
Live auditions had always felt like some weird little song and dance
to me. You had to wait for hours with other actors and then have
some chit-chat and be charming, then buckle down and do the
audition . . . It didn't relate at all to what it was actually like to go
and film a movie. So I started treating these self-taped auditions
like I was investigating a role, like I was going to work. And I *really*
work on them now. I memorise them backwards and forwards.
Some people say you're not supposed to do that, but everybody

has a different theory. I film them at home and it's an interesting process. It's made a huge difference to my career in the last couple of years. Almost every single audition I send in, I come into contention for the role.

The tape that you sent me was amazing.

In a perfect world I tape them with another person. But sometimes I haven't had anybody available to do it with, which only works if it's a monologue or with just an occasional interjection from another character. But I've taped myself alone and heard the other dialogue in my head, reacted to it and then gone in and dubbed the other person's lines on top. Even those have worked. Talk about film trickery.

Or perhaps the fluidity and advantages of technology?

Yeah.

Let's assume you like the director, you like the script, you find it interesting, original and truthful, in all the ways that you've said, you've got the role and you start to prepare. What are the key aspects of preparation for you?

That varies, depending on the role and the world of the film. There are some roles where it's mainly reading, for example, and there are others where it's listening to music. Sometimes it's like a total immersion experience; you know, I go off fishing if I'm playing a fisherman. It's been completely different every single time around. But the best of all worlds for me is knowing about a role at least a couple of months in advance, because that way I can ingest the world of the movie slowly, even when I'm not doing anything particular to research the role. Because I'm always thinking about it. In fact it becomes totally obsessional, it's on my mind all the time, even if I'm just going through my everyday life. I also really enjoy the education part of it. There have been roles where I've been required to speak French, or play piano, or ride horseback or play polo. Things that just become *actual*, where you have to – in a really disciplined and regimented way – go back to school. And that's great, because there's a structure provided for you, so it doesn't just depend on the wanderings of the mind. Beyond that, there's a process of just living with the character and the world of the film.

What you're describing is quite a private process. How much preparation do you ideally like to do with the director?

I guess that depends on the role. In your case, you had such a familiarity with the world of the film, and it was such a specific milieu of society and such a specific period, that I felt listening to you talk about it was very satisfying. I loved hearing about it. That's really what you're looking for: details, whether you find them yourself or have them provided by someone else. But as an actor you always want to surprise the director a bit, so whatever process you share with them in preparation, you don't want to give away your performance yet. You want to surprise yourself as well, on the day, so you both know where you're heading with the character, based on what starts happening. Then it just continues to develop.

What about the process of how the relationship gets built between actor and director?

Well . . . you want to feel loved, you know. All actors want to feel loved. I really think the best directors, even the ones who have 'bully-ish' tendencies, tempers, or are difficult personalities – all the things that you associate with certain 'tricky' directors – of those, the ones who are the best, who make really great movies with great performances, love actors. They love their vulnerability and their weird foibles and superstitions. They can't get enough of it, in some way. The ones that are unimpressed by it, and suspicious of it, and think that it's either self-indulgent or threatening, are the least successful. I think actors need to feel shined on.

Shined on by the loving gaze of the director? Or something less specific?

It's different from one person to another. I felt that you adored your actors. All of them.

I do.

. . . and you expressed it. You're not a sentimental person, but you are an affectionate person and you were able to express that, quite overtly, in a wonderful way, and I think that your actors benefited from it. Some people don't like to touch other people, or be physical in any way, but that doesn't mean that they wouldn't be capable of making their actors feel loved. You can tell, no matter what the director does, whether they are fascinated by the actors' process and by every element of film-making. Especially the performances. Because you want to feel that the director is fascinated and amazed by what you're doing. Even if what you're doing might be a mistake, if you're trying something that doesn't work.

Do you like to rehearse? In whatever way you define that.

It's a tricky thing. I guess, it depends on the film. Look! Both movies and theatre are trying to get to the same thing, which is 'spontaneity', and on the whole, they go about it in completely opposite ways. With a play, you go through a long period of rehearsal. At first it's a purely intellectual process, where you sit around a table and discuss the work and its context. Then you start to blunder through it and find moments of spontaneity. But generally, by halfway through the rehearsal process, it's starting to feel sort of . . . dead. And then you start to know the play so well that you're able to forget about it all again, forget that you learned it and just rely on the fact that you've done the work, and it's all there within you. You don't have to show it, or prove it, because it's all there, from the weeks and weeks of repetition and experimentation. And then, at best, you eventually get back to the point where you're performing on stage and having moments of discovery every night because you're so loose and comfortable. Now, with a film, because you rarely have that kind of time, you're just trying to get to the final stage, immediately. And often – just as in the theatre when we have a burst of spontaneity that gets replaced by the middle period and then comes back again – you're trying to capture that first reaction on film, that first instinct. So the middle ground of rehearsing a movie I feel is a tricky, dangerous thing to do. If you have a lot of time, and can *really* work on scenes in the way that you would in a play . . .

But what is a lot of time?

I don't know. A few weeks I guess. If you had all your actors together for a rehearsal process – something that you've created in a way that's particular to you – then you could really achieve something. You could create a world where everybody feels they're in the same film and has a level of comfort with each other, the way that you do when running a play for a long time. Of course sometimes you have horrible experiences with other actors, but generally when you've spent that much time together you trust each other and you're able to improvise together. I don't mean with the dialogue, necessarily, but with your performances, in ways that you might not be able to if you're working together for the first time. I guess what I'm saying is, it's all or nothing.

Speaking of improvising, have you ever found that useful in a film, either in the moment of shooting or in the process of discovering the part?

I've done a lot of roles that have had accents that are different to mine. So I used to think, 'Oh, don't make me improvise because I'm still working out how to speak.' But I've changed my mind about that. I think it's good for there to be a situation that's uncomfortable for everybody, with that level of fear. If everybody is in it together.

A state of alert 'present time-ness'?

Of course, that's what you always want. I have had times where I've felt very, very safe, and also had that kind of feeling, but I think it's important to push yourself into a feeling of discomfort, in order just to face it head-on.

I feel exactly the same way about directing. I've come to welcome discomfort because it's a measure of moving beyond limits. I know I'm growing at that moment. So when I see feelings of discomfort in an actor, I try and remain extra-calm and welcoming, because I know something's happening.

Well that's the reaction that I would hope for. As far as using improvisation in filming, you just have to be clear about what you're trying to do, what the purpose of the scene is. If the director has that, and if the actors are aware of that too, then the scene can have a driving force. If two people come into the scene believing one thing about each other and go out believing something else, then at some point in the scene, that discovery has to be made. If you have certain parameters like that, then it can be great, because you're not just rambling, or trying to come up with funny lines.

What about appearance? Working from the outside in; clothes, hair and all those things?

Totally, my style! *[both laugh]*
    I just *love* costumes and physical transformation. It's been a *big* part of my performances. Even in roles that haven't necessarily been

wildly different from myself, I feel that the subtlest little details about what you wear and how you do your hair say so much about the character. And it makes you feel one way or another depending on those choices. It's one of the first things I think about. What does this character look like? How does he dress? Is he somebody who cares a lot about his appearance, or not? It sets me on the road. For example, *Face/Off* (1997) was a role I designed myself, everything from the clothes to the hair to the glasses. I had based it on Robert Crumb's brother, Charles Crumb. John Woo never saw me until the first day I arrived on set. What had been written was a younger version of Nicolas Cage, a wild, flamboyant club-going guy who wore leather pants. And in fact when I'd gone to my fittings initially, that's the gear that they had for me, but I said, 'No, I wanna look like Woody Allen,' so they had to go shopping for corduroys and sweater vests. Anyway, I showed up on the set and it was the first time he'd seen me. He just looked me up and down and said, 'OK. But . . . you have machine-gun,' *[both laugh hysterically]* and I was like, 'Fair enough man! It's a good twist!'

What about the work from the inside out? Tracking the inner life and the inner contradictions of the character?

'Contradiction' is a great word. To me the most important thing is playing a role from the point of view not of *behaviour* but of character. You always want there to be at least two completely contradictory things in the character that co-exist. Not necessarily with the need for explanation. It's more interesting, it creates tension, it's surprising and it gives you a broader range of possibility within the character so that you're not having to restrict yourself to certain choices. You know, 'Oh, the character wouldn't do this,' or, 'The character wouldn't do that.' Everybody behaves differently from one situation to another, or with one group of people or another. But I think what you're really talking about is something less tangible and less planned out. The inner life of the character comes in that build-up period where it's just sitting with you and you start to get more and more specific about the thoughts and feelings and memories that the character might have had. Or even the physical objects that might have some resonance with the character. It's all about finding specific things that have *emotional* resonance, that make you *feel* something just by thinking of them, or looking at them, or hearing them. Things that have an emotional resonance for that character and for you *as* that character.

Which is more important as signposts to this inner life: the text – the written lines – or the subtext, what the character might be thinking or feeling, but is not able to say . . . you know, the gap?

You're saying that the inner life *is* the gap between the text and the subtext?

I'm asking what that means to you.

Ah. That's interesting. Look! Most people rarely say what they mean. An age-old thing that Uta Hagen made famous, is to ask: what do I want? And that remains a very good way to start thinking about a scene in a way that isn't entirely dependent on the text. Obviously there's plenty to be gleaned from the text itself, but you need to work out what you want in the scene. I had an acting teacher once who had, I think, an even better way of putting it, which was, 'How do you want to make the other person feel?' That's so cool because it makes everything that you're doing active. It takes the attention off yourself because you're concentrating on trying to make the other person feel a certain way. That could be to make somebody feel loved, humiliated, interesting, stupid, or funny. Those are all things that you channel through the text, but the text could be anything. It's fascinating when you deal with text that's doing the opposite of what you're trying to make somebody feel.

A text that is rich with subtext.

Right.

What about when you're working with aspects of a character which are not, on the surface of it, lovable or likeable? How do you approach that?

[long pause] I think that you always have to love the character. A lot of actors will say that and I think it's true. You can't ever judge the character. It's always good to find the humanity in someone. Even people who have done the most appalling things, if you were to sit down and talk to them, you would find that they're human beings and are capable of all kinds of conflicting emotions. Their impulses and their reasons for doing things are so complex and affected by so many different things. So I look for moments to bring out what is most human and identifiable in a character, even if he's a villain in the story. That doesn't mean that I think that one should try and sugar-coat or avoid. There need to be other moments that totally indulge the character's worst fears or instincts. Maybe the most challenging situation morally or ethically that I've had as an actor was playing a real person who's suspected of one of the most horrific crimes of the century, but who has not been convicted and whom many people think is innocent. Others are convinced he's guilty. He probably did do some very abusive things to people in his family, whether or not he was guilty of the real heinous crime. He was also capable of being romantic, affectionate, protective and loving of his wife and children, despite also having real capacity for rage. I knew that everything I did was going to be scrutinised in terms of did he or didn't he . . . So from one scene to the next I wanted to seem capable alternately of great warmth and kindness and then of murder.

Do you think of yourself as a character actor, and if so, what does it mean to take on another self?

I do think of myself that way. The term has all kinds of resonances because of the way that it's used in Hollywood, which basically means a supporting actor.

I see, so it's a euphemism for them?

Yeah. When you say somebody's a character actor in Hollywood, it means one of those guys who pops up in little parts and who has a moustache or whatever.

But what does it mean to you?

To me, it means . . . you know, all of my idols. Robert DeNiro, Daniel Day Lewis, Sean Penn, Robert Duvall. These are people who in almost every role, transform themselves both physically and behaviourally. Their whole essence changes. And I think that I became an actor to get away from having to be myself. My instinct always propelled me towards playing characters that had something, at least at face value, that was very different from me. I felt it gave me freedom.

Do you think there is any such thing as a fixed self?

No. I think that we change as we grow. I've just worked with Christian Bale and I've never encountered him when he's not got some character going. And he tends to keep it alive throughout the process of filming. I don't know who he is beyond whatever he's playing and I sometimes feel the same way. I have so much uncertainty about myself and how to interact with the world and I change my mind about it constantly. I've never had a fixed identity in that way, which, by the way *[long pause, sighs]* some people would say you have to have, to be a movie star. I remember Nic Cage saying to me, when I was in *Face/Off* with him, 'You know, I mean Alessandro, who do you wanna *be* man? I mean like, you know, who *are* you? What's your *deal?*' *[SP laughs]* And I was like, 'I don't know what you're talking about, I have no idea, I don't know what I wanna be, I just wanna play a lot of different characters.' And he was like, 'Well, you better figure it out,' and you know I never really did. Some great actors have strong personalities that come through in all of their roles. There's some part of them that you can see in every one of their performances, even though, technically, there's all of this mastery that obscures it.

Do you experience that 'double presence' yourself? That you are you – and not you – at the same time when you're working?

Yeah, more and more. Putting a performance together for me has always been like scavenging, collecting things from my own experience that I could use. But recently I feel that I've been able to let my own voice come through, even when I'm trying to play somebody who sounds very different to me.

In the shoot, what do you feel you really need from the director?

First of all you want to feel there's an environment where, even if you're on a short shoot, and you're in a rush, you can try things that won't work or do things that might be totally misguided – or even terrible – if they ended up in the film. *[SP laughs]* You want to feel that the director even encourages you to do that, and is going to protect you by knowing how to get rid of all that stuff when they're editing. You want the feeling that there's a little bit of messiness, that everything isn't too tight. And then as far as the way you want to be directed, that's so much to do with the different personalities of different directors, but generally you want to be nudged. You don't want it to be laid out in prosaic terms, you want to be given a hint. Sometimes there's something that's called for which is technical and that's different. But if it's a quality or a feeling, you just want them to say something that gets to the heart of the matter. And then ask you to interpret it in a way that feels personal to you.

Does it matter to you whether the director is looking at you or at the monitor during a take?

No, I think that's something that's up to the director, how they like to witness the thing. I'm not even that aware of where the director's looking while I'm doing the take.

How aware are you of the lens? Or the presence of the camera as a channel to the audience?

I try to not be aware of the lens, in the sense of how it's catching my face, because then your performance gets affected by trying to play to the camera in a certain way. But the director needs to be aware of that because the slightest change of angle can affect the power that a performance has in a given moment.

Absolutely.

But on the other hand, I do feel as an actor you have to feel open to the lens. It's as if you want the lens to see inside you.

Yes.

In film acting, unlike stage acting, you also have to hide a bit from the lens. You can't give it all away to the lens or else it becomes pushed. It's paradoxical.

Do you feel the lens has to come and find you?

Yeah, I guess.

How do you feel about watching yourself in the finished film?

Increasingly, I don't like it very much. There are a lot of films I've been in that I've never even seen. *[both laugh]* It makes me feel uncomfortable. The experience that you have watching your own performance is so different to the experience that other people have watching it that it almost seems useless. By the time the film's made, the performance isn't for you anyway, it's for the audience.

Are you aware of the audience while you're filming? Or a future, imaginary audience?

I'm always surprised when, after being in the cloistered environment of making a film, suddenly there are hundreds of people watching it. The feeling is that you've been in another world. You often forget while you're filming that every little thing you're doing is going to be projected for hundreds of people. In terms of story-telling, you want things to be clear, you want the story to play. And there are certain choices you need to make, as an actor, in order to tell the story.

What about when the film finally comes out into the world, and there are premieres, publicity junkets and critics. What is that transition like for you?

The nice thing, once the film's all done and people are watching, is that you feel you can sit back and be interested by the way that people respond to it. Of course there's pressure and it affects your career and all that kind of thing but, as far as the emotion of it, you feel kind of detached. At least I do, because so much time has gone by. I don't mind doing all the promotional stuff, especially if it's for something that I feel passionate about, and want people to see, but it's something that I've never quite been a master at. Some people are just so brilliant at self-promotion, and I'm not.

You mentioned earlier that you felt your experience of being a producer has changed your feelings about acting and also about directors. What do you think has shifted by moving across into that other role?

Oh, God! It comes back to what I was saying earlier, confirming that the movie really belongs to the director. Everybody is there to try and facilitate that, including the actors. I guess it also makes you appreciate what the actors have to go through even more because, from a producer's standpoint, you're dealing with so many things, that trying to make things comfortable for the actors is not necessarily the top priority. *[SP laughs]* You feel for the actors who have schedules changed on them in the blink of an eye and have to come in and give a performance. But really, the bigger picture is that it's all down to the director.

Happiness on set: lucky bonus or necessity?

It always seems that the happiest sets made the worst films. *[SP laughs]* But no, it's great if you get along with everybody. Happiness is such a relative term. In film-making, you're never happy. You're energised and you're excited, you're alive and you're curious, you're adrenalin-soaked and all those things, but that's different from happiness. I don't think I've ever been happy on a film, but I have had all those other feelings.

TIMOTHY SPALL

I once saw Tim dancing late at night in the cafeteria at the Dinard film festival – a French festival celebrating British cinema – where I was showing *Yes*. He and Simon Abkarian improvised a wild duet that had tears of love and laughter streaming down my face. But I had often wept whilst watching Tim on the screen: his quality of tender humanity, so radiantly evident in films such as Mike Leigh's *All or Nothing*, (2002) made watching him feel like I was connecting with a dear and intimate friend, whose aspirations and failures left me heartbroken.

I tried writing a role for him in a script that didn't quite make it, but when I wrote *Ginger & Rosa* I started to visualise him as Mark, one half of an adorable gay couple, the only force of stability in a rocky personal and political environment. He came to our first meeting armed with an entire and credible back-story for Mark, and we took off from there.

Two years later he climbed the steep stairs to my studio in East London for this interview, entirely transformed. He was deep in preparation to play Turner in a new Mike Leigh film and even his way of looking at me had become the steely, penetrative gaze of a painter. As usual, he had me practically crying with laughter and I felt a familiar melancholy when it was time for him to leave.

That's a dinky one ain't it? *[indicating the recording device]*

It is a dinky one.

Looks like you can do your nasal hair with it as well. *[laughs]*

[SP laughs] OK. Right then. What's more important to you, the script or the director, when you're deciding whether to do a film?

Considering that you get more scripts from directors that you don't know, the script is always something that is very, very important. If it's a really good script from a director that you've never heard of, you have to make a massive leap of faith. Then you go and meet them and really that doesn't tell you very much. As we know – not always – but talk is cheap. You can get an idea but it's difficult. But if you get a good script from a director whose work you know and like and admire then that is a far easier decision to make. But sometimes if it isn't an offer then it's very frustrating because you think, 'I really want to do that!' and they might not offer it to me, you know? So definitely, definitely the script is paramount. If I got a script that I thought had problems but I knew the director was good I would always want to know whether the part was still in development. Was there any wiggle room in the character being developed more? And then a director, if they're good, will tell you straight and honestly if they think it can be done. Or they say, 'If you read it again you'll realise the character is more important than you think.' Actors all want big parts, you know. *[laughs]* They never say, 'Oh please give me the smallest part!' They want a really nice role and it's not just about showing off. There's more to it than that.

But sometimes the script is interesting, the director is interesting, it's only one scene but you think, 'My goodness me! I can't see any reason – if it works – that I would not do that.' Because what comes with it is very important, very textured. Two classic examples come to mind. There's Vanessa Redgrave in *Atonement* (2007). And there's Orson Welles in *The Third Man* (1949). They are scintillating moments and never forgotten. It's like a painting, isn't it? In the foreground there's a wonderful, gorgeous, evocation of beauty and in the background there might be something really strange and that's the thing that draws your eye.

You've mentioned 'good director' several times – what makes one good from your perspective?

You know if you're working with a good director. A good director is like a good author. They don't usually write any characters that don't speak to the audience, even if they only turn up for a second. A good director would want that person to be imbued with meaning and to emanate humanity. That's what a good director does. I suppose that's called art: understanding that nothing is wasted. In a great script every character will have some form of wealth. There's that story, you know, about *A Streetcar Named Desire*. Right at the end there is an old lady selling flowers, all she says is, 'Flowers for sale, flowers for sale.' Somebody meets her in a bar in New Orleans and asks, 'What are you doing at the moment, Gladys?'

and she says, 'Oh I'm doing a Tennessee Williams play.' 'So what's it about?' – and she says, 'Well it's about this old woman who goes around selling flowers.' *[Laughs]* Now you could put that down to someone who is completely misguided, or there's another way of looking at it which is, 'I might not be playing the lead but I'm the lead of my own part.'

But you know when a script is weak. It's when it's hard to read. And you know what makes it even harder is when potentially it could have been good. Then the energy you have to expend to try and make it work in your head –

– it's exhausting –

– and you feel like crying at the end of it because you know it could have been good. But to go back to your original question: you know when you do get a good script. When you sent me your script and I knew you were directing it, I read it and I thought, 'Praise the Lord.' And then we had a meeting – a long, long meeting. Some directors know who they want straight away, some have to consider it because of the ensemble they want to put together. I knew that you needed to cogitate . . . but we had a really good meeting and I think you told me at the time that you would like me to do it.

I did.

And I was delighted. The script obviously meant something personal to you and it meant something to me as well.

What are you usually hoping for in that first meeting with a director? What qualities are you hoping to find?

Speaking for myself – and I think it might be typical of a lot of actors – is that we are this peculiar mixture of chutzpah and insecurity. So even if we're showing ourselves with lightning-style confidence, we're shitting ourselves inside. We're hoping the director is not going to look at us like, 'Oh my God, I've made a mistake.' You're hoping that what you tentatively start sharing with the director, the director will understand, and it will become a dialogue, an exchange. It doesn't have to be a long conversation. It doesn't have to be in depth. It might just be, 'Oh, I thought I would do it like this.' And then a very good director sees it and if they don't like it they won't just say, 'No that's crap.' They'll say, 'That's interesting,' and they will find another way of introducing a different approach. An actor knows when a director knows that an actor knows that a director knows – all those telepathic things. It's like improvising an emotional riff, in a benign way, about trying to create something that suits both of you. Or sometimes there's conflict. I've been in horrendous situations where I've felt like the director hasn't liked what I've been doing and hasn't been able to tell me why. But sometimes a director doesn't have to say anything. I've worked with directors who say nothing at all.

Right from the beginning?

I'll give you an example: I had a small part in one of the first films Clint Eastwood was directing. I was thinking, 'Oh, Clint Eastwood, I've been watching him since I was a kid.' I was playing the Bush pilot. I was in this little airplane with him and we did a take. He said 'OK, cut.' Then he said *[imitating Clint Eastwood's voice]* 'OK . . . OK, yeah . . . Let's go again.' *[both laugh]* And that was his direction! I thought, 'That's alright!'

But did you get it? Did you get what the message was?

Yeah, yeah! I got it!

So it's not necessarily about the words anyway? It's a quality of resonance. Right from the beginning.

Yes. There's a telepathy: you catch a look in people's eyes. Long before I came to see you, I tried reading the script and coming up with all sorts of scenarios of what the character's background was. And everything I said you mostly agreed with and if you didn't, you said, 'Ah yes, or perhaps this,' and then all of a sudden I knew I was with someone who I was going to have a dialogue with. Although eventually we didn't talk enormously about it, we mostly just did it. I remember you saying a wonderful thing in a scene where Ginger has come round and she's dealing with a terrible loss. We were like surrogate uncles really, the gay couple, the two Marks. And you said to me that for her being with them was like cake. When you feel insecure and you go into an environment where the whole feeling of the place is one of an old-fashioned, inexplicable comfort that assuages feelings of fear. Cake. It just made absolute sense. And these two guys you know, they'll probably go down in history as two of the fattest, ugliest queens!

No. Everyone loves them!

Do they?

They love them! Everyone wants Marks. That's the thing that people say to me: 'Where are my Marks?'

And I knew that's what you were after in those characters. I knew that's what they were representing. And also what you were saying was 'look this was nineteen-sixty . . . '

Sixty-two.

So this was pre-Wolfenden?

Yes.

So here we are, two – I don't even think they used the term homosexual in those days – two 'perverts', in the eyes of the law. These two men were surrounded by attractive, gorgeous, bright young radicals, all fucking up their own lives. And these two clever, middle-aged, homosexual men who loved each other represented wholesomeness in a world that was about to obliterate itself. They just happened to be what a lot of people would regard as perverts in both regimes, both the Soviet Union and the Western world, but in this story they represented stability, salvation and the simplicity of their love. There is poetry in that simplicity. I think that's another thing that you look for in a script. The poetry in the simplicity and the banal. There can be an evil in the banal or poetry in the comic, or tragic-comic. With you I always felt that we were on the same – I don't like saying the same page because it's such an over-used word – but we were in the same ether.

That's a good word, ether. And telepathy. These are quite ephemeral concepts but for us they are completely real, am I right?

I think they are! To outsiders they can sound pretentiously mysterious but collaboration has to have all these elements. It can't just be mathematics. There are of course technical things to deal with but the mathematics is the easy part. It's the conjoining of the artistic collaboration that needs these qualities that are difficult to define.

So in that first meeting with the director – any director – it's really about evaluating as fast as possible what the quality of the relationship might be.

Yes.

What clues are there?

We got on immediately – but it doesn't have to be like that. Some directors are quite aloof, some directors are quite grumpy, some directors are quite explosive, some directors are noisy, pissed off or just pissed! *[laughs]* As long as you know that those conflicting personalities are all pulling on the same rope, it works.

What do you wish that all directors understood about actors?

We're frightened babies. Frightened but very clever babies. I was thinking about it the other day: 'My God, I'm so childish. Isn't it time I grew up?' I brought up three children, I've got three grand-children but I'm still childish. But sometimes I think that actually as an actor you can't be anything else. You know the term 'play'. You play a part. It's all about playing and it's about identification. You can watch a little girl playing, completely immersed in setting up an entire planet in front of her and being every different character. It's what you do as an actor. It's only trying to transfer all of that child-ish openness and creativity and invest it in what is written down in a script. You meet some actors and they're playing kings and you feel . . . 'My God this man could rule a continent!' And then all of a sudden you catch something in his eye. Or you see the back of his neck and you think, 'You still wish your dad loved you more.'

I'll never forget the time I was working with Bertolucci on *The Sheltering Sky* (1990). I was sitting in the caravan out in the middle of one of the bleeding deserts and a lovely actor came in and we were waiting to shoot a scene. He was a lovely jolly actor. He was gay and camp and very funny and we were having a laugh, being funny together, and then he started talking about his childhood and he began to cry. He said, 'My dad used to hit me and all I wanted him to do was love me and cuddle me.' It really broke my bloody heart. You've always got to remember that someone might seem absolutely confident but what people present as their personality is only the skim off the top. What makes them the way they are is the interesting thing. All that stew of their life. I suppose that's why you've got to keep the lid on. Lots of people go around doing an impersonation of being grown-up. You see them at conventions: 'I'm a man, I'm a suit,' and you know they've had to screw the lid down as a kid. The actors with all the lids open can be a massive pain in the arse. But if you can keep the lid on loosely, you can keep opening it up when you need to. I'm sure you've worked with a few actors where the child never stops. All they want is attention all the time. That's predicated on insecurity.

What about yourself? Have you ever been in a situation like that where you just can't get an actor to do things the way you want them to?

I've never really found myself in that situation. If one can smell something going off the rails you've got to stop the clock and deal with it immediately.

Come at it from a different way.

Yes, or find out what's really going on. There's always a reason. And always a way. But you need to have built up trust, built a relationship.

Some directors like to come up to you and scream in your face.

Do they?

Well, I've never had that but I have seen it. I've seen people get very annoyed and shout and be rude.

Do you think that's ever effective?

No, no. It's never effective. It destroys people's confidence. It's a waste of time. Pointless, pointless, pointless. Because as I say, most people are not fucking it up on purpose. They're fucking up because they don't know what they're doing. Or they're doing it wrong because they're scared and need help. They don't need screaming at, you know?

I agree. What about any other misconceptions about the actor's inner process? Are there things that you need to keep hidden?

When you think about conjurors and magicians – and there are some brilliant ones around – we all know it's a trick but the one thing they never do is tell you how they do it. That's why it succeeds. Same as professional wrestling; we all know it's choreographed but if you told a professional wrestler that they just make it all up, they go mad, they would be incensed. But with actors, because of the 'making of . . .' movies and because people are intrigued by the cult of celebrity, we get asked to tell all. It's tied in with all the bullshit fashion, selling things, perceptions of beauty, all that. Actors tend to be sucked into a world where if they are perceived as beautiful or in some way representative of what people aspire to, they are seen as more special than they actually are. So it pulls them into an over-inflated self-image. I don't think it can be helped. I think it has happened more and more recently because of the way advertising has become so much subtler at doing what it does.

Do you feel that you have avoided some of that?

I can safely say to you that I am not wearing one article of clothing that has been sponsored. I don't get calls from Chanel. I once got a shirt from someone who I was sitting next to who worked for a shirt company. But I'm neither the shape nor am I the type of actor that attracts that kind of thing. It's aspiration and association. The world has always had its models but advertising has bolted itself on more cleverly to film and television than it used to.

Incredible changes.

There's almost a tacit – I wouldn't say conspiracy – but there's a tacit agreement between television, film, the music industry and magazines and retail. You can't blame people making money out of them. Somebody says, 'Oh, you're nominated for an Oscar, do you fancy wearing an £18,000 watch?' 'Yeah alright, thank you, if you've got one going!' *[laughs]*

It's never happened to me! But I can't remember what the original question was . . .

The actor's process, and then whether you had escaped the whole machine that you started talking about: advertising, celebrity . . .

Yes. I actually find the word celebrity a bit offensive.

It is offensive.

It's become meaningless, you know. It just means a person who is celebrated. To me what I am, apart from being a person, is an actor. I am a depicter.

How important is detailed preparatory work on the script with the director for you? As a depicter?

One has come to terms with the fact that it doesn't have to be crucial. In fact, rather alarmingly, it has become an exception to the rule. You really don't get much time these days. You know, sometimes I've been in things where I've just turned up on the day and you just have to do it. When I first started you used to rehearse things properly. Sometimes you over-rehearsed things in the old multi-camera days and it all looked a bit turgid, like a hybrid between a play and a film. But I do think – although it's always a bit nerve-racking – that a read-through is important. I've always thought they are a necessary evil as it often feels like a protracted exercise in getting the sack. *[laughs]* But I think it is crucial. Though sometimes it's a crucial luxury. And of course if it's a low-budget movie, a really low-budget movie – and there are lots of them about, low- or no-budget movies – the only time you ever have to talk about it is the time when you met them eighteen months ago in a caff. I did a film where we had an hour's conversation and eighteen months later we shot the scenes one after another. Big dialogue scenes.

What about the look? Clothes and so on. How important is that to you in the preparatory process?

Very important. Working with Mike Leigh, we learned how to prepare – it's all part of the organic deal with him, building as you go along. For months. But more often after you've had your conversation with a director, the next person you meet is the costume designer. There's always a bit of discomfort because you've got to get undressed in front of people, which is a bit embarrassing, particularly people you don't know. I'm just flagrant now. As long as I've remembered to put me underwear on and it's clean, I've stopped worrying about me tits and all that, I don't care any more. *[laughs]* I've got hair on me chest so at least I'm a man. But then when you start putting the clothes on you start thinking, 'Oh yeah, yeah.' Do you remember when we did Mark and we put those glasses on and that hat, all of a sudden: bang! There was this man. You could see he had lived in America because of the hat and from his glasses that he was terribly English, and there was something about him that was cosmopolitan. He had a sort of homeliness about him and a touch of the dandy about him.

One thing you have to remember if you're doing a period piece is that the clothes were cut differently, which makes your posture different. The cut of a jacket, the fact that you very rarely took it off. All these things that we've forgotten, all these etiquettes. And the fact that you wore a tie, all these details that contribute to the accuracy and the authenticity of what somebody from a particular period is like. Now you watch a lot of period stuff and men often wear hats in the wrong way and girls walk in period clothes as if they're in jeans. The choices of what clothes a character chooses to wear and how he wears them, physically, are vital. And I have played a myriad of characters who wear horrible clothes . . . *[laughs]*

Clothes that represent a lack of taste, a pretension, a terrible mistake with their choices, such as someone who is trying to wear the clothes much too young . . . all of those things that I think most actors would avoid because they don't want to look like shit. But to me looking like shit is sometimes crucial – *[laughs]* – absolutely crucial. It's different with a wish-fulfilment character – you know, some people have got to look really cool, they just have to. But my characters tend to be the way that people actually are, not the way you would like them to be. You don't want to be distractingly awful but whatever you do, you must you serve the character, not serve yourself. And by serving the character you're serving the authenticity of the script and then you're serving the principle of the art of the piece.

How consciously do you draw on, or reference, your own life, when you're working on a character?

All the time. All the time. My life is the only life I've had, as far as I know. And it's been quite varied and eventful. I've had the luck to travel a lot, I've had the luck to have children, I've had the luck to have grandchildren, I've had the misfortune but then the eventual luck to have had a life-threatening disease which went away through a mixture of love and expertise. I have an imagination and an enquiring mind. I spend a lot of time looking at things and registering them. I'm very sentimental, in the purest sense. I can find things heartbreaking that I see in the street. I'm not trying to make myself out as some kind of shaman but I do think that you've got to keep looking, keep your mind open, keep understanding. For example, sometimes when you're in a bad mood you don't give a fuck about anything. If you're playing someone who's always nice, you're playing a saint. You're playing St Francis of Assisi. But if he had an infected haemorrhoid *[laughs]* and a pigeon shat on his head, he's not going to be happy about it, he's going to be pissed off.

The contradictions are very important. There's no such thing as a truly bad person, there's no such thing as a truly good person. Hitler has got to be one of the most evil men in living memory or in the history of the world. But I remember watching some footage from the very last days of the war when the Allied troops were coming, just before he went into his bunker, and a whole row of troops had been pulled out. Some of them were kids of about twelve or thirteen, some of them were men in their seventies, and he was just going along the rows talking to them. There was a little boy, and Hitler ruffled his hair. I thought, 'You are Hitler, you are a man who has committed in your name some of the most heinous crimes in the world,' but there was a look in his face at that moment that I felt pity for.

Let's talk about the shoot. Let's assume you have had some rehearsal, you've got the costume, you've done your preparations. What do you really need from the director when you're shooting?

I used to wing it quite a lot when I was a younger, lazier actor. I didn't learn my lines as well as I should have done. Now I learn my lines very, very well and I think a hell of a lot about the way that I'm going to do it. I will speak it aloud on my own but I very rarely run lines with anyone, not even my wife. It's a private process. And then when we come to shoot it, when the lovely men and women with the machines turn up, we know it starts to become a technical exercise as well, so we have to find our marks and we sometimes have to change our performances, depending how far away the camera is from us or how close it is. So all of these processes can affect what I've thought about previously. And obviously you're always working against the clock. But that's not always a bad thing because it sticks a squib up your arse and it makes you get on with it, it means you can't piss about.

But there's usually a lovely moment – and sometimes it can happen straight away or sometimes it takes a few days – where everybody gets to know the rhythm of the shoot. There's the rehearsal, then the cameraman comes in to see the rehearsal, the sound guys attach the radio mike. It all becomes a collaboration. I remember as a young actor arriving on set and feeling it's all big blokes with machines shouting at each other about four k's, five k's, and I don't know what they're doing. They all look like blokes I went to school with. Aargh! Now I see that it's all part of the process. You do sometimes feel small and the director's often distracted, dealing with everybody. You've got to realise that you are then part of capturing something that doesn't exist. You've got, if you're lucky, about three or four times to get it. And that's when you can really lose your bottle. Because you know – particularly if it's a great big close-up and you're getting it wrong – that one day you're going to be sitting in a cinema and your head is going to be forty foot high and you're going to think, 'Oh for fuck's sake, I shouldn't have done that.' *[laughs]*

Somebody said to me, 'You have to trust the process.' And it becomes a process – not like the process of making sausages – but a process that is constantly evolving. We know there's a great big fucking monster with a whip called Time behind us but you just have to say to it: 'Hang on a minute. We're playing the game. We know you're the monster with the whip but you're going to get fuck all if you keep whipping us until we get it right.' So to me that's what the shoot is. And the director is directing this process. In charge. The guvnor. So you know that if the director is feeling that it's working and is happy with what you're doing you have to trust. It becomes a shared experience.

How aware of the camera are you when shooting?

I know where the camera is. I know that it is the audience and I know that it is the capturer. That bit of metal with a lens, and a clockwork thing and whatever is in it now – computers; that is the thing that is capturing it all. It is the fishing rod, the trawling net and the flipping microscope that catches the disease or cures it. It's easy to sound pretentious but I know where it is, without analysing it. I vaguely know what lens sizes are. I don't really take much interest in that. Someone said to me, 'You either know everything or you don't know fuck all.' I know quite a lot but I don't want to know all the ins and outs of it. But I know that everything I thought about the character, everything I've worn, everything I'm saying is for that fucking thing. It's for the camera. That snooping, sneaking, snoopy gatherer. That bloody interloper. The interloper of utmost importance.

You've got your interloper, you've got who you're relating to in the scene. What about the actual eyes of the director? Does that make a difference to you? Are you aware of them?

Oh yeah. Oh yeah. There's a modern strange thing that's happened because of the use of playback and monitors. Now in America they've started to call it 'video city', haven't they? You know, where the scene is taking place over here and there are seventeen people over there with about ten monitors and people pressing buttons. I like it when the director's close by, like you. I need to see what the director's face is doing when they're watching the scene. To me it's very important.

So it's like a triangle actually: camera, actor, director.

Oh yeah. Totally. Absolutely. As I say: 'That is the trinity.' And of course the other thing is the attempt to behave how a human being would with another human being.

In the midst of all that.

Yes.

Do you necessarily trust your subjective experience as you're doing it or do you feel that the director needs to carry the outside eye, the objectivity? Let me give you an example: you think it's the best – or worst – take that you've done, the director doesn't agree – or vice versa – and later on you see the result and find out that actually there wasn't a correlation between how you felt at the time and how good or bad it was.

I think you can safely say all of the above. An actor is obsessed with his performance, fundamentally about getting it right. During the process you often take your eye off the ball of the whole thing. You shouldn't do but you often do. You're just playing a part and you don't know the consequences elsewhere in the film.

So how you feel in the moment is not necessarily the criterion for whether it's good or bad.

No, because you can do something where you think, 'God, that felt like that was really spot on,' and then a director says to you, 'Well, actually that one you just did was good, but two takes ago was *really* good. It was way less on the nose.' Because the thing is that subjectivity can make you overdo things, even overdo naturalism, in a weird way. Some people do things for an effect.

Which at the time gives a full feeling, a big experience, but can push the audience away. Sometimes a better performance actually feels less strong to the actor but draws the audience in.

Well, that's why the trust in the director's view is very important. I have grown to know that feeling – and it doesn't have to be all about emotion, it can be a feeling of blankness or whatever – is secondary to the trust I have with the director. I went through an experience recently, on a comedy of all things, in which I was playing one of the main characters, and it all went wrong. I felt that I lost the confidence of the people who employed me and I felt that the director was going through the motions. I had nowhere to turn. I relied on the kindness of some people who knew I was in agony.

They got me through. To illustrate how important this connection with the director is, even if it's one of tacitness – this experience was the loneliest I've ever felt professionally. And the most distraught and desolate I've ever felt. It was crippling. Of course the thing turned out to be a massive fucking success. *[laughs]* But it left a massive, massive sore in my guts.

Did you feel that the director was absent?

Yeah. I think, yes. I think he felt that other people had been sacked around him and that he was the one that should have got sacked.

Oh right, so he was scared. Which brings us to a happy shoot: necessity or lucky bonus?

Lucky bonus. I've done films that have been a hoot. A love-fest from beginning to end that have turned out to be the biggest piece of shit in the world. And I've done several agonising 'Oh my God, do I have to get out of bed this morning and go to that shithole' ones that have turned out to be massive successes. And they're often comedies. So it's exactly what you said, a happy bonus. And you know it's bloody wonderful if you have a great time and it turns out to be a great film but they don't always go together.

Is there a metaphysical element to the aspect of your job we sometimes call presence?

Metaphysical. It's a very, very interesting question. I just need to think about it for a second. You could say that it's become one of those 'macrobiotic' sort of words – the channelling of things. The channelling of the elements of being human. The best acting never looks like acting, does it? In a weird way it's the opposite of acting. It is inhabiting something that doesn't exist until you do it.

Do you think it's also possible that the best directing doesn't look like directing?

In my experience that is the case. It's a given that what we're trying to do is alchemy. It is a bit of wizardry. OK, it's technical, it's concrete, it's physical, it's artwork and sometimes it's bloody tedious, but in the end, without the alchemy, it's nothing. That little bit extra, that is almost indescribably subtle, is a product of all of the telepathy, all of the leaps of faith, all of the runes being cast in the right or the wrong way. All these things are metaphysical. They are. OK, they are the product of the human intellect, but sometimes I do believe . . . I don't want to live in a world that doesn't have magic in it. I just don't like the idea of that. I was watching something the other day. It was Robert Mitchum in one of those war films where he's looking after a nun. There was a corny old scene but there was something about it that was sincere. He was apologising. He was handsome. And he was very, very funny. And I thought: that's magic. That's turning base metal into gold.

Afterword

Talking with the actors I have worked with on such different films felt like bringing them together into one space, a space flooded with the strong working memories that lead to a very particular form of mutual affection. I relished the opportunity to connect with each of them again and examine what we do. I was struck, once I had finished editing the interviews – a process that felt intriguingly similar to my work on their performances in the cutting room – by how many times the actors revealed their basic needs to be so simple. Again and again they expressed, each in their own unique way, that the work they do leaves them vulnerable and exposed, often afraid, and that what they most need from the director is simply kindness.

How is it that directors can forget such a basic human principle? It seems as if the pervasive atmosphere in which we all work, or attempt to learn new skills, is judgemental. 'Mistakes' are seen as failures rather than steps along the way of discovery. If a new director could remember only one thing from this book that would help their work with actors beyond measure, it would be this: be kind. Remember that a performance does not usually arrive fully formed: it is a process of evolution. For this evolution to take place, the actor needs to be able to experiment in a non-judgemental, enthusiastic atmosphere and the director needs to develop a quality of compassion for the testing processes involved.

Trust was a key word, again and again. The trust described is twofold: the actor needs to feel they can trust the director humanly, and will thrive in a safe, open, respectful atmosphere, but also needs to trust that you know what you are doing. They can only surrender to the process, concentrate on the task in hand, if they know that you are doing your job with total commitment and even a degree of ruthlessness. Kindness, in that sense, is secondary to a consistent and determined directorial vision. Actors may want to have a good, enriching experience, but above all long to be part of a good film, something that was worth the effort and commitment and fulfils the hope and expectation they invested in it.

I was intrigued to find that most – though not all – of the actors I talked with relished the idea of rehearsal, though with some caution about the danger of losing spontaneity. My own emphasis on working on the 'why' rather than trying to establish the 'how' of a performance is a guide to how to navigate around this fear.

I was surprised to find that whilst some actors preferred to be watched by the director during takes, others preferred not to be aware of his or her presence. There was a significant split in the needs and desires expressed, which means, yet again, that the director needs to take a flexible, adaptable and individual approach.

The time and energy the director needs to give to all aspects of a film – how it looks, sounds and is structured – means that actors may sometimes feel neglected during a shoot. This is far less likely to occur if you have had some meaningful time together in preparation. I was surprised to learn how, on most films, the actors usually prepare for their roles alone. I have rarely experienced actors resisting my involvement in – and enthusiastic engagement with – their preparation process, but it seems this is relatively rare. I began to wonder whether some of what I experience as essential (sharing as much as I can with the actor, being present at costume fittings, drawing out memories and experiences, etc.) might, for some of them, feel like an invasion of their private exploratory territory. But what I aim for is a state of respectful interdependence in which the need I have for their work – and the need they have for mine – is seen as a source of strength rather than weakness.

Also I began to wonder, when some of the actors expressed

puzzlement as I questioned them about being looked at, whether some of the invisible things I think I am doing (creating a force-field of attention with my focused gaze, for example) are illusory. Like prayer or private vows of intention and motivation, these things are hard to measure, and their effectiveness is open to question when examined objectively. Nevertheless I continue to believe that these subtle, interior questions of attitude, will and desire on the director's part do have an effect. I am quite sure that my love of actors and their process does land somewhere in them and is useful. It also leads me to a state of empathy and resonance with them that I hope transmutes into a quality of performance on screen.

Every actor mentioned the pressure of time – the high-tensile speed of a shoot – as a challenge to doing good work, though one or two relished it. Dealing with the apparent lack of time is something all of us working in film have in common, whatever our job. We try to do our best work on little sleep and with scarcely a moment to reflect. Mastery of time – learning to work accurately at speed, without panic or the feeling of being rushed, or rushing others – is a vital skill for a director to acquire. Essentially it is a matter of keeping track of priorities, which means continually, repeatedly, attempting to return to first principles. Why are we doing this? What is truly necessary to tell the story? Where is its core? Often the answers to these questions will be revealed in the work with the actors.

I was reminded by some actors' responses that the director's hand is always there, but need not be heavy. Some of the actors refer to the need to 'play' or be 'playful', even though we are often working on the most intense emotions: the longings and losses experienced in every human life. The director's passion for cinema – its visual magic, the power of words, the articulacy of action, the potent meanings in objects and environments, the rich layers of sound, the glory of colour, the play of light and shade – must be accompanied by a passion for understanding the actor's task in embodying the fragile, complex humans who move through the shadowy, impermanent conditions of everyday life. Laughter helps to puncture any over-seriousness, and we laughed a lot during the interviews, as we often do in rehearsal and during shoots.

When I questioned the actors closely, their deeper ambitions had nothing to do with fame, 'celebrity' or measurable achievement. I love them for that. The nearest word to describe what we seem to be seeking to touch together in our work is 'truth', though that word – like beauty – has become imprecise through over-use. What does it mean to be 'true' when definitions of what is real or authentic vary according to genre conventions or the film-maker's intentions? Nevertheless, as the world of the film evolves, one begins to sense what is working, what seems transparent, truthful or right; the consequence of a deeper impulse.

I asked many of the actors whether they experienced a hidden sense of purpose that others might not understand or recognise in their work. Each person had a different frame of reference – religious, secular, professional or personal – in which to answer the question. I gradually realised I might be pushing them to express something I believed myself. It was as if I was trying to make the interviews themselves an extension of our working relationship: my voice coming through theirs, my thoughts transmuted through their bodies. What I wanted to get at was the paradox of cinema – that we work so hard on the practical, concrete, visible and audible details of this ephemeral form, precisely in order to evoke an immaterial, invisible and unhearable universe of human experience. This is what makes cinema, for me, magical and inexhaustible.

Acknowledgements

This book could not have been written without the rich, sometimes testing and often joyful experience of collaborating with actors. I learnt how to direct by working with each and every one of them. Sandy Daley and Nicholas Quennell lent me an 8mm camera when I was a teenager and got me started. I was fortunate to experience early collaborative relationships with Jacky Lansley and Rose English in which the boundaries between performer and director were blurred and often interchangeable. Together we discovered that these 'identities' are simply an agreement to occupy one role or the other. Lindy Davies and I compared notes and offered mutual solidarity from our different yet overlapping directorial perspectives. David Mitchell and David Hass inspired me with their intelligent and passionate enthusiasms. Walter Donohue has been a sure-footed editor, exercising good judgement and inspiring confidence. Sarah Chalfant read and encouraged in all the right ways. Christopher Sheppard, as always, has been a solidly positive presence throughout my doubts. Hunny and my mum nurtured my fascination with performance in all its forms in addition to giving me life and love, without which there is nothing.

Picture Credits

All images © Adventure Pictures.
Photographed by Helen Leoussi: xiii; by Roger Perry: xiv, xx; by the author: xvi, 10, 16, 33 (bottom), 49, 52, 143, 161, 223, 236, 254, 273, 352; by Moune Jamet: 1, 96, 112; by Liam Longman: 5, 48, 125, 128; by Christopher Sheppard: 21, 33 (top), 129, 137, 139; by Babette Mangolte: 22; by Nicola Dove: 30, 36, 47, 59, 72, 74, 75, 76, 92, 101, 102, 106, 122, 183, 198, 294, 313, 335, 378, 397; by Richard Kalvar: 40; by Peter Mountain: 50, 83; Alexei Rodionov: 107 (right).
Plate Section: *Orlando* images photographed by Liam Longman; *The Man Who Cried* images by Peter Mountain; *Rage* images by the author; *Yes* and *Ginger & Rosa* images by Nicola Dove.

Filmographies

The actors interviewed in Part Four, between them, have an extensive body of work. Beside their films with the author, their acting credits include:

Simon Abkarian: *To Take a Wife, Khamsa* and *The Army of Crime*.

Riz Ahmed: *Shifty, Four Lions* and *Ill Manors*.

Joan Allen: *Manhunter, The Contender* and *The Crucible*.

Annette Bening: *The Grifters, American Beauty* and *The Kids Are All Right*.

Steve Buscemi: *Fargo, Reservoir Dogs* and *Boardwalk Empire*.

Julie Christie: *Darling, McCabe & Mrs Miller* and *Away From Her*.

Lily Cole: *The Imaginarium of Doctor Parnassus, The Moth Diaries* and *Snow White and the Huntsman*.

Judi Dench: *Shakespeare in Love, Iris* and *Philomena*.

Alice Englert: *Beautiful Creatures, In Fear* and *Singularity*.

Elle Fanning: *The Door in the Floor, Somewhere* and *Super 8*.

Christina Hendricks: *Mad Men, Drive* and *How To Catch A Monster*.

Jude Law: *The Talented Mr Ripley, Artificial Intelligence: AI* and *Cold Mountain*.

Alessandro Nivola: *Face/Off, Laurel Canyon* and *Junebug*.

Timothy Spall: *Secrets and Lies, All or Nothing* and *The King's Speech*.